More praise for Life Beyond #MeToo...

"Work Is Love Made Visible . . . and violence is its opposite. This book gets to the roots of sexual harassment and violence and coaches us to move into a more loving, safe future."

—Sarah McArthur, Marshall Goldsmith, Frances Hesselbein,
co-authors, *Work Is Love Made Visible*

"The epidemic of violence against women must end. ***Life Beyond #MeToo*** casts a vision for freedom from violence and discrimination and gives tools for you to start taking action to change the world."

—Miriam Barnett, CEO, YWCA Pierce County

"This important book addresses in depth how countless women have learned disempowerment through generational patterns and individual experiences of victimization. It also explores deeper issues that allow for a culture of oppression and victimization, shares how communities can support victims as they develop backbone power, and helps individuals to be overcomers. Life Beyond #MeToo is a must read for both men and women. In order to shift from the 'Old Normal' paradigm, we must all have different conversations, take different actions, and be committed to the 'New Normal.'"

—Dr. Anne Brown, RNCS,
author, *Backbone Power: The Science of Saying No*

"In *Life Beyond #MeToo: Creating a Safer World for our Mothers, Daughters, Sisters, and Friends,* Christine Rose allows those harmed to finally speak truth by sharing their stories of abuse. She sheds light on how abuse has negatively impacted women all over the world in this thoroughly researched account of sexual abuse and the #MeToo movement. She points out the lengths that abusers will go in order to have their way with the victims of their depravity, as well as the shame, guilt, and responsibility they place on them. Christine Rose identifies the ravages against women and the cost by discussing the physical, emotional, and economic impact of abuse. Of most importance is her message about healing past traumas, especially in the Christian church, and one of empowerment for girls and women to live life to the fullest."

—**Kelly James, PhD, LPC,** national certified counselor, certified professional coach and associate professor at Oral Roberts University Graduate Counseling Programs

"Working moms are bearing the high costs of gender discrimination. *Life Beyond #MeToo* helps us see how to get to the roots of the problem and start addressing it in this generation."

—**Christine Michel Carter,** #1 global voice for working moms, consultant for brands and agencies, speaker on millennial moms and black consumers at Minority Woman Marketing LLC

"Conversations are key to changes both in the workplace and out. We will not heal our hurt or brokenness by hiding our pain. *Life Beyond #MeToo* offers help to start conversations that can change the world."

—**Lorie Reichel-Howe,** CEO, ConversationsInTheWorkplace.com

"Thank you so much for the opportunity to read your incredible book! It has changed my world. Your words and stories brought tears to my eyes and gave me goosebumps. I am now blessed with a deeper perspective of how widespread sexual discrimination is in our world today. I also have a larger, more educated view of the numerous forces at play and a renewed appreciation of the power of the #MeToo movement and the recent cascade of events that are shifting societal norms in pursuit of greater equity and safety for all. The book is a call to action for all leaders to turn the tide of toxic workplaces in favor of cultivating healthier, more productive workplaces.

Most importantly, I value how this book is a guide and conversation starter that can inspire us collectively to co-create a new way of being together in a 'New Normal' where all human beings are respected, valued, and able to live fuller, safer lives."

—Samia Kornweibel,
CEO and certified Leadership Circle coach,
LifeLens Coaching & Consulting LLC

"This book is a call to action, and Christine puts her heart on the line in a pursuit to help others recognize that a change is needed, and the time is now. Thank you for this bold and daring work."

—Jennifer Barron, BSW, MA, MBA,
Community education manager, Centene Corp.

"The tides of cultural change are moving strongly in our current times. People are looking for how to cope and choose a better path to the future in these movements but face their own uncertainties. Christine Rose identifies and clarifies the mess of sexual violence in our culture with new illumination and what can be done about it. Not simply a commentator, Christine provides coaching strategies and an innovative approach to leveraging the transformational power of the #MeToo social media event."

—Robert Dunham,
co-author of *The Innovator's Way: Essential Practices for Innovation,*
founder of the Institute for Generative Leadership,
former VP at Motorola Computer Systems and
COO at Action Technologies

L🌹FE BEYOND #MeToo

CREATING A SAFER WORLD FOR OUR MOTHERS, DAUGHTERS, SISTERS & FRIENDS

L✤FE
BEYOND
#MeToo

CREATING A SAFER WORLD
FOR OUR MOTHERS,
DAUGHTERS, SISTERS & FRIENDS

Christine T. Rose

REDEMPTION
PRESS

Published by Redemption Press, PO Box 427, Enumclaw, WA 98022

Toll Free (844) 2REDEEM (273-3336)

ORDERING INFORMATION

Quantity Purchases: Special discounts are available on quantity purchases by corporations, educational institutions, associations, and others. For details, visit www.lifebeyondmetoo.com.

Individual purchases: To order additional copies of this book, please visit www.lifebeyondmetoo.com or www.redemption-press.com.
Also available on Amazon.com and BarnesandNoble.com
Or by calling toll free 1-844-2REDEEM.

Redemption Press is honored to present this title in partnership with the author. The views expressed or implied in this work are those of the author. Redemption Press provides our imprint seal representing design excellence, creative content, and high quality production.

All Scripture quotations, unless otherwise indicated, are taken from the *Holy Bible, New International Version*®. *NIV*®. Copyright © 1973, 1978, 1984 by International Bible Society. Used by permission of Zondervan. All rights reserved.

ISBN 13: 978-1-68314-812-8 (Paperback)
978-1-68314-814-2 (ePub)
978-1-68314-813-5 (Mobi)

Library of Congress Catalog Card Number: 2019916278

Set in Adobe Garamond Pro by Redemption Press.
Cover design by Samuel Pierce
Interior design by Nate Myers

Contents

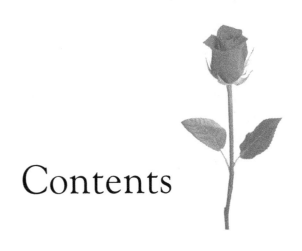

Acknowledgments

I've been blessed with an amazing team to put a book together to share the vision of a safe world for our mothers, daughters, sisters, and friends. I would like to gratefully acknowledge:

- My daughters, Marian and Megan, you are my inspiration and hope for a better future. I love you forever.
- Sabrina Matson, your friendship and encouragement got me started on this book.
- Vivien E. Rose, Ph.D., your research assistance, countless conversations about the book, and willingness to share your deep knowledge of women's history were instrumental to this work. Your care and practical assistance were also gifts from the Divine.
- Julia Miller, your support, love and prayers were invaluable to see this project to the finish line.
- Samuel Pierce, thank you for your ability to see my vision and for the beautiful cover art.

- The brave and brilliant women and men who contributed your stories and content, you have my sincere gratitude.
- The team at Redemption Press: Athena Dean Holtz, President and CEO (chief everything officer) for believing in this project; book coach Inger Longelin for your help to get a strong start; project manager Hannah McKenzie, editors Tisha Martin and Rachel Newman, and managing editor Dori Harrell for your skill and care to bring the book to publication; graphic designer Nate Myers for polishing the cover and interior; Codey Forsell, bookstore web page creator; and Pamela Harding, COO, whose help with details is keeping at all legal. Thanks to all of you.
- Thanks to Vincent and Amy Davis at Warrior Book Marketing for your work to get out the good news about New Normal.
- Martha Bullen and Debby Englander from Steve Harrison's Quantum Leap program, thanks so much for your coaching and great advice.
- Thanks to the Life Beyond #MeToo Facebook community for joining in the vision to change the world.
- Special thanks to my prayer team for your ongoing support for me and this work.
- I'm deeply grateful to my ICF mentor coach Theresa McKenna and to the community of amazing peer ICF Washington coaches who have encouraged me in my coaching journey. Without you all I wouldn't have the foundation I needed to do this work.
- Thanks to all the radio hosts and producers, and podcasters, who have helped me share the hope for a New Normal.
- Alyssa Milano, thank you for your "tweet heard round the world."

Even with all the help and support, perfection is unattainable. Any errors of attribution or accuracy are mine alone.

There is not room in this book to recognize each person and organization working to create this kind of change, but I'd like to thank every person and each organization that has worked toward a New Normal and is doing the lion's share of the work today. You are our (s)heroes! Your vision, blood, sweat, and tears have moved us closer to New Normal, and we owe you a debt of gratitude.

Introduction

What Is This Book About?

In October of 2017, an onslaught of social media posts using the hashtag (#, a tool to categorize social media posts) MeToo opened the door for millions of women, and countless men, to share deeply personal stories of sexual harassment, abuse, and violence via the internet. It created an unprecedented opportunity to advance culture change to create a safer world for our mothers, daughters, sisters, and friends. This book takes a coaching approach to the #MeToo space, addressing both personal transformation and global cultural change for each person willing to join the conversation and pursue change with an open, honest, and respectful heart and mind. As a credentialed International Coaching Federation (ICF) business and executive coach, I work with business leaders to accelerate growth in their lives and in their organizations. Through coaching, my clients come to deeply know themselves and their teams and are free to align with their values as they live in relationship with self and others. I facilitate discovery, awareness, and choice to empower people to achieve their great contributions, love their lives, and grow successful companies with vision, strategy, structure, and accountability. Often my clients' personal stories have contributed to subconscious scripts that impact their choices and actions, and coaching has helped them consciously shape new beliefs.

Through reading this book, I hope you'll gain knowledge, insights, and tools for creating change in your own life and in your community. By the end of this book, you will be empowered to find your own solutions to the situations you face, allowing you to foster the changes you want to see. While addressing immediate problems, you will develop an ability to create ongoing transformation.

Each chapter opens with a #MeToo story, published exclusively in this book. The names and identifying details are changed to provide anonymity. Stories may trigger some things for some readers, so please do what you need to care for yourself if memories or feelings arise. Each chapter closes with questions for personal reflection or as conversation starters in a group setting. Add your own questions if you wish. Take time to think about each question and use them to develop your own understanding of the issues addressed in this book.

The first eleven chapters deepen your awareness of what #MeToo is and where the conversation has been taking us. You will get the big picture of where we as a society and culture have been in the past, and you will be invited to be part of "New Normal" with a global shift in how we view and treat all people.

Chapters 11 to 15 address the possibility of change. You'll gain a sense of how you and your family, your workplace, and other institutions in society can engage in self-reflection, connection, and contribution toward world transformation. In chapters 16 and 17, you'll be encouraged to pursue personal growth and healing to empower you to make your own contribution to the New Normal, a world free from sexual discrimination and violence. The book closes with a chapter of hope.

By the time you finish this book, you will have the tools necessary to understand yourself and others better and will be armed with knowledge and power to step in and create change. You will be better able to deal with discrimination, harassment, and sexual violence. And you will be equipped to help others. While the coaching tools and information presented may be useful to many, this book does not offer professional counsel or legal advice. If you are in need of counseling or legal assistance please contact a licensed professional.

Who Is This Book For?

This book is an invitation to every person who wants to live in a world that is safe for all people. It is relevant to virtually everyone who cares about any human being, including themselves. This is for those who do not know how to begin to think about or talk to others about #MeToo or about the trauma that is endemic to humanity. I especially invite anyone who has been

- abused as a child or teenager or has experienced sexual violence as an adult at home;
- a perpetrator of, or impacted by, sexual discrimination, harassment, or violence whether at home, in the workplace, at school, in their faith community, or in public;
- a consumer of pornography or the sex trade or influenced by someone's addiction to pornography, use of prostitutes, or involvement in sex trafficking; or
- a parent, educator, leader, member, or volunteer who takes seriously their role in shaping the minds and characters of young people.

I invite you to consider opening up your mind and heart to new information and new opportunities to connect with others. This book is a gift for you, or someone you know, that could change a life and possibly change the world.

One Person
at a Time

The late afternoon sun cast long fir-tree shadows across the sidewalk on the south side of the street, making it darker than when my classmate Sandy and I had walked after school to her family's white colonial two-story to play with her dolls.

An autumn breeze blew rust-mottled maple leaves across a driveway, and my light-yellow sweater didn't seem heavy enough, nor did the robin's egg–blue elastic-waist pants I'd chosen before school. My dark sneakers and white anklet socks gathered dust from the trodden trail behind the school as I hurried around the corner out of Sandy's neighborhood and onto a narrow path next to a tall chain-link fence. Mom had said it was okay to take the short way home.

It would take me past a playground with a portable, past the multipurpose room and library, and past a cluster of classrooms. I would cut through the school grounds, cross the big playfield, pass through a narrow gate in the school's chain-link fence on the opposite corner of the school property, cross the street, and walk two more blocks to home.

Though I shivered with the autumn chill, I was excited to tell Mother about my first visit to Sandy's. No time to stop on the playground, as it was late and I had to get home before dinner.

From two classrooms away, I heard basketballs slapping the pavement in the breezeway. I turned the corner and noticed two tall boys who looked like giants compared to my brothers. I hurried toward the south wall when one of the boys let his ball bounce away.

He leered and shouted at me, "Hey, little *girl!*" Unzipping his blue jeans, he barked, "Stay where you are and pull down your pants!"

I froze.

The boy moved menacingly toward me. Confused, I stared as he pulled down his jeans with one hand and grabbed himself with the other. The other giant boy dropped his basketball, started unbuckling his belt, and edged my direction.

My heart pounded in my chest. I couldn't breathe. The hairs on the back of my neck stood up. I didn't understand what was happening and didn't know what to do.

The first boy was closer now, just a couple steps away. The second boy was still five steps away by the breezeway wall. If I tried to run back to Sandy's, the boys would for sure catch me. The other direction, behind more classrooms, was empty and hidden. The only way out was to run past them through the breezeway toward home. As I darted past the first boy, he reached toward me, brushing my sweater with the fingertips of his free hand.

Out of the corner of my eye, I saw he had started chasing me, his jeans and underpants falling. My brain yelled, *Run!*

As I raced across the breezeway, the second boy began to chase me too, but I dodged him and ran as fast as I could on cement walkways until heavy footsteps and breathing echoed behind me. I ran downhill until the sounds were muffled by grass and faded completely.

Even though I felt the danger had ended, I continued running across the field and slipped through the gate at the far corner of the schoolyard. For the first time ever, I forgot to look both ways before crossing the street. A car honked and swerved, and it wasn't until I was on the other side of the street that I dared to look back. The big boys, their pants on, laughed as they sauntered up the hill.

I ran the rest of the way home in tears. Wiping my tears with the back of my sleeve, I told my uncle what had happened.

He chuckled. "Boys will be boys." He poured a glass of milk and gave me a cookie, even though dinner was on the stove.

Mealtimes in my family home were big, noisy, and chaotic, but my uncle didn't mention my experience.

Neither did I, and it was the last time I asked for permission to visit anyone at that school. I was five years old.

#MeToo, Angel

That little girl was me. My mother's nickname for me was Angel.

Over half a century after this story took place, I write this book now as a human being with a spirit, soul, body, and voice that is ready to be heard. While the first #MeToo story I remember was at age five, I grew up in a home with three sexual abusers (now deceased). I've accomplished a great deal of counseling and healing and now spend little time thinking or talking about my experiences. Although they established a broken pattern that led to many problems in my life, I've been able to face and overcome these experiences and rebuild my past from its shaky foundation to a solid foundation for my present and future.

Later, I will open more windows on the effects of sexual violence, but I will do a bit of self-revealing here. My past has been quite a train wreck because I had a "broken-people picker." I'm not proud of the results—several promiscuous years before marrying the wrong person for the wrong reasons, a few affairs that bookended many faithful years of marriage, and a return to promiscuity after divorce. I had offered my body to people who never once treasured my soul. If their intentions were to exploit me, I was an easy target. And if covert video surveillance had been installed, my behaviors could have turned me into someone's porn against my will.

I regret my past decisions but understand the brokenness that led me there. Yet if I could go back and relive the past knowing what I know now, I'd make different choices. Years of counseling and years of the awareness of God's faithful and compassionate love helped me get much-needed perspective, significant healing, and balance in my personal life.

Then as a coach, I spent years rebuilding my personal and professional foundation. This work set a new course for the positive life I'm living today and gives me great hope for others whose lives have been impacted by sexual discrimination, harassment, abuse, and assault. With this solid ground beneath my feet, I'm able to share my thoughts and a few of my own experiences from a place of strength.

I've been victimized by criminals in my own home growing up, and I've experienced ongoing harassment, stalking, criminal violations, and gaslighting as an adult. I'm a daughter, sister, mother of two adult daughters, aunt, and friend to girls and women in a world where stories are rarely shared and burrow deep into unhealthy cultural patterns that severely damage girls, boys, women, and men. I'm a community member spending resources to help people deal with the aftermath of their adverse childhood experiences (ACEs), including sexual abuse. I'm a resident of a state that has a commission on women, which restarted after #MeToo to address needed changes. And I'm a citizen of a country whose policies impact not only how violence is dealt with but also funding for programs to help victims of sexual violence. As a member of the global human community, I'm aware of a worldwide scope of devastation from sexual violence that seems to exceed our capacity to measure, fathom, or understand, and that goes back through the ages.

I'm a person of faith who believes Jesus was the sinless Son of God who surrendered His life on a cross for the forgiveness of all humanity's sins, rose from the dead, and will return one day holding final authority over all. I trust God with my broken past as I focus on the present and future, seeking to walk humbly in the Divine Presence who sees all and offers compassion and forgiveness to those willing to accept these gifts. There is a great need for healing and change in the Christian church, and I often feel out of place among its 2.2 billion[1] members, as sexual abuse scandals and other offensive actions done by self-professing Christians are abhorrent to me. As a grateful, redeemed sinner who depends daily upon the cleansing and healing of the Holy Spirit and the mercy of God through the work of Jesus on my behalf, I equally respect the humanity, dignity, and perspectives of those who do and do not share my faith. Willingness to see things from others' perspectives is critical in a coaching conversation.

As a business coach, to the degree my clients need to work on deep healing, I refer them to counselors. When they need legal or financial advice, I refer clients to legal or financial professionals. Clients may work with me on reframing assumptions and creating strategies, goals, or action plans to help them move toward a better future. I have the privilege of seeing transformations, and the starting point is always in my clients. My mastery of coaching skills is always in development, and any other subject-matter expertise isn't as relevant, except to the degree that it helps cultivate curiosity and offer powerful questions that open new ways for my clients to think, be, and do.

While I support nonprofits helping victims of sexual violence, this strategy seems as futile as taking cuttings off a huge tree while ignoring the roots that continue to thrive. I hope this book adds to the existing body of work to create root-level change.

I have argued with porn users that the global porn industry objectifies people. Most of the individuals who show up in pornography on computer screens around the world aren't acting out or acting upon their hearts' deepest desires, but rather, their involvement in that unfortunate industry minimizes their potential to offer their highest and best contributions to the world.

I have wept after reading celebrities' histories of sexual violence. News stories about human trafficking, of girls and women who are kidnapped and locked in cupboards or sheds or chopped up and buried on rural farms, tie my stomach in knots. Sexual discrimination, harassment, and abuse scandals within the church, business corporations, the arts and media, and politics are rampant. Avoiding these stories is impossible if you're plugged in to society, so numbness creeps in.

There's something deeply wrong and rotten about this world that allows such negative things to happen. The issue unveils a heavy weight of injustice. I believe my (and your) responsibility requires more than silence, which is complicit agreement with all that is wrong.

President John F. Kennedy quoted Edmund Burke as saying, "All that is needed for evil to triumph is for good men to do nothing."[2] We are to blame.

After the topic came up during a visit with a girlfriend the summer of 2018, I said, "I need to write a book." I believe our world is sitting on a pivot point, a windowsill of time to talk about and develop strategies to change what has been overlooked and accepted for far too long and to work together to create lasting change. I'm grateful this work is already happening on many levels. It must continue and increase until we reach a New Normal where all humans are treated with dignity and respect.

My passion is to empower girls, women, and all who support them to live their best futures. This requires identifying, examining, and discarding any parts of "default mode" that are not useful. Coaches don't come equipped with all the answers. In fact, quite the opposite. We see our clients as brilliant, creative, and able to generate solutions, growth, and the changes they're seeking through our engaging in questions that help them connect, gain self-awareness, create vision, design strategy, move into action, and accomplish change through accountability.

This book is one tool to help you coach yourself through your experiences to make sense of your own life beyond #MeToo. I use the pronouns "they" or "her" as I refer to victims because the vast majority are females. I recognize many males have been victims too, and encourage you, as you read the book, to replace pronouns in a way that serves you. In any case, I hope you'll engage and gain awareness (and self-awareness) by considering each question, connecting in conversations with others about this topic, contributing to a shared vision, offering your thoughts and actions as strategies are developed, adopting new habits, and working with those in your community who are adding structure and accountability to create change. Your value is immeasurable. Your contribution is needed.

I believe the following:

- #MeToo begs for global (individual and corporate) self-awareness, calling for honesty, repentance when needed, forgiveness, and willingness to be vulnerable in ways that will rebuild trust.
- We as individuals and as a society need to rebuild trust, connect and align from a place of awareness, create a united vision, and develop and enact strategies with accountability to create transformation until the transformation becomes innate, unchanging, a New Normal.
- We need a new vision for how girls and women (and all humans) can be and are treated with dignity and respect. We need to examine old strategies and to create new strategies for defining and requiring new standards for human behavior. We need a worldwide call to action, demanding accountability that leads to a New Normal. Global transformation will have its starting place in one person at a time. I am that one person. So are you.

Questions to Thoughtfully Consider and Discuss

1. Were the actions of the big boys in Angel's story sexual harassment, abuse, or assault?
2. What do you think about how Angel's report of her experience was handled?
3. What was your exposure to the onslaught of #MeToo stories in October 2017?
4. How have the stories impacted you or your community?
5. What might facilitate learning about this topic?
6. What are your thoughts about people who've made mistakes and their ability to learn from them and recover?
7. How open are you to looking at others' perspectives?
8. What are your best practices to develop and grow in your own knowledge and awareness?
9. Who is accountable for the wrong in our society?
10. What about silence might make it complicit agreement?
11. What are your beliefs about #MeToo?

What Was That All About?

Marcus dropped in to talk to the shop owner on his monthly visit. He was a vendor, handsome, charming, and friendly with the owner. Marcus looked me over and began asking questions about me. He learned I walked two miles to get to work every day after school. He started dropping by the shop weekly and always took a few minutes to chat with me. Black like me, he called me "sister" at first, but after a while he started calling me "baby."

A few months later, he came by at the end of my shift and offered me a ride home. "I'm going right past your house anyway, baby." I accepted. He started swinging by the shop parking lot a couple times a week to drop me off a block from my house. After a few weeks, he brought me a soda and a snack. When the school year ended, I started working an earlier shift. He would pick me up when my shift was over around one o'clock.

One day he asked if he could take me to lunch. I was thirteen; he was twenty-two. My mom reluctantly allowed me to go. Marcus took me to a local steakhouse and chose a table near the back. Then he leaned over, started rubbing my back, and told me I was the most beautiful girl he'd ever met. After lunch he laid an open-mouth kiss on me and grabbed my butt. He took me back to my house, kissed me goodbye, and told me he was in love with me.

After that, in addition to driving me home and kissing me, he started calling me a couple times a week to check up on me. He told me he wanted to marry me. A few weeks later, he drove past my home to his apartment. When I asked where we were going, he said, "I want to show you where I live." He gave me alcohol and trained me exactly how to give him oral sex. He told me not to tell anyone. "They won't understand the love we share, and we could get in trouble." He took me to his place every week, sometimes twice a week, and demanded oral sex. I invited him to join our family dinner. He said he had night school and his schedule wouldn't allow it.

At the end of the summer, I quit my job to focus on school and sports. He called occasionally, but when he asked me about getting away to see him, I told him I couldn't. Two years later, he sounded angry and jealous when I told him I had met a boy my age.

Four and a half years later when I was a freshman in college, Marcus called me during my winter break and asked if he could see me "for old times' sake" and bring me a Christmas gift. "Remember, beautiful? We were going to get married." My high school sweetheart and I had just broken up, so I agreed. I was eighteen; he was twenty-seven.

He came to the house where I was housesitting. He looked old. I opened my gift, wine, and he poured me one glass while I brought cheese and crackers from the kitchen. He talked about himself for half an hour. I felt sick. I got up to go to the bathroom and fell unconscious. When I came to hours later, I was on the floor in pain. He was on the couch watching a movie. It occurred to me it was the first time a man had seen me naked.

He got up, walked past me and out the door, and instructed, "Don't tell anyone. It would be useless. I'll tell everyone you asked for it." I was speechless. He said no one would believe me. "You let me in. This is all you." The door slammed shut. I wrapped myself in a blanket, ashamed, and cried for the rest of the night. I never told. I tried to forget it all.

#MeToo, Terri

Terri's story was unique to her but common in the scope of human events, an example of sexual abuse and assault in one tragic tale. The #MeToo firestorm opened millions of stories like Terri's, hidden in dark corners of hearts harboring brokenness and pain. Whether it happens at work, at home, in public, in church, at school, or anywhere else, a story like Angel's or Terri's damages emotions and shreds community. Generally, the perpetrator demands silence. These stories not only keep the victim silent; they silence the listener, because they're saturated in shame. We'll look at specifics later, but for now, it's important to realize that while a story like Angel's or Terri's or any of the others in this book might be shocking to the victim, to their families and friends, and even to people in their communities who learn about what happened, these stories are commonplace. In 2017, social media called forth millions of stories. Let's examine #MeToo to unite on an understanding of what's taken place and what it means.

A Brief History of the #MeToo Viral Social Media Firestorm

History is recorded using words. The famous poet Ralph Waldo Emerson in his 1837 poem "Concord Hymn" memorialized the start of the Revolutionary War with the words "the shot heard round the world."[1] Unless you're disconnected from current events and the media, you're probably familiar with the social media tsunami following actress Alyssa Milano's "tweet heard round the world," which read:

> Me too. Suggested by a friend: "If all the women and men who have been sexually harassed or assaulted wrote, 'Me too' as a status, we might give people a sense of the magnitude of the problem." (@ Alyssa_Milano 1:21 PM—Oct 15, 2017[2])

#MeToo was tweeted over 53,000 times in twenty-four hours and more than 500,000 times by October 16.[3] On Facebook, #MeToo was used by more than 4.7 million people in 12 million posts during the first twenty-four hours.[4] Forty-five percent of users in the United States had a friend who had posted using the hashtag.[5]

While women have shared their stories collectively many times before, #MeToo is unique in anti-sexual-harassment social media movements because of the celebrities who started and contributed to the stream of tweets. Michael Cornfield, an associate professor of political management at George Washington University and the research director for the Peoria Project (a nonprofit research project conducted by Catalist LLC) said, "Celebrities get involved in issue advocacy all the time, but not in such visible profusion. That means that the #MeToo explosion is not only going to be hard to forget, but hard to replicate."[6]

Globally, #MeToo spawned similar social media firestorms in multiple languages, including Arabic, Farsi, French, Hindi, and Spanish. Twitter users in the US, France, the UK, Canada, and India were the most prolific #MeToo campaigners. By March 2018, #MeToo or its equivalent had been used in eighty-five countries to bring attention to harassment and violence and to work for change.[7] The #MeToo social media event created impact and longevity that's being felt around the world today.

Tarana Burke originally launched the "me too Movement" as part of her work in Just Be Inc., the nonprofit organization she founded in

2006. According to Just Be Inc.'s website, the "me too Movement" is focused on young women of color like Terri who have endured sexual abuse, assault, or exploitation (S.A.A.E.). In Just Be Inc.'s informal survey of programs across the United States, they found that few were equipped to deal with young women of a variety of ages and races who were victims of molestation, incest, or exploitation. Just Be Inc.'s definition of exploitation includes events that may not be reported or responded to in communities of color.

On its website, Just Be Inc. highlights its work to address all sexual victimization in these communities:

> Young women who are, for example, severely harassed daily in school or made to commit to sexual favors or perform sex acts under duress can be severely traumatized by their situations, and the effects can be just as damaging as being raped or otherwise sexually assaulted. Our work is meant to address the nuances of being, what we call a "S.A.A.E survivor."[8]

In her TED Talk at TEDWomen 2018, Ms. Burke said, "As survivors, we often have to hold the truth of what we experience, but now we're all holding something, whether we want to or not."[9]

While social media certainly facilitated the rapid rise of the viral social media wave that called attention to the prevalence of sexual violence, many prior movements and actions paved a way and built a foundation for its longevity.

In May 2014, #yesallwomen posts also had women sharing their experiences about sexual violence and sexism after a mentally unstable, self-proclaimed *incel* (involuntarily celibate) man in Isla Vista, California, killed six people and injured fourteen more near the campus of University of California, Santa Barbara, before dying by suicide. He wrote and spoke about hating women prior to his actions.[10] The #yesallwomen hashtag was a response to #notallmen, a Twitter stream of men calling attention to the fact that not all men are misogynists and not all men are murderers. #Yesallwomen responded with the point that while not all men are violent, all women are constantly on alert because of the (sexual and other) women-focused violence of some men. #Yesallwomen was tweeted 1.2 million times in four days.[11] Here are two examples published in the *New Yorker*:

> #YesAllWomen because "I have a boyfriend" is more effective than "I'm not interested"—men respect other men more than my right to say no.

> Because if I know I will be out til after dark, I start planning my route home hours, even days, beforehand #yesallwomen.[12]

Other hashtags, such as #TimesUp, #WhatWereYouWearing, #YouOkSis, #SurvivorPrivilege, #WhyWomenDontReport, and #WhyIDidNotTell also encouraged survivors to share their stories. Soon after news broke in March of 2014, the viral social media campaign #BringBackOurGirls spread around the world, calling for Boko Haram to return 275 girls they had abducted from Chibok, Nigeria. The hashtag was record setting and attracted support from Michelle Obama, the Pope, Malala Yousafazi, and other people of influence.[13] #BringBackOurGirls continues to be used years later, but it did not prevent an estimated 7,000 abductions of girls and women (plus boys) nor secure the safe return of those kidnapped from Chibok. Boko Haram routinely abducts children (both girls and boys), but the mass kidnapping drew attention on social media because of its magnitude.[14]

As a response to #MeToo, Hollywood celebrities founded the #TimesUp movement, Time's Up Now (a 501c4 social welfare organization) and the Time's Up Foundation (a 501c3 public charity) on January 1, 2018.[15] During 2018, over 3,400 women and men were connected to legal resources through the Time's Up Legal Defense Fund.

Two-thirds of those who contact the fund identify as low-wage workers. Over 800 attorneys have joined the network, and top attorneys across the country are taking on cases. According to the Time's Up website:

> As a first program to address safety in workplaces beyond the entertainment industry, we launched the Time's Up Legal Defense Fund, which is housed and administered by the National Women's Law Center (NWLC). The Fund connects those who experience sexual misconduct including assault, harassment, abuse, and related retaliation in the workplace or in trying to advance their careers with legal and public relations assistance. . . . Together, we are seizing this unprecedented moment and transforming it into meaningful and institutionalized change across culture, companies and laws. And we're just getting started. [16]

Criticisms of the #MeToo Movement

Criticisms of the movement abound from a variety of perceptions and perspectives. As a coach, I'm interested in addressing criticisms while encouraging open conversation, and in crafting solutions.

One critique of #MeToo is that it's been co-opted by white women. Black women activists including the Jim Crow era rape survivor Recy Taylor set a pattern followed by Tarana Burke when she launched a campaign to speak out against sexual violence and oppression.[17] Minorities and men certainly contributed stories in the social media movement, but questions still arise about whether the #MeToo social media phenomenon failed to give adequate attention to minorities, males, and transgender people. Their voices are equally worthy of being heard. Why did it take famous (mostly white) people to create the momentum we witnessed in 2017? Are minorities' contributions to the movement embraced, or is the critique valid? Is the problem of sexual violence much worse for women than for men? What about different racial groups? What about self-described nonbinary people?

Sexual violence definitely hits some communities harder than others. In the US, approximately 40 percent of black women report coercive sexual contact by age eighteen. Almost 8 percent of Latinas will be raped by a spouse, partner, or ex-partner during their lifetime. American Indian and Alaska Native women are much more likely to be victims of sexual violence committed by a stranger or acquaintance rather than a family member or intimate partner. Approximately 70 percent of perpetrators are non-Native. Indigenous women are the victims of rape and sexual assault at a rate that is three and a half times higher than any other race in the United States.[18] In a 2010 survey conducted by the Urban Indian Health Institute and Centers for Disease Control and Prevention (CDC) documenting experiences of sexual violence among indigenous women living in Seattle, 94 percent of the 148 women interviewed reported they had been raped or were coerced into sex at least once in their lives.[19]

In January 2018, StopStreetHarassment.org commissioned a 2,000-person survey (a nationally representative sample of adults in the USA) on sexual harassment and assault, conducted by GfK. The survey results found that nationwide, 81 percent of women and 43 percent of men reported experiencing some form of sexual harassment and/or assault in their lifetime. Verbal sexual harassment was the most common (77 percent of women and 34 percent of men). Over half of women and 17 percent of men said they were touched or groped in an unwelcome way. Of those surveyed, 27 percent of women and 7 percent of men survived sexual assault.[20]

The problem of sexual violence against women is global. One in three women in the world report having experienced sexual violence.[21] While the violence men experience is real, the number of women experiencing sexual harassment, abuse, and assault is far greater. Stories of sexual violence are not limited to any race or gender. All voices are needed to accelerate positive change.

Other Criticisms of #MeToo

Some criticize that the movement claims victimization equally, regardless of severity of harassment, abuse, or assault a victim experienced. Attorney and former ACLU Board Member Wendy Kaminer wrote,

> Thinking people make distinctions between a hand on your knee and a grope up your skirt, between a sexual attack by a supervisor and a pat on the butt from a guy in a bar just as they distinguish pickpockets from home invaders. #MeTooism condemns such distinctions as reflections of rape culture.[22]

Another criticism is that claims of victims are not credible. In an interview with the *New York Times*, Kevin Cramer, Republican senator from North Dakota, suggested the #MeToo movement had gone too far. "That you're just supposed to believe somebody because they said it happened," he said of the movement, which has seen a number of women come forward with accusations of sexual assault, abuse, and harassment.

"The world got to see close up how ugly it can be when you go too far,"[23] Cramer continued, in reference to Supreme Court Justice Kavanaugh's confirmation hearing. Cramer appeared to claim the movement was more about victimization than empowerment. "They cannot understand this movement toward victimization," Cramer said in a statement in reference to his wife, daughters, mother, and mother-in-law. Former Senator Heidi Heitkamp rebutted. "It did not make my mom less strong that she was a victim," Heitkamp said. "She got stronger and she made us strong. And to suggest that this movement doesn't make women strong and stronger is really unfortunate."[24]

Another critique of #MeToo is that it classifies all men as wrong and all women as right. Angelina Chapin, an editor at the *Huffington Post*, wrote, "The social media campaign is, of course, intended as a wake-up call for men. If every woman you know has been harassed or assaulted, then every man you know has likely made a woman feel unsafe."[25]

Carina Chocano, a contributing writer to the *New York Times Magazine* and author of the book *You Play the Girl*, wrote in *Rolling Stone*, "This is not an individual problem. This is a systemic problem. There are no two sides. 'Personal responsibility' doesn't factor in."[26]

This puts even well-intentioned men on the defensive. Some men with lifelong track records of respecting and working with women are afraid of offending any woman even by what they had in the past considered a way of adding value, a compliment such as "You look nice today." Their criticism is that #MeToo is removing the possibility of positively recognizing gender differences in public.

Another criticism is that the movement doesn't require action from men to create systemic change; rather, it's a movement started by women and fueled by women's stories, and in the end it will make little difference because it doesn't include men. #MeToo hasn't clarified exactly what changes need to be made or what part men have in making them. Critics say not only are men disengaged from creating change, but they don't see a need for it. Angela Chapin wrote in the *Huffington Post*, "It's not enough that we spend our lives being constantly harassed and violated by men; we also have to explain to these men why their behavior is problematic and, often, illegal."[27]

In an editorial article in Bustle.com, location independent writer Alyssa James wrote,

> At this point, if a person isn't aware of rape culture, it's because they don't want to be. . . . Sexual harassment and assault are more than isolated incidents perpetrated by bad people. . . . It's a systemic issue where the failure to punish people who commit assault feeds a culture of male entitlement and violence. . . . The people who need to take action are the ones with the power and privilege to do so without risk: in this case, men. . . . I understand how this viral hashtag can be empowering for some, but for me this is yet another "movement"

that pushes survivors to be the drivers of change and educators for men. Men who will inevitably get credit for doing what they always do: the bare minimum.[28]

Some may consider Ms. James's opinion off the mark. As a coach, I'd like to encourage you to think about what you believe about #MeToo being a systemic issue and who needs to take action. Are the critics right, or are men included? Do men understand what's happened and what needs to change? Are men in fact engaging in creating change?

A Moment, a Movement, or a Generation?

Social movements are defined as a specific type of group action where large, informal groups of individuals or organizations work for or against change in specific political or social issues.[29] Responses to Tarana Burke's creation of the "me too Movement" and Alyssa Milano's use of the hashtag inviting the world to self-report experiences of sexual harassment and violence have clearly shown again that sexual discrimination and harassment, abuse, and assault against women are perpetrated in epidemic proportion, impacting all of society.

In July 2018, President Trump mentioned #MeToo in terms of a generation at a rally in Great Falls, Montana. Imagining himself sparring with Senator Elizabeth Warren on the debate stage (about her claim to Native American ancestry), he told the crowd that he would toss her a DNA kit, "But we have to do it gently *because we're in the #MeToo generation*, so we have to be very gentle."[30] Whether a moment, a movement, or a generation, from Facebook friends to presidents, #MeToo has certainly caught our attention.

Things between Men and Women Will Never Be the Same

The March 2018 cover title of *Oprah Magazine*, "This month's big question, Where do we go from Here? What we know for sure: Things between men and women will never be the same," points to Oprah

Winfrey's "What I Know for Sure" essay at the end of the magazine, in which she wrote,

> And for women who've tolerated varying degrees of misogynistic behavior for so long, we just accepted it as normal. The normalization is over. The power of #MeToo has allowed every woman to see that the struggle is not hers alone. Our voices raised together can lead to systemic changes in the workplace and our culture. We're on the precipice of something larger than we know. A shift in the way we view ourselves. And in the way the world views us."[31]

After watching Ms. Winfrey deliver her acceptance speech at the 2018 Golden Globes in which she called for an end to injustice, ultraconservative former White House chief strategist Steve Bannon told reporter Joshua Green,

> This is a definitional moment in the culture. It'll never be the same going forward. The anti-patriarchy movement is going to undo ten thousand years of recorded history. You watch. The time has come. Women are gonna take charge of society. And they couldn't juxtapose a better villain than Trump. He is the patriarch.[32]

I sincerely hope that the time has come for deep, lasting culture change. We may all have an opportunity to see this change happen in our lifetime.

A Small Drop in the Ocean

In opening remarks at the Human Rights Forum held at Carter Presidential Center on June 25, 2013, President Jimmy Carter said, "The abuse of women and girls is the most pervasive and unaddressed human rights violation on earth."[33] If you've studied history, you'll agree that #MeToo is raising awareness, but despite its magnitude, it is a mere drop in the ocean of complaints from women about men's enforcing sexual power against women. Every generation of women has its stories, and every generation has kept its silence.

Some of the complaints about infringement on women's rights turned into movements. The women's rights movement in the United States

[was] launched July 19 and 20, 1848 in Seneca Falls, New York. Thirty-two men and 68 women signed a Declaration of Sentiments based on the Declaration of Independence, calling for the end of "absolute tyranny" of men over women. Among the economic, political, legal, educational, religious, and social means of maintaining this tyranny was women's inability to vote. The national movement to gain that right spanned 72 years and multiple generations.[34]

The second wave of the women's rights movement in the US took place in the 1960s and early 1970s. Workplace sexual harassment was defined in Title VII of the Civil Rights Act of 1964. Sexual harassment in educational facilities was defined in Title IX of the Education Codes of 1972. This period also brought the growth of rape crisis centers, movements against date and marital rape, and legal and advocacy work against domestic violence.

Women and girls today are living the legacy of women's rights that seven generations of women before us have given their best to achieve. Alice Paul, that intrepid organizer who first wrote out the Equal Rights Amendment in 1923, said, "I always feel the movement is sort of a mosaic. Each of us puts in one little stone, and then you get a great mosaic at the end." Women, acting together, adding their small stones to the grand mosaic, have increased their rights against all odds, nonviolently, from an initial position of powerlessness. (Bonnie Eisenberg and Mary Ruthsdotter, the National Women's History Project, 1998)

The third wave of feminism, led by Gen-X women whose foundations were the work of the original women's rights movement and the second wave, started in the mid-1980s. They organized to work toward gender, racial, economic, and social justice.

#MeToo may be a transformational third-wave event marking the collective release of women from the burden of shame from others' sexual harassment and violence against them. Or it may show itself to be a new social movement leading to adoption of new practices and laws that will eventually solve the global, cultural mess of sexual harassment and violence. Time alone will tell. In any case, it pays to be clear on the words being thrown about and agree on their meanings and significance.

Questions to Thoughtfully Consider and Discuss

1. What words would you use to describe Terri's experiences?
2. What are valid reasons for not reporting? What is a victim's responsibility to report crimes against their body?
3. What are your thoughts about the various critiques of #MeToo?
4. What is positive about #MeToo?
5. What, if anything, is important about #MeToo? Why?
6. What assumptions are you holding about sexual harassment and violence?
7. What other perspectives exist that may differ from yours?
8. Where's the power in #MeToo? Where's the power in ridiculing #MeToo?
9. What do you believe are the goals of #MeToo?
10. Describe ideal relationships between men and women in society.
11. What is the next thing you need to do after considering the information you have read and the questions you've pondered in this chapter?

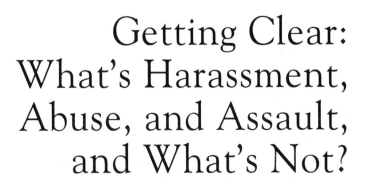

THREE

Getting Clear: What's Harassment, Abuse, and Assault, and What's Not?

After the sales call, I slid into the driver's seat of my car, put my purse on the floor behind my seat, and buckled my seat belt. My recently promoted sales manager, Cal, buckled his. I pulled out of the parking lot, listening to Cal assess the last call.

As I drove up to an intersection and put on the brakes, Cal interrupted his monologue and ogled the elegant raven-haired woman crossing the street in front of my car. She wore a tan raincoat over a black skirt that was cut just above the knees, a white sweater, and a red scarf, carried a black laptop case, and was wearing black three-inch heels. His stare and the uncomfortable silence lasted through twelve flashes of the *Walk* sign on the other side of the avenue. Cal licked his lips. "Now, that's a fine pair of legs," he critiqued out loud, his train of thought about the last sales call completely missing the station.

I thought, *Hello, businesswomen are a hell of a lot more than a pair of legs!*

Cal turned toward me. He scanned my legs, from my skirt hem just above my knees down to my navy pump on the brake pedal and the one hovering over the gas pedal. He smiled, put his left hand on my right thigh, and offered me a look of consolation along with his appraisal. "You know, you're sexy, Janiece. All the guys on the sales team would love to tag you. Hell, I'd even go for you if I weren't your boss. But to be brutally honest, you're above average . . . but she's a goddess! She must work out! Did you see those thighs? I wonder who she works for. Maybe we should follow her and do some cold-calling."

"Cal, get your hand off me." I flinched and hit the gas. "You already know we're just barely going to be on time for our next appointment on the other side of town."

I wasn't sure what I could say. He was my new manager, and we hadn't begun to establish a solid working relationship yet.

Jaw tightened, I looked straight ahead, focusing on driving. Cal rubbed his hands together and gazed wistfully out the window behind me, then rotated his torso to look out the back window as the woman in the raincoat entered an office building. It took him another half mile after she disappeared to return to his thoughts about the last sales call.

I lost all respect for this man and couldn't have cared less about his sales-management expertise, so I remained silent. We made two more calls, and he was jovial with customers, but Cal didn't look me in the eyes the rest of the day. He saw nothing wrong with his behavior or comments, or if he did, he didn't admit or apologize for it. He simply reviewed the calls. I couldn't wait for the workday to be over. I never reported him, but I started looking for another job that evening.

#MeToo, Janiece

Did Cal's unwelcome looking over, touching, and commenting about Janiece's body and his loss of focus on the job constitute sexual harassment? Sexual assault? Sexual abuse? None of these? Something else? If you're like most people, the laws governing sexual misconduct aren't as familiar to you as other laws that might impact you more frequently, such as laws against using your cell phone while driving. Perhaps you skimmed over your employee handbook or walked right past the EEOC poster in your company's break room. It's possible many of us are not completely clear on what would fall under the definition of sexual harassment in the workplace and in other public places or how sexual harassment and discrimination differ from sexual abuse or sexual assault.

In a coaching conversation, it's essential that coach and client have a clear understanding of what the client means by the words they use. Coaches listen and ask questions to clarify what exactly the client wants to communicate. To have meaningful conversations, all involved must look at sexual discrimination, sexual harassment, sexual abuse, and sexual assault and come to an agreement about what those words mean. If it's outside your realm of experience, it's even more essential for you. Please don't skim over this chapter. It may seem tedious or uncomfortable, but it will raise awareness and help facilitate honest conversations that can lead to change. Note any thoughts that come to your mind as you are taking in this information.

What Is Sexual Harassment?

The legal definition of sexual harassment is helpful to assess and define questionable behaviors like Cal's in the story here. Title VII of the Civil Rights Act of 1964 states:

> It shall be an unlawful employment practice for an employer . . . to discriminate against any individual with respect to his compensation, terms, conditions, or privileges of employment, because of such individual's race, color, religion, sex, or national origin. (Title VII, Civil Rights Act of 1964)

Anyone who's not sure what sexual harassment is can check the legal description in the Civil Rights Act: "Sexual harassment, specifically targeting members of a sex, is a form of harassment which can range from hostile work environment to unwelcome physical contact to quid pro quo demands for sexual contact for a job, evaluation, or promotion, to retaliation for complaint of, testimony of, or other opposition to work-related discriminatory practices."[1]

Sexual harassment is a form of sex discrimination prohibited by Title VII, which also makes it illegal to retaliate against a person for complaining about or reporting discrimination, filing a charge of discrimination, or participating in an employment discrimination investigation or lawsuit. Title VII applies to employers with fifteen or more employees, as well as federal, state, and local governments; employment agencies; labor organizations; and those receiving government funds for any government purposes, including contractors, grantees, or schools. Sexual harassment consists of (but is not limited to): unwelcome sexual advances, requests for sexual favors, or other verbal or physical conduct by or directed at either gender, if they are used to sexually coerce or to create a hostile work environment. (The "hostile environment" standard also applies to harassment on the bases of race, color, national origin, religion, age, and disability.) The behavior does not have to be of a sexual nature. It can include offensive remarks related to a person's sex. For example, making offensive comments about women or men in general can be deemed sexual harassment.

There are two general categories of sexual harassment: quid pro quo and hostile work environments. Sexual harassment may include unwelcome sexual advances, requests for sexual favors, or other sexual language, conduct, or expression when:

1. Submission to the conduct is an explicit or implicit term or condition of employment (quid pro quo);
2. Submission to or rejection of the conduct influences employment decisions affecting the individual (quid pro quo);
3. The conduct has the purpose or effect of interfering with an individual's work performance or creating an intimidating, hostile, or offensive work environment.

Examples of sexual harassment may include (but are not limited to) persistent unwanted courting, unwelcome touching, physically restricting an individual (cornering), sexual innuendos, pranks, teasing, hazing, and other sexual talk such as jokes, personal inquiries, and gender-based remarks intended or perceived as put-downs.

Harassment may show up in more subtle ways that make a workplace very challenging for the victim.

> Offensive conduct may include, but is not limited to, offensive jokes, slurs, epithets or name calling, physical assaults or threats, intimidation, ridicule or mockery, insults or put-downs, offensive objects or pictures, and interference with work performance. Harassment can occur in a variety of circumstances such as the following: The harasser can be the victim's supervisor, a supervisor in another area, an agent of the employer, a co-worker, or a non-employee; The victim can be anyone affected by the offensive conduct; Unlawful harassment may occur without economic injury to, or discharge of, the victim.[2]

Examples of harassment also include (but are not limited to) remarks, gestures, physical contact, or display or circulation of offensive or explicit written/printed materials, pictures, or other items which could be considered as derogatory, abusive, degrading, or demeaning or have the purpose or effect of interfering with an employee's work performance or creating an intimidating, hostile, or offensive working environment on the basis of one of the protected categories identified above. It also includes more subtle forms of behavior, such as offensive posters, cartoons, and caricatures when they contribute to a hostile working environment. Petty slights, annoyances, and isolated incidents (unless extremely serious) will not rise to the level of illegality. To be unlawful, the conduct must create a work environment that would be intimidating, hostile, or offensive to reasonable people.[3]

Reports of harassment are on the rise. The Equal Employment Opportunity Commission reported a 13.6 percent increase in sexual harassment claims from fiscal year 2017 to fiscal year 2018.[4] According to a 2018 study, 38 percent of women and 13 percent of men reported being harassed at work.[5] Less common is harassment at school: 30 percent of women and 14 percent of men reported having been harassed in primary or secondary school, and 16 percent of women and 6 percent of men said they were harassed at a college or university.[6]

Street Harassment

I've heard it all, from "Hey baby, smile!" to "I can make that . . . purr!" Harassment happens all the time in public places. According to the nonprofit organization Stop Street Harassment (SSH),

> the most common place to experience sexual harassment is a public space like the street or a store, with 65 percent of women and 19 percent of men reporting harassment in such places. This includes but is not limited to catcalls, sexually explicit comments, sexist remarks, homophobic slurs, groping, leering, stalking, flashing, masturbating, and assault. Most women and some men will face gender-based street harassment by strangers in their life. Street harassment limits people's mobility and access to public spaces. It is a form of gender violence, and it's a human rights violation.[7]

Street or public harassment happens all around the world. In a recent study, 65 percent of women reported being harassed in public spaces. That's approximately 104 million women in the USA.[8] We'll get into the impacts of harassment later in the book, but consider the facts you've read about harassment. Have you ever experienced or witnessed harassment? Have you ever been a harasser? Sexual harassment can happen to anyone.

Sexual abuse goes beyond harassment. Sexual abusers target the most vulnerable, those who are either too young or incapable of protecting themselves from the perpetrator's behaviors.

What Is Sexual Abuse?

Given the prevalence of sexual abuse and how many abuse stories surfaced during the #MeToo firestorm, it's important to know what sexual abuse is and how to recognize it.

According to *Merriam-Webster Dictionary*, sexual abuse is:

1a: the infliction of sexual contact upon a person by forcible compulsion
   b: the engaging in sexual contact with a person who is below a specified age or who is incapable of giving consent because of age or mental or physical incapacity
2: the crime of engaging in or inflicting sexual abuse. [9]

Like harassment, sexual abuse is perpetrated against a person and lacks consent of the victim. Consent is the differentiator between sexual acts that are legal and those that are illegal. Because children (and some adults with a physical or mental incapacity) are unable to give consent with an adult's mature perspective, sexual abuse has been recognized specifically as a type of child maltreatment in US federal law since the initial congressional hearings on child abuse in 1973. The details of sexual abuse laws vary by state, but certain features of these laws are common to all states. Sexual abuse is illegal in every state as well as by federal law in the United States.[10]

I was abused beginning at age seven. Twenty-eight to 33 percent of women and 12 to 18 percent of men were victims of childhood or adolescent sexual abuse.[11] Incidences of sexual abuse that do not include touch and other types of sexual abuse called covert sexual abuse (including role distortions and boundary violations) are reported less often, which means the number of individuals who have been sexually abused in their childhood may actually be greater.[12] Out of the yearly 63,000[13] child sexual abuse cases substantiated, or found to have strong evidence, by Child Protective Services (CPS), 80 percent of perpetrators were a parent, 6 percent were other relatives, 5 percent were "other" (from siblings to strangers), and 4 percent were unmarried partners of a parent.[14]

All my abusers were male, as are the vast majority of sexual abusers. Out of the sexual abuse cases reported to CPS in 2013, 47,000 men and 5,000 women were the alleged perpetrators.[15] In 88 percent of the sexual abuse claims that CPS substantiates or finds supporting evidence of, the perpetrator is male. In 9 percent of cases, they are female, and 3 percent are unknown.[16]

My psychologist told me that my abuse had been severe. According to Dr. Dan Allender's book *The Wounded Heart*, sexual abuse may consist of behaviors that range in severity from mild to extremely severe. Dr. Allender says,

> Sexual abuse often follows a typical sequence of stages: (1) development of intimacy and secrecy, (2) enjoyment of physical touch that appears appropriate, (3) sexual abuse proper (physical contact or psychological interaction), and (4) maintenance of the abuse and shameful secret through threats and privileges.[17]

There may be exceptions to the general pattern, but the stages are present in most cases.

I've forgotten much of my childhood. It is quite common for people who were victims of childhood sexual abuse to disconnect from or lose memories of the abuse. One of the distinguishing elements of sexual abuse is betrayal. Most victims are abused by someone they know, most often a parent, close relative, or trusted adult in a position of leadership in their life. One effect of betrayal is refusal to trust, and another impact can be loss of memories.

Jennifer J. Freyd's book *Betrayal Trauma: The Logic of Forgetting Childhood Abuse* explains psychogenic amnesia, the phenomenon of lost memories of abuse at the hands of a parent or caregiver. Betrayal trauma blocks memories and information that would interfere with one's ability to function within an essential relationship such as that of a parent and child. Freyd writes,

> Survivors of childhood abuse and betrayal trauma have learned to cope by being disconnected internally so as to manage a minimal kind of external connection. But with adult freedom and responsibility come the potential to break silence, to use voice and language to promote internal integration, deeper external connection and social transformation. Through communication—integration within ourselves and connection between individuals—we can become whole: embodied, aware, vital, powerful."[18]

With an opportunity to connect and share stories, often for the first time, #MeToo has helped some adult survivors of childhood sexual abuse to tend their wounded hearts and seek healing.

What Constitutes Sexual Assault?

Sexual assault is the most severe type of sexual violence. Sexual assault is defined as follows: illegal sexual contact inflicted upon a person without consent or inflicted upon a person who is incapable of giving consent (because of age or physical or mental incapacity) or inflicted upon a person who places the assailant (such as a doctor) in a position of trust or authority. These crimes include attacks or attempted attacks generally involving unwanted sexual contact between victim and offender. Sexual assaults may or may not involve force and include such things as grabbing or fondling. Sexual assault also includes verbal threats. Sexual assault consists of a wide range of victimizations that may be separate from rape or attempted rape.

In 2018 the legal definition of rape in the United States was defined by the Department of Justice Uniform Crime Reporting (UCR) Program as "penetration, no matter how slight, of the vagina or anus with any body part or object, or oral penetration by a sex organ of another person, without the consent of the victim."

According to the US Department of Justice's Office of Justice Programs' Bureau of Justice Statistics 2016 report, rape is defined as "coerced or forced sexual intercourse. Forced sexual intercourse means vaginal, anal, or oral penetration by the offender(s)." This category could include incidents where the penetration was from a foreign object such as a bottle. It also includes attempted rapes, male and female targets, and both heterosexual and same-sex rape. Attempted rape includes verbal threats of rape. Depending on which US political party is in office, definitions may change.

The statistics about rape vary. RAINN (Rape, Abuse & Incest National Network) is the nation's largest anti-sexual-violence organization. RAINN created and operates the National Sexual Assault Hotline (800.656.HOPE, online.rainn.org, or the Spanish website rainn.org/es) in partnership with more than 1,000 local sexual-assault service providers across the country and operates the DoD Safe Helpline for the Department of Defense. RAINN also carries out programs to prevent sexual violence, help survivors, and ensure that perpetrators are brought to justice. According to RAINN, every ninety-eight seconds, a person is sexually assaulted. Male-perpetrated sexual victimization is a chronic problem. Of the women who reported rape or sexual assault in the National Crime Victimization Study, 96 percent were assaulted by men. There are, however, women perpetrators who assault both men and other women. In *Scientific American*, Lara Stemple and Ilan H. Meyer wrote, "Women who commit sexual victimization are more likely to have an extensive history of sexual abuse, with more perpetrators and at earlier ages than those who commit other crimes."[19]

RAINN reports that by far the greatest number of victims of sexual assault are women. According to their website,

> as of 1998, an estimated 17.7 million American women had been victims of attempted or completed rape. Ninety percent of adult rape victims are female. Young women are especially at risk because 82 percent of all juvenile victims are female. Females ages sixteen to nineteen are four times more likely than the general population to be victims of rape, attempted rape, or sexual assault. Women ages eighteen to twenty-four who are college students are three times more likely than women in general to experience sexual violence. Females of the same age who are not enrolled in college are four times more likely.[20]

Men also experience sexual assault. As with sexual violence against women, the majority of sexual violence against men is perpetrated by heterosexual males, who use sex as a weapon to dominate. The numbers show,

> as of 1998, 2.78 million men in the US had been victims of attempted or completed rape. About 3 percent of American men, one in thirty-three, have experienced an attempted or completed rape in their lifetime. One out of every ten rape victims are male." In their most recent report, Centers for Disease Control found that "nearly one in five women and one in seventy-one men have been raped in their lifetimes."[21]

If men are wondering why rape is such a big deal, imagine having a 20 percent chance of being raped instead of a 1.4 percent chance of being raped, with all of the impacts and costs to the victim. If one of every five of the guys you socialize with or work with were going to be victimized, instead of one in seventy-one, it would be a very big deal to men too.

RAINN reports that sexual assaults are decreasing in the United States but that perpetrators are still for the most part not being held accountable for their crimes. "While we're making progress—the number of assaults has fallen by more than half since 1993—even today, only six out of every 1,000 rapists will end up in prison."[22]

What do the numbers look like outside the US for sexual assaults? How do other countries handle punishment for this crime? What about harassment and abuse statistics outside the US? Are the statistics similar? Given the low percentage of those doing time for their crimes, it may come as no surprise that many victims choose not to report the assault. This is also true for harassment and abuse. Let's examine some of the reasons for keeping silent.

Why Don't Victims Report?

There are many reasons for not reporting assault, not the least of which is fear of greater harm to oneself or loved ones. I was the victim of sexual assaults from multiple perpetrators, but I didn't report a single one, and none of the perpetrators ended up in prison.

A 2013 study found that rape is grossly underreported in the United States.[23] A 2014 report by the Department of Justice estimated that only 34.8 percent of cases of sexual assaults are reported to the authorities.[24] Another 2014 study determined that police departments eliminate or undercount rapes from official records in part to "create the illusion of success in fighting violent crime."[25]

Harassment is also underreported. In a 2018 survey, of those who experienced sexual harassment, less than 10 percent of both women and men said they had filed an official complaint or report about the experience.[26]

Sexual harassment in the workplace often goes unreported for other reasons. There is lack of confidence in the company's willingness to enforce policies, fear of threats and retaliation by the perpetrator and by the organization, and fear of not being believed and compounding the pain, shaming the victim.

Sexual harassment in public places is also unreported. If the time and hassle to report is not worth the results, if the perpetrator of the harassing behavior is unlikely to face any significant consequences, if the victim fears a risk of escalation, then she (or he) is unlikely to report the incident. When shame or blame is placed on the victim after reporting the harassment incident, it makes perfect sense for the victim to ignore the incident and move on with her life, but that doesn't remove the experience of harassment. The harassment wound remains and is compounded by the lack of support for the victim.

The reasons victims of harassment, abuse, and assault don't report vary, depending on the circumstances, but there are common threads. In cases of childhood sexual abuse, the child's brain is not fully developed. Abusers are frequently related to the child or are close to the child's family or are in a position of leadership. The perpetrators are skilled in reading opportunities, in luring and grooming the child, and in gaining silence after or throughout the abuse through threats, fear, or other manipulation of the child's developing brain.

In my case, I was told by one abuser that if I ever revealed the abuse, he would go to jail and die, and it would be my fault. Another told me it would kill my mother, who had been sick for most of my life. Another simply said, "Don't ever tell. You'll be sorry if you do." As a child, I had limited ability to assess the risk of threats. Other abusers threaten death to the child, their pets or family, or worse. To a child who has no choice but to live with her abusers, silence about her traumatic experiences seems a small price to pay to be sure worse things don't happen to her or to others. Keeping the secret may appear to be the best or only option. And when there are deeply traumatic experiences, abuse memories may not resurface until triggered, years later, as an adult.[27]

The Common Thread—Lack of Consent

A quick review of the paragraphs above about sexual harassment, sexual abuse, sexual assault, and rape reveals a common thread: lack of consent. Consent comes from the Latin roots *con*, meaning *with or together*, and *sentire*, meaning *to feel*. When someone voluntarily chooses to go along with another's actions, they give permission or agreement, *consent*.

Laws vary in each US state regarding the age of consent for sexual intimacy. Laws seek to protect those who are incapable of consent because of their stage of brain development, consciousness and awareness, mental capacity, or other limitations. Consent cannot be given if someone is under the influence of drugs, if they are intoxicated by alcohol, if they are asleep or unconscious, or if they have Alzheimer's or another disease that impacts their brain function. Getting a person drunk so you can have sex with them is an example of nonconsensual sex. According to consent laws, you can be found guilty of incapacitating victims by using substances prior to engaging in sexual acts that render the victim incapable of giving consent. The moment someone enters a state where consent is not possible, sexual acts are no longer consensual (there is no more consent from that person). Nonconsensual sexual acts are assault. Nonconsensual sex is rape.

Crying Wolf—How Pervasive Are False Accusations?

For those who are bearing the costs of a false accusation, whether damage to your reputation, loss of a job or relationships, or even a felony, I'm truly sorry that you've suffered. If you and the purported victim are both clear on what happened and there was clarity about consent (including legal age and no mental incapacity,) injustice stinks. The only redeeming results are that you may become vigilant to avoid situations where lines are blurred, and possibly you will have more compassion for others who have suffered in the same way. The good news is that the way others treat you in your past does not have to define your future. Please keep reading, there is material in upcoming chapters that you may find useful.

That being said, false reports are the exception. It's more likely a victim doesn't report to the police. About two of every three victims don't file police reports. The prevalence of false reporting is low, between 2 and 10 percent. The National Sexual Violence Resource Center reported:

> A study of eight US communities, which included 2,059 cases of sexual assault, found a 7.1% rate of false reports (i). A study of 136 sexual assault cases in Boston found a 5.9% rate of false reports (h). Researchers studied 812 reports of sexual assault from 2000–2003 and found a 2.1% rate of false reports (g).[28]

As of July 2019, I could find no current, peer-reviewed research that offers consistent data on how many reports are true versus how many are unsubstantiated. Nor is there current research where authors can look for data and draw different conclusions about the prevalence and nature of unsubstantiated reports. The words *false* and *unsubstantiated* have different meanings. If something is false, it's patently not true, whereas unsubstantiated may mean there is not enough evidence, such as too few witnesses available in a certain jurisdiction or rape kits were not used or the rape kits were improperly used, or DNA testing was not done to support the victim's testimony or report. When current statistics about crime reporting offer differing results, it may be an indicator that more studies are needed to acquire data that are consistent and accurate. This information would help legal authorities and the general public agree about how many reports are not substantiated and why. Whether reported, substantiated, or not, there's ample evidence that sexual discrimination, harassment, abuse, and assault have a cost for the victim and society.

Questions to Thoughtfully Consider and Discuss

1. What is your personal experience with sexual harassment?
2. What responsibility do companies have to prevent harassment?
3. What do you do with harassment that is subtle?
4. Who bears responsibility for providing safe streets and public places?
5. What is your experience with sexual abuse?
6. What is your personal experience with assault or attempted assault?
7. Considering what we know about abuse trauma, how long should victims be given to seek legal restitution?
8. Under what conditions, if any, is there ambiguity about consent?
9. If there is not positive consent or there are questions or mixed signals, what should a person do?
10. What actions will you take as a result of reading this chapter?

FOUR

So What's the Big Deal?

Don used to joke around with everyone on what we called "the crew." There was a feeling of camaraderie that made work fun at this summer job in door-to-door sales in neighborhoods not far from my home. Don was sales manager and part owner of the company and made up nicknames for each person on every crew. Most were sarcastic. I didn't know most of my co-workers' real names. Everyone called the boss Big Don.

Don often stared at me, but he hadn't given me a nickname. My second week with the company, Don invited me to sit in the front passenger seat of his Cadillac when we went out on sales calls. Some co-workers were annoyed. They considered it a place of honor and had been vying for that spot. Even if someone finished their calls before me, Don always saved that seat for me.

One day Don announced, "Come on, everybody, we're going for pizza. RC, you sit in the front."

I headed for the back door of another driver's car.

"Where you going, RC? I told you to sit in the front of my car." Don looked directly at my crotch.

I asked one of his crew leaders if she thought he was talking to me, and she assured me he was. I complied that day but started looking for other drivers after my calls.

Over the next month, Don got more and more friendly. One evening at dinner, he came over and rubbed his thigh against my leg. "What's the matter, RC? Don't you want to ride with Big Don?"

I inched away. "I just want to share the honor with others on the team."

He scowled.

"What's RC for?" I asked.

Don burst out laughing. "Rib Crunchers! You know those gorgeous thighs would crunch any college boy's ribs. That's why you need a real man like Big Don!" He leaned in to me. "Let's you and me ride together tonight, RC." Even team members whose first language wasn't English knew it was clearly a proposition.

Don's raucous laughter drew the stares of several team members. I was relieved when a crew leader stepped up and asked Don a question. Blushing, I picked up my plate and moved to a different table.

After that evening, I steered clear of Don, but the easy camaraderie with the team turned into strained silence. I needed the money for school, so I couldn't quit. On my last day, Don ogled me. "I'm sure gonna miss those RC legs, kid. Come on back next summer. If you want the job, it's yours."

Later I learned that my sales had earned me a free four-day vacation prize in a sales contest, but I declined because Don would be there.

#MeToo, Tami

Often the response of those who can't relate to stories like Tami's is callous questioning: That was a long time ago, so what's the big deal? Why can't you just get over it? Why is this coming up now? Why can't you move on? What difference does it make? But even for the victim of what may be considered the least significant form of sexual discrimination or violence, there is a loss. To minimize or deny this damage is to compound the original loss.

Severity and depth of impacts to the victim depend on the nature of the offense, the environment and relational closeness of the perpetrator, the age and maturity of the victim, and the degree of care that was received at the time of the wound. Being raped by an acquaintance, while severely damaging, is less damaging than being raped by a family member, and both are significantly more severe than the catcall of a stranger on a street corner.

Impacts can be immediate and long term. One immediate impact is the adjustments victims must make to find a sense of safety. In a 2018 survey on harassment, 23 percent of women and 12 percent of men said they changed a regular routine or travel route to avoid repeated harassment.[1] Few studies have attempted to calculate the magnitude of damage experienced by targets, perpetrators, and society at large resulting from sexual harassment, abuse, assault, and rape. I hope that by reading this chapter you will see the tip of the iceberg, and it will cause you to stop and consider the costs of these actions to the victims and to society.

The Damage from Sexual Harassment

In addition to losing out on earnings (her trip), Tami was demoralized by the harassment she endured at work and by the resulting ostracization from her co-workers. Harassment often takes an emotional and psychological toll on the victim. In a 2018 survey, 31 percent of women and 20 percent of men who reported being harassed also reported feeling anxiety or depression as a result.[2]

When harassment happens early in a person's career, as it did to Tami, the impacts can snowball and be cumulative over the course of their career. Dartmouth Associate Professor of Sociology Jason N. Houle wrote about a 2011 study on the impact of sexual harassment that happens early in one's career: "Consistent with stress research, our quantitative analyses indicate that harassment is a stressor that has a positive and linear relationship with depressive affect for both men and women, even after controlling for past depressive symptoms, harassment experiences, and other workplace stressors." [3] The data showed that the effects of harassment are lasting, in part because of the increased stress. Houle reported "a growing body of high-quality research has consistently shown negative effects of workplace harassment on mental health."[4] Sexual harassment leads to symptoms of depression for women and men. The study said that harassed workers feel annoyed, angry, and conflicted and that these emotions lead to self-blame and self-doubt.

It's essential for all of us to know how deep the impacts of sexual harassment and violence truly are and how long lasting. Like Big Don in Tami's story, harassers don't consider the impacts of their words or behavior. If they stopped to count the cost to the individual, to their business, and to society, they might make different choices about how to use their words or their bodies. After we count the costs of sexual harassment and violence, we will look into how we all can influence the Big Dons in our lives to start counting the costs and making better choices. For now, please stay with us while we're looking into the impacts to victims.

Far beyond immediate stress from harassment, a victim faces impacts going further than the human psyche. In allowing ongoing harassment and sexual violence in the workplace, society pays long-term costs for injuries inflicted by the perpetrators. Physical impacts and economic costs to the victim are compounded by very high costs to business and society at large. Apart from the financial costs, victims pay physical costs that we can barely imagine.

Physical Impacts

Impacts to health of victims are deeper than any initial physical wounds of sexual harassment or assault. In more than a dozen other studies over the past decade, researchers have documented other physical symptoms caused by sexual harassment, such as headaches, gastrointestinal problems, and disrupted sleep.

Epidemiologist Rebecca Thurston studied female sexual abuse and harassment victims. In her research she learned that stress from the trauma of sexual harassment over time is like a poison, stiffening women's blood vessels, worsening blood flow, and harming the inner lining of their hearts.[5]

Often people think harassment is a one-time event, but as in Tami's story, it happens over a period of time. The ongoing, prolonged stress creates lasting physiological reactions, increasing long-term risk for heart attacks and strokes. An article in the *Chicago Tribune* referred to a six-year study that consisted of 1,654 employees at a midwestern university, published in the 2005 *Journal of Business and Psychology*, finding that those who experienced sexual harassment were more likely to be sick or in accidents after they had experienced the harassment. Years later, the harassment continued to elevate rates of illness, injury, and accident.[6]

Long after the harassment ends, depression, anxiety, PTSD, and other disorders continue. Studies show sexual harassment increases risk of substance abuse and alcoholism. Harassed women develop eating disorders at a higher rate than the general population, and even those who are present in harassment situations experience lasting effects from the trauma.[7] Even if they're not paying for healthcare themselves, victims can be impoverished by other costs they don't deserve to bear, including long-term financial impacts.

Economic Impacts

Harassment can reduce the victim's earnings. After experiencing sexual harassment, nearly one in ten women sought a new job assignment, changed jobs, or quit a job because of the abuse, as did one in twenty men.[8] Women harassed early on in their careers often accept lower-paid or underpaid work so they can leave a hostile work environment, and many never recover the momentum lost on their career journeys; men with disrupted work histories, however, often do not take lesser-paid jobs.[9]

If an employee is given a poor evaluation, is not considered for jobs, or is demoted for refusing to give quid pro quo, or if the employee left because of a hostile work environment, it's likely they will experience a decrease in standard of living, increased medical expenses, and increased counseling and mental health expenses. The victim is not the only one who is negatively impacted by financial loss due to harassment. Go deeper and you'll find the costs spread far wider than we normally think. Our employers and their customers also pay dearly for some people's misbehavior.

Costs to Business

Financial costs extend not only to the victim but also to witnesses who experience retaliation, illegal under law, as well as to businesses. A typical Fortune 500 corporation that tolerates sexual harassment incidents will lose $14.02 million annually (adjusted for inflation) because of absenteeism, decreased productivity, increased healthcare costs, and employee turnover.[10]

The California Coalition Against Sexual Assault released a report in January 2018, *The Cost and Consequences of Sexual Violence in California* (Miller, Fulton, & Lee 2018), detailing the financial costs of responding to sexual violence without consideration of investment in prevention. In 2012, tangible costs associated with sexual violence in the state of California (including medical care, mental healthcare, property damage, victim services, and adjudication) were over $9 billion, while intangible costs, including lost work productivity and lost wages, were over $130 billion.[11]

The National Academy of Sciences released a report, *Sexual Harassment of Women: Climate, Culture, and Consequences in Academic Sciences, Engineering, and Medicine*, that documents many researchers' speaking up about the harassment and abuse they have faced throughout their careers. Many women working in scientific careers tolerate harassment as part of this career choice.

Harassment also negatively impacts scientific scholarship. It is impossible to measure the costs of lost creativity and innovation in psychologically and physically unsafe workplace cultures where harassment is tolerated. An article in *Scientific American* by Seattle 500 Scientists, a community of women scientists in the Salish Sea area—which includes Vancouver, British Columbia, and Seattle, home to many large employers such as Starbucks, Microsoft, Google, and Amazon—asserts,

> The pervasiveness of harassment, abuse, and bias has a real cost for both individual scientists and for the overall advancement of science. Tolerating bad behavior means wasted tax dollars, disrupted scientific advancements, and weakened innovation. And those who perpetuate this culture of harassment and bias are not just jerks whose bad behavior can be separated from their otherwise good scholarship, but a real and serious impediment to scientific progress. [12]

If there are hidden costs in the scientific community, there are hidden costs in other disciplines, and we will learn more about them later. For now, it's important to recognize that harassment is prevalent and costly to our society.

The Damage from Sexual Abuse

Sexual abusers are motivated by their desire to control, possess, get revenge, or destroy. In *The Wounded Heart*, Dr. Dan Allender describes what happens when a child is abused or assaulted. There is usually (but not always) an effort on the part of the abuser to "groom" the child by creating a false relational intimacy, followed by what seems like life-giving touch, a seduction that breaks the child's will, and threats or promises from the abuser gaining the silence of the victim. The victim feels profoundly powerless, resulting in a loss of a sense of pain by a process of splitting, denial, and memory loss. This can lead to a loss of a sense of self, where the child shrinks back from the hunger and thirst for all that makes them feel alive. Numbness allows them to survive, and they can carry this numbness into adulthood. This is often followed by a loss of judgment about relationships. A child who feels extremely powerless grows up believing she is deeply inadequate.

In a healthy, nurturing environment where children are treated with sensitivity and compassion, there is rarely abuse. The betrayal an abused child or teenager experiences comes from not only the sexual abuse but also the failure of the family to create a nurturing, safe home, leaving them with no refuge. A betrayed child internalizes damage. This leaves them hypervigilant, filled with suspicion of others' motives, and relationally distorted, which makes deep relationships nearly impossible. They lose hope for intimacy, strength, and justice, and they see themselves as deeply flawed.

A child may feel or be unaware of an internalized ambivalence that comes from having authentic need for a relationship met by an abuser who creates at the same time the deepest harm possible through betrayal. The ambivalence leads to intense shame and contempt that may be directed at self, others, or both. This leads to a fear of pleasure and desire (for almost anything), an increased chance of revictimization, and ongoing patterns of compulsivity or addictive behavior. As a result, the person who was abused may have a subconscious image of self as a whore. Victims of sexual abuse often fight depression; sexual dysfunction; addictions; compulsive disorders, including eating disorders; stress-induced physical symptoms; low self-esteem; and unhealthy ways of relating to others.[13]

Healthcare costs are 16 percent higher for women who were sexually abused as children and 36 percent higher for women who were physically and sexually abused as children. Additionally, sexual abuse often has a negative impact on children's educational attainment, later job performance, and future earnings. Sexual violence survivors experience reduced income in adulthood as a result of victimization in adolescence, with an average lifetime income loss estimated at over $255,000 ($241,600 in 2008).[14] The perpetrator isn't considering any of these costs when he makes his personal gratification a priority. The victim's family, friends, and co-workers are usually unaware of the damage and high costs the victim is paying for the perpetrator's decisions.

We've looked at a non-exhaustive list of some of the consequence of sexual abuse to the victim and the greater community. Given the high costs to sexual abuse victims and the ongoing impacts to their future educators, employers, families, and communities, it is increasingly clear that sexual abuse can no longer be considered "someone else's problem."

The Damage from Sexual Assault

Of all crimes, rape carries the heaviest cost to the victim. In the US alone, the total estimated cost is $127 billion a year (excluding the cost of child sexual abuse). In 2008, researchers estimated that each rape cost approximately $151,423, including care for the victim, tests and time spent by medical staff, facilities costs, administrative costs, and more. The same study found that violence and abuse constituted up to 37.5 percent of total healthcare costs, or up to $750 billion.[15]

According to a 2011 study, "Sexual assault is associated with greater psychological harm than any other crimes."[16] Eighty-one percent of women and 35 percent of men who report assault report significant short- or long-term impacts like PTSD.[17] There is also an increased risk of future victimization. Both female and male victims are more likely to be assaulted at a future time than those who have never been assaulted.

Military Sexual Assault

The Uniformed Services University Center for Deployment Psychology highlights how particularly damaging sexual assault is in the military. Victims and perpetrators are part of a small, trusted community of people who are supposed to be there for you in a life-or-death situation. Violating a fellow service member shreds the fabric of the military culture, which can be essential for survival. Victims of military sexual assault (MSA) often know, work with, or live in proximity to the assailant. The aspect of closeness of a community that works, plays, and lives together makes it much more difficult to report MSA. Fear of reprisal from the perpetrator, who may be in a position of greater authority; fear of losing out on advancement opportunities; and fear of being shunned by the community all make the choice not to report seem to be the better option.

The psychological consequences of MSA, including PTSD, depression, substance abuse, insomnia, and even suicide are compounded if the assault is same sex. According to USU/CDP,

> following the assault, heterosexual male survivors often report concerns regarding their masculinity and sexual orientation. Although the assault was clearly an act of power and dominance, male survivors often feel that they were targeted for being effeminate or standing out in some way. It is important to provide psychoeducation on male rape myths and emphasize that the assault was not consensual. Healthcare providers should also underscore that, even if the MSA survivor experienced some sexual arousal during the assault, this does not imply willing participation.[18]

Family and loved ones of those who are harmed by assault also deal with extra stress and the emotional, mental, physical, and financial costs of supporting the victim through whatever they need for healing, especially if they are able to offer support. In the many cases where the victim does not report or may not disclose the assault for cultural reasons (in some cultures it can lead to the death or shunning of the victim), relationships can go through turbulent periods as the family and friends may experience an inexplicable distance and lack of trust from the victim.

Below the Waterline

Data in this chapter represents the tip of the iceberg of negative impacts of sexual harassment and violence in the United States alone. The global damage is vast and cannot be calculated but is real, nevertheless, and grows daily as sexual discrimination, harassment, abuse, and assaults continue. Once inflicted, damage to the victim can't be undone, and relational costs and damages to human potential extend below the waterline, far beyond known costs that impact the victim, families and friends, healthcare systems, and businesses, and therefore impoverish economies—local, regional, national, and global.

It's fair to say the world is paying ridiculously tremendous unnamed costs when we tolerate sexual discrimination and violence. Beyond physical, emotional, psychological, and financial, costs are paid in relationships and in the fabric of our cultures. In my own case, years of personal counseling helped me arrive at an understanding of how the wreckage has impacted me and others without my knowledge. I can't put monetary value on what we have lost as a result of the damage incurred from growing up in an abusive home. I failed to contribute to my fullest potential: in my family and friendships, in the schools I attended, in the workplace, and in my community. By not living up to my potential, I missed decades of contributing my creativity, energy, talents, and resources, which were diverted or impaired due to the sexual abuse and violence I've lived through. What is the cost the world pays in lost potential from tolerating sexual discrimination, harassment, and violence?

I'm grateful for the healing I've experienced so far, and I'm committed to contributing to my fullest potential for as many years as I have left, yet I can't help but wonder, if this is true for me, how many billions of others are also affected? Victims. Families. Friends. Schools. Workplaces. Communities. Countries. The world. I wonder what our world could look like if every single human lived in an environment free from all sexual discrimination and violence.

As we continue to tolerate harassment, abuse, and assault, the world is paying countless hidden costs. The #MeToo movement is a pivotal moment in history that calls us to examine, assess, and decide whether the costs are worth any perceived gains. Things are changing.

Questions to Thoughtfully Consider and Discuss

1. Do you have a #MeToo story? How have you been impacted by sexual harassment, abuse, or assault (personally or through someone close to you or at your workplace)?
2. What harm is there in street harassment?
3. In addition to legal costs, what does an employer who tolerates harassment risk losing?
4. What does sexual abuse do to a family?
5. How do legal definitions, such as that of rape, impact society?
6. How does consent fit into the equation?
7. In what ways does rape cost society?
8. Who pays the costs of sexual violence?
9. What is the cost to society's ignoring the impacts of sexual violence?
10. What value is gained by limiting sexual expression to consensual situations?
11. Based on what you read in this chapter, what will you do or change?

FIVE

Part One:
What's Changed?

I moved to a smaller town at the age of thirteen. My parents were both busy, and I was befriended by the older, childless couple that managed the townhome complex near the beach where we stayed while my parents were shopping for a house. The couple earned my parents' and my trust by buying me trinkets and serving me treats. They took me to the beach, on shopping trips, and to restaurants. Being new in town and moving in at the start of the summer, I had no friends my age, so my parents were happy I was being entertained and didn't question the couple's motives.

That fall I started school and met some people who smoked pot. It was my first experience, so I got very high and very scared. I called the couple, and the wife sent her husband, the Captain, to pick me up.

When I got into the car, he asked me a couple of questions, then all of a sudden, he had his hands all over me, down my pants, and in my shirt. He was old and panting and sweating. I managed to struggle away, fall out of the car, and run. I was ashamed, so I never told anyone, ever. I was frightened and hid most of the time until we moved, which thankfully was shortly after! This is the first time I've told this story to anyone.

#MeToo, Nellie

I love vacations near the water, especially walks on the beach. Each day the beach carries signs of change. Rocks move. Shells and driftwood appear in new places. Occasionally, a major storm or tsunami will hit, and the margins of the beach will move significantly. Cataclysmic seismic events can move or remove the entire coastline. The impacts to the ecosystem are dramatic and longstanding. In a January 2018 article, *New York Times* contributing writers Natalie Proulx, Christopher Pepper, and Katherine Schulten stated, "The #MeToo movement has inspired a 'tsunami' of stories, from newspaper front pages to social media to private conversations between friends and relatives. It is, many believe, a watershed cultural moment."[1]

Like waves, ongoing actions and new initiatives taken in light of this movement appear to be having an impact. The ocean of change is too big to survey in this book, and I predict the changes will continue to ripple around the world long after it goes to print. So let's start by looking at a few changes that have already occurred: an increased openness to conversations around the topic of sexual violence; a backlash coming from a variety of sources; increased media exposure; impacts in the arts and culture; and increased movement in business, politics, and law, both nationally and globally. It's too early to tell if the waves of change will be significant enough to make a lasting change in the pattern of human relationships.

Openness to Conversations

If the goal of the #MeToo movement was to open conversations around the topic of sexual harassment and violence, it's been accomplished. A 2018 study by the Pew Research Center found that the hashtag was used more than 19 million times on Twitter since Milano's original tweet, more than 55,000 uses per day. The analysis shows that 29 percent of the #MeToo tweets during these periods were written in another language, with Afrikaans (7 percent of the total), Somali (4 percent), and Spanish (3 percent) comprising the greatest numbers of non-English tweets mentioning the hashtag over these time periods. [2]

Google's "Me Too Rising" project[3] tracks and visually displays search activity around #MeToo globally. Data shows this hashtag has been searched for all over the world. A Google search of "#MeToo conversations" on October 20, 2018, yielded approximately 35 million results; "Sexual harassment," 112 million; and "increased conversation around sexual harassment," 12.8 million. TED Talks offers a playlist featuring at least six TED Talks on the subject of sexual violence.[4]

Conversations about discrimination, harassment, and violence are leading change. Numerous articles tell you how to talk with your children about the movement and about sexuality free from violence. Articles online and in newspapers offer advice for parents about how to have conversations on this topic with their children.[5] Parents and educators are being equipped with curricula for speaking to young people about this topic. In January 2018, the nonprofit Stop Sexual Assault in Schools (SSAIS) launched #MeTooK12, "a campaign to promote awareness and inspire action to counteract pervasive sexual harassment and sexual violence in K-12 schools."[6] SSAIS claimed in 2018 to be "the only organization specifically created to address sexual harassment/assault and K-12 students' rights. With the increased attention on sexual assault on college campuses, it's time to address the epidemic of sexual harassment and assault impacting younger students."[7]

In addition to schools, this movement is making its way onto stages and into speeches engaging audiences for change. In a speech at Georgetown University's Law School on September 26, 2018, US Supreme Court Justice Ruth Bader Ginsburg (RBG) referred to the difference in her generation and today's women's freedom and courage to speak out about harassment: "These #MeToo complaints, every woman of my vintage has not just one story but many stories, but we thought there's nothing you can do about it. . . . Boys will be boys. So just find a way to get out of it."

RBG was encouraged by the fact that "Women nowadays are not silent about bad behavior."[8] The Harvard Business Review (HBR) did a podcast in March 2018 entitled *Work After #MeToo*.[9] HBR Editor Amy Bernstein said,

> This #MeToo moment is stunning to me because it represents such a sea change from the world I entered in 1982 when I graduated from college and went to work at a network news operation in New York. Sex was everywhere, but no one ever talked about harassment, and it never really entered my mind. And I am pretty sure that if a 20-something-year-old woman had brought up an unwanted advance in the office where I started at, she would've tanked her career. The change is that today I believe the complaint would be taken seriously.[10]

In November 2018 I had the privilege of being on a panel discussion at a small business conference. Conversations included creating safe company cultures. I've been invited by radio talk show hosts to discuss this topic on the air and have spoken to local Rotary clubs on creating a culture free of harassment and violence. From the grassroots level, around the world, conversations continue about sexual discrimination, harassment, and violence, and what to do about them. These discussions energize listeners and leaders to take action to create safer workplaces. At the same time, we've seen a backlash, and it's real.

The Backlash

There's no denying that conversations have led to a backlash, and not just by men who ridicule #MeToo but by those who fear the power of a woman's accusation, and some women who align with these men. In a joint survey by *Glamour* and *Esquire* magazines of 1,147 men (in the US), results published on May 30, 2018, 41 percent of men had not heard of #MeToo, 47 percent had not discussed it with anyone, and 31 percent had talked about it with a female friend. Eighty-four percent of men were worried that allegations of sexual misconduct would harm the reputations of men who don't deserve it.[11]

> The majority of men we surveyed in very top jobs still hadn't heard of Me Too. About one-third of men ages 18 to 55 say they're personally worried about being wrongly accused of sexual harassment at work. (Those with self-reported incomes over $100K were significantly more likely to be worried.) The data also shows that younger men are more likely to say Me Too will improve workplace equality.[12]

Discussing this book with male business associates raised issues about the costs of male responses to #MeToo within business relationships. One said he believes men in general are afraid of offending women, and they fear being in a position that might require them to defend themselves over a false accusation.

Another friend is an investor in a privately held company. Of its approximately 200 employees, over 90 percent are males. During the last six months of 2018, he observed that relationship dynamics changed in the company, estimating that 60 percent of communication was lost because male employees wouldn't say a word more than absolutely necessary to female employees. "The silence is deafening. The men are petrified of being accused of any impropriety that could impact their careers," he said. It resulted in severely strained working relationships between the males and females in the company. The communication problems are impacting relationships with customers, as much of the nuance of positive casual work relationships is missing from communication, and customer needs fall through the cracks. The owners are reticent to address the problem because so far, the males have denied there is any difference in their communications with the women who work directly with customers.

These men are not the only ones backing away from women in the workplace.

Across industries, "several major companies have told us they are now limiting travel between the genders," Johnny Taylor, president of the Society for Human Resource Management, told the *Chicago Tribune*, citing execs who tell men not to go on business trips or share rental cars with women co-workers. UCLA psychologist Kim Elsesser, the author of *Sex and the Office*, sees a nascent "sex partition." If men start to back away from women, at least in professional settings, it's difficult to see how that will aid the feminist cause.[13]

Another sign of backlash is an increase in the numbers of people who believe that false accusations of harassment are a bigger problem than unreported or unpunished attacks on women. In September 2018, males disavowing contact with females to avoid the (minimal) risk of false accusations hijacked use of the hashtags #HimToo and #HeToo.[14]

In November 2017, YouGov polled 1,500 Americans about sexual harassment (for the *Economist*). In September 2018, it conducted a similar poll. The share of American adults agreeing that men who sexually harassed women at work twenty years ago should keep their jobs rose from 28 percent to 36 percent. The proportion who think that women who complain about sexual harassment cause more problems than they solve grew from 29 percent to 31 percent. Eighteen percent now believe false accusations of sexual assault are a bigger problem than attacks that go unreported or unpunished, compared with 13 percent in 2017.[15]

On Tuesday, October 2, 2018, during the process of approving Brett Kavanaugh as Supreme Court Justice, President Donald Trump spoke of the possibility that men whose behavior is "exemplary" for their entire lives are presumed to be guilty should women accuse them of sexual misconduct to the press.[16] Trump, speaking to the press, said,

> It is a very scary time for young men in America, where you can be guilty of something you may not be guilty of. This is a very, very—this is a very difficult time. . . . What's happening here has much more to do than even the appointment of a Supreme Court justice.[17]

The Republican majority approved the appointment. A resurgence of the MeToo hashtag followed the testimonies of Kavanaugh and Dr. Christine Blasey Ford, who testified that Kavanaugh had assaulted her in high school. The Marist Institute for Public Opinion conducted a poll to see how people responded to the different testimonies of Ford and Kavanaugh. After hearing no evidence except the testimonies of the parties involved, of men, 39 percent believed Kavanaugh, and 37 percent believed Ford. Of women, 52 percent believed Ford, and 27 percent believed Kavanaugh. By political party, 80 percent of Democratic men believed Ford, as did 74 percent of Democratic women. Among Republicans, 77 percent of men believed Kavanaugh, as did 73 percent of women. Independent men split 39 percent to 35 percent, siding slightly more with Ford, but a solid majority of independent women believed Ford, 56 percent to 24 percent.[18]

The appointment was newsworthy for many reasons, one of which was the impact of #MeToo. In an October 2018 article in *Quartz* magazine, Ephrat Livni wrote,

> It seems that the story of #MeToo has turned into yet another opportunity for men to talk about themselves—how they've suffered as a result of accusations, or redeemed themselves and deserve our

attention again, or how the world's gone mad and lost its standards, or how they are allies and not bad guys. Whatever the response, men retain cultural dominance, so much so that a man like Kavanaugh, accused of attempted rape, can trigger fears that boys won't get to be boys anymore if women keep telling their stories."

Men's fear of accusations in a #MeToo era crosses racial barriers. Victor Morton wrote an article published in the *Washington Times* on October 19, 2019, which says in part:

Vernon Robinson, co-founder and treasurer of Black Americans for the President's Agenda, launched a full-force attack on the #MeToo movement in an interview with *The Washington Times* late Thursday evening, stating that black men will be harmed by junking the presumption of innocence and instead categorically believing all sexual misconduct accusers.

Fear spread beyond the workplace to relationships between the sexes in general. Mark Kern, a video game developer, tweeted new rules for navigating relationships:

Guys, first moves are over. Women, it's all you now. You have to call us, send us gifts, do all the asking out and paying for dinner, make the first move, and provide consent paperwork in triplicate for the goodnight kiss. We quit. (@grummz)[19]

Either the backlash is even stronger or #MeToo is getting little or no attention in the Middle East and countries with a strong culture of male dominance, including Mexico, Italy, India, and China. In Germany, for example, Nadja Schlueter, wrote in *Jetzt* magazine, a publication of the (Munich, Germany) *Süddeutsche Zeitung*, October 18, 2018,

#MeToo has become a joke since appearing a year ago; and almost always among men, robbing the words and issue of its "seriousness, weight, and relevance." [Because sexual violence isn't typically perpetrated by women against men in Germany] for women there is nothing funny in the words.[20]

The movement is not without its share of female critics: "I'm going to really hate myself for saying this, but I think by women speaking against all these things, it makes them look weak when they are very strong women," actress Lindsay Lohan said.[21]

A group of 100 women signatories on a letter published in *LeMonde* critiqued the French version of the movement, arguing that it leads to accusations that immediately silence men without giving them a chance to defend themselves. The letter explains that a woman's freedom to say no to a sexual proposition can't exist without the

freedom to bother. "We consider that one must know how to respond to this freedom to bother in ways other than by closing ourselves off in the role of the prey," the letter says. "Incidents that can affect a woman's body do not necessarily affect her dignity and must not, as difficult as they can be, necessarily make her a perpetual victim. Because we are not reducible to our bodies. Our inner freedom is inviolable. And this freedom that we cherish is not without risks and responsibilities."[22]

Caroline De Hass led a rebuttal from French feminists:

The signatories of the Le Monde article are deliberately confusing a relationship of seduction, based on respect and pleasure, with violence. To mix everything is quite practical. It allows everything to go into one basket. If harassment or aggression are "heavy flirting" then it's not too serious. The signatories are wrong.[23]

#MeToo wasn't about romantic relationships between the sexes. It was about coming out with long-hidden stories of harmful behaviors that victims had experienced in the hope of exposing how big the problem is and possibly creating change. Men fear losing their power; women fear never having any.

Fear

When people operate from a place of fear, we stop operating from a place of contribution. When it comes to the issues brought up by #MeToo, fear is like a cyclone, knocking down or sucking both men and women into the chaos. Women fear nothing will change and that the violence and discrimination will continue.

Men have told me that their biggest fear is a false accusation. Statistics indicate that false accusations of assault are less common than unreported assaults and about equal to the number of reported assaults that are not prosecuted. Some men fear loss of relationship with women, loss of respect, loss of socioeconomic advantage, and loss of power.

What if the relationships between people don't equate to a zero-sum game with winners and losers? What if we're better together? Conversations with men, women, and those who are self-described as nonbinary will help people hear and understand others and consider the costs they are afraid to pay in the midst of change. Whatever your beliefs, there is ample opportunity to discuss how humans interact, and there have been abundant changes taking place since October of 2017.

Questions to Thoughtfully Consider and Discuss

1. What, if any, changes have you personally experienced as a result of #MeToo?

2. What is your response to the #MeToo movement?

3. What is #MeToo really about?

4. What do the men you know have to say about #MeToo?

5. What do you think about the statements "If it doesn't cost anything to sexually harass somebody, things will never change. Men have to become afraid of the consequences"?

6. Is it true that men tend to protect other men? If so, what will it take for the girls and women they know to live a life completely free from sexual harassment, abuse, or assault?

7. How open are you to conversations about ending sexual harassment, abuse, and assault?

8. Have you experienced any backlash?

9. What changes have you seen or implemented at your workplace as a result of #MeToo?

10. What is local government's responsibility for stopping harassment and violence against girls and women?

S I X

Part Two:
What's Changed?

I was nine years old, playing alone in my front yard.

"Hey, Juanita, d'ja wanna screw?" one of the neighbor boys asked, holding out his fist, palm down. I looked up with curiosity. The gang that had been playing ball on the street circled around. I thought maybe they wanted his screw.

I didn't care much about screws and was a bit puzzled about why anyone might think I'd want one or why they'd even talk to me, for that matter. The gang leader was my brother's age, thirteen years old. All the boys laughed, circling in closer. I couldn't fathom why there was so much excitement over a stupid screw. My Papi kept jars of them in the garage.

"Tell him *sí*!" several of the boys chimed in.

"Tell him *no*!" a couple of the boys yelled. I didn't say anything. I stared at the closed fist. Suddenly he reached over and gripped my arm.

My older brother Andres shouted from about ten feet away, having just come out of the garage.

The leader scanned the landscape nearby. He didn't seem to hear or notice my brother.

Andres shouted. "Leave Juanita alone." He grabbed my other arm and yanked so hard my shoulder joint snapped, pulling both of us back a few feet.

I felt like I was in a tug of war. "*Ai*! What's that for?"

As Andres pulled me away, the boy retreated, scurrying like a rat toward the street, followed by the others.

Andres shouted, "Guys. You leave my sister alone!" To me, "Juanita, come on. Play inside from now on. Don't you ever play alone outside anymore. It's not safe for girls." And he didn't let me go until I was in the house.

When Mama asked about the bruises on my arms, Andres told her he grabbed me to get me out of the dirt in the garden. When I looked at him, he glared at me. Mama never knew about the boys, and Andres never told her anything.

#MeToo, Juanita

There have always been allies, but one of the changes since October 2017 is the emergence of previously silent allies who recognize that discrimination and violence against women should not be the norm and who are doing what they can to create change in their workplaces and in their communities.

Andres didn't appreciate the circumstances requiring him to step up to his sister's defense, and he wasn't keen on sharing his courageous actions with his family. He didn't want to get any neighbor boys in trouble, and he didn't want to draw attention to his sister's vulnerability. He was a protector. Did he act like an ally? #MeToo has given allies of the world ample opportunity to step up, voice their thoughts, and help change culture. In a September 2018 article, "What Men Should

Know about #MeToo: It's about Them," *New York Times* writer Maya Salam reported about the "New Rules Summit held in Brooklyn in September 2018."

> "Here's what men don't get about the #MeToo movement: It is not about women, it's about us," Wade Davis, a former NFL player turned educator and activist, said at the summit. By "us" he meant men. Women "are laying themselves bare to awaken us, so we can do better," he said to a crowd attending the panel "How to Be a Male Ally."[1]

Urging men to awaken and be allies, as Mr. Davis has been doing, is an ongoing theme since #MeToo captured media attention all around the world.

#MeToo Waves in the Media

Media hasn't dropped the ball since things started rolling in 2017 with the social media #MeToo firestorm. The attention in some media outlets started out in 2017 as a list of prominent entertainment and media personalities, including Harvey Weinstein and Bill Cosby, who were accused of sexual harassment. The list included men who worked at ABC, AlterNet, Amazon Studios, CBS, ESPN, Fox News, Minnesota Public Radio, NBC, National Public Radio, New York Public Radio, *Paris Review*, the *New Republic*, and VOX Media.[2] Many more powerful media personalities and leaders were suspended or asked to take a leave of absence, pending investigations.

Increasing conversations about #MeToo, sexual harassment (online and face-to-face), and sexual assault fueled media coverage, which in turn created more opportunities for conversation. The media added stories daily referencing #MeToo and calling attention to the problem of sexual violence. In the US, media sources including *Hollywood Reporter* and BuzzFeed changed their organizational structures to handle increased tips about sexual misconduct.[3] According to the Women's Media Center Report on #MeToo,

> the #MeToo movement has revealed previously hidden patterns of sexual harassment, wage discrimination, and hiring policies that excluded and intimidated women. . . . It has also led to an increase in discussion of other women's rights issues, such as gender equality, reproductive rights, and the wage gap. Our study found that between eighty and seven hundred articles a month focused on the #MeToo movement itself, rather than mentioning it in the context of a story about a specific sexual assault case. In February 2018 alone, over 55 percent of stories about sexual assault mentioned the movement, and for four months in 2018, this proportion remained over 50 percent.[4]

The Canadian Press's annual survey of news editors and reporters voted sexual harassment as the most compelling story of 2017 (the fentanyl crisis came in second).[5] In response to the survey, Joshua Freeman, web journalist for Toronto CP24TV, said,

> No other story this year seems to permeate everyday life for men and women across the social spectrum. It cuts to the way that men and women interact with one another on a daily basis and raises questions about how far we think we've come versus where we actually are when it comes to sexism, professionalism and our ability to navigate our own sexual impulses with maturity.[6]

Mexico's women joined in the #MeTooMx movement, engaging the media and some of the country's top actresses. According to a GirlUp. org guest blogger, Fernanda Garza, the response in Mexico has been "controversy, scandal, and public debates on what is actually considered sexual harassment or assault within the context of our country. Nonetheless, women all over Mexico are fighting back, and aiming to re-educate the way a *machista* society interprets 'simple actions.'"[7]

In the United Kingdom, Liam Hackett, an activist, reality-TV-show host, and entrepreneur best known as the founder and CEO of the global equality and anti-bullying charity Ditch the Label, got clear on whose responsibility it is to stop sexual violence. Hackett aligned with the #MeToo message when he wrote, "Stop policing the bodies of women and stop teaching young girls how 'not to get raped.' Start teaching young boys about consent and fight against the toxic masculinity that underpins rape culture #metoo."

The *Irish Times* published an editorial agreeing that conversations on #MeToo are challenging yet essential. Emer O'Toole, researcher, writer, associate professor of Irish performance studies at Concordia University, and author of *Girls Will Be Girls,* wrote for the *Irish Times,*

> [It's] hard work, this #MeToo moment, necessitating many difficult conversations. Sometimes it feels like my interlocutor wants to find virtually any explanation for hundreds of thousands of women coming forward to share stories of harassment other than the simple fact of sexist abuse. Yet, if we don't have these conversations, I'm afraid that discourse will polarize, that this extraordinary feminist moment will be swallowed by misogynistic backlash. We need to direct the flow of molten #MeToo rage and let it cool into a foundation that can support structural change. The interactions required to do so are emotional, exhausting, yet vital.[8]

Sweden eclipsed other Scandinavian countries in terms of responses to #MeToo. In addition to the termination of TV- and radio-show hosts' contracts, the firing of journalists, and politicians being publicly accused and resigning, over 60,000 women united to demand change. And more than 10,000 female doctors gathered in support of the #utantystnadsplikt, the movement against harassment, rougly translated "No more secrets." The Swedish Secretariat for Gender Research posted an article dated March 8, 2018, detailing the impact of #MeToo in

Sweden, Iceland, Denmark, Finland, and Norway. According to the article,

> Christian Groes, Associate Professor at Roskilde University's Centre for Gender, Power and Diversity, said #MeToo has received an enormous amount of media attention in Denmark, including discussions about whether or not it is okay to publish the names of alleged perpetrators. According to Groes, there has been a tendency for men to want to protect other men. Personally, he believes that the publication of names fills an important function. It helps transfer the stigma from the victim to the offender. If it doesn't cost anything to sexually harass somebody, things will never change. Men have to become afraid of the consequences.[9]

Australia's media also talked about sexual harassment after #MeToo. Australia's popular news website the Conversation posted a series of articles from March to September 2018 on #MeToo themes. In one article, Hannah Piterman of Deakin University wrote,

> Women are still treated as second-class citizens in a country that purports to uphold equality of opportunity for all. Sexual harassment is regarded as commonplace in their work environment. And it is on the rise in Australia: as many as one in five women in Australia report sexual violence.

Women in Senegal and Nigeria reported that the fear of being associated with the topic kept them from responding to or posting about #MeToo. One woman deleted hers out of fear that her family might find out.

> "Sexual harassment is so endemic in society that it is almost a right for men in Nigeria," said 39-year-old Faustina Anyanwu, who posted on Twitter about experiencing harassment when she worked as a nurse.

"It is almost impossible, in fact, unimaginable for a woman to report such cases," she told the Thomson Reuters Foundation. "Culturally, the woman is ostracized and will not be married."[10]

In South Africa, sexual harassment is rampant and has launched a sense of fatalism. Femicide in South Africa is five times higher than the global average, and sexism is tolerated across the country. According to South African author and satirist Marianne Thamm:

We as women, as girls, must each day step into the world and deal with perpetual and constant clear and present danger. As you can glean from the #MeToo campaign, the abuse not only emanates from the unwelcome glances, but touches and whispers from men we know or who are directly in our orbit. The fear is with us always, everywhere.[11]

In other African, Asian, and Middle Eastern countries where there is not cultural or governmental support for women's rights, #MeToo has been silenced, ridiculed, and criticized. In Russia, after a member of the Duma (a legislative body in the ruling assembly of Russia and of some other republics of the former Soviet Union,) Leonid Slutsky was accused of sexual harassment with little response, RBC media outlet, TVRain, and Echo Moscow Radio stopped sending correspondents to the State Duma. Hours later, Russian newspapers *Kommersant*, *Vedomisti*, and *Novaya Gazeta* joined them, with other private print and online publications. The Duma responded by canceling accreditations for the boycotting media organizations. The independent Russian Union of Journalists escalated the boycott by issuing an open letter to the Organization for Security and Cooperation in Europe (OSCE) with over 500 journalist signatories, exhorting the Duma to stop dealing with Slutsky and to condemn his behavior.[12]

Around the globe the media has responded one way or another about this issue. The media and encourage or undermine change. Notice what the media is covering in your locality and your country. How are their stories reflecting or impacting the culture? The #MeToo headlines have decreased over the past two years. Are you seeing any changes in the way news is reported in your local media? What are your community news writers contributing to culture change? You have the ability to impact stories and the culture by sharing relevant stories. Write letters to the editor or opinion pieces when there's a relevant news story. Share the truth about the damage sexual violence does to our culture, and contribute to culture change.

Cultural Changes after #MeToo

#MeToo rests on generations of ongoing work to publicly recognize sexual discrimination and harassment, define and codify it, draft change legislation, and open conversations about discrimination. One of the most powerful changes #MeToo has made is to create a deeper recognition of the scope of the problem. The famous women who have helped #MeToo gain traction were not the only voices. Millions of powerless, nameless women around the globe have reached the mad-as-hell-and-not-going-to-take-it-anymore! stage. For example, in a December 21, 2017, story in the *Harvard Gazette*, staff writers Christina Pazzanese and Colleen Walsh reported,

> Ann Marie Lipinski, curator of the Nieman Foundation for Journalism at Harvard, said she suspects the response is a combination of women simply having "had enough," along with the celebrity of many of Weinstein's accusers, including actors Ashley Judd, Rose McGowan, and Angelina Jolie. Their status drew widespread attention to the issue, but it's a "frustrating fact" that famous women were deemed more credible and were more readily heard than the mostly unknown accusers of Cosby or Trump. "For all those women working night shifts in hospitals or stocking things in grocery stores or working in a lot of industries where there is more anonymity and not the same level of public scrutiny or, in many cases, fame, it must be pretty

frustrating to feel that your complaints are not being taken with similar seriousness," she said.[13]

Theater arts organizations were impacted by #MeToo, as they have since been rooting out perpetrators of sexual misconduct. *American Theatre's* entire September 2018 issue was devoted to investigating sexual discrimination in the performing arts. The issue identified powerful people in the theater community who were terminated because of sexual misconduct. It highlighted the fact that in theater, people are expendable because there are hundreds of actors waiting to take your place; it's very difficult to speak out when harassment or assault does occur.

In an online article in *American Theatre* magazine, Diep Tran, current senior editor of the magazine, also agreed that there is fear and a need to work together to create change in the industry:

> Any theatre grappling with sexual harassment that wants to rehabilitate its institution would do well to take a multi-pronged approach. While misconduct may originate with one person, one incident at a time, it is too often enabled and exacerbated into a pattern, a culture, by a system of silence, fear, and complicity. That's why it will take the efforts of everyone working, brick by brick, to challenge and dismantle this system and create a better, more accountable, more inclusive culture in theatres around the country.[14]

The music industry has had its own #MeToo moments; there seems to be, however, no long-term negative effects for most famous musicians who've been accused of harassment and violence against women. Michael Arcenaux, culture columnist for WIRED magazine, listed several offenders and identified the current absence of accountability in the music industry by saying, "Misogyny is everywhere—and if it's difficult to make men accountable for their actions, that task becomes exponentially more difficult when that man is a celebrity."[15] Mr. Arcenaux may have nailed it when he added, "The problem holding the music industry back from real change isn't conspiracy—it's complicity."[16]

The art world also felt the ripple effect of #MeToo as galleries, including the National Gallery of Art, canceled exhibitions of famous artists who had been exposed for sexual misconduct. Prior to #MeToo, shows opened on the merit of the artists' work, without regard for any humans who were violated by the artist. The movement clarifies the truths that sexual harassment is evil and that art created by harassers and abusers is not worthy of exhibiting. An article in the online magazine the *Conversation* by Irina Aristarkhova, Associate Professor at the Penny W. Stamps School of Art & Design at the University of Michigan, addresses the issue of sexual harassment when it comes to the arts: "#MeToo has changed the public view on sexual harassment. Indeed, the public debate surrounding the decision by the National Gallery of Art to cancel two exhibitions has been as much about the value of human beings as it has been about the value of art."[17]

#MeToo Waves in the World of Business

The impacts of #MeToo are also seen in businesses across North America and will likely be seen around the world as the movement spreads. More companies are looking at their sexual harassment policies and working to prevent sexual abuses and make reporting easier for employees. In 2017 Claire Schmidt founded AllVoices, an online anonymous reporting service, to help companies aggregate results of anonymous reports to address environmental harassment at a workplace without sharing any specifics about identity with the company or any outside legal authority. The goal is to protect the individual reporting while encouraging culture change.[18] Savvy entrepreneurs like Schmidt are addressing the need for anonymous reporting options.

Technology is also being used to support workers who face harassment regularly. In July 2018, Chicago implemented an ordinance requiring hotels to provide panic buttons for their workers to protect hotel staff working alone in a guest room from sexual harassment. When a worker presses a button, the supervisor and HR Department receive alerts giving the employee's name and location. Seattle and New York already require panic buttons, and the technology is spreading to other cities. The American Hotel & Lodging Association and several major companies including Hilton, Marriott, and Hyatt announced plans by 2020 to be sure hotel workers throughout the entire US are equipped with panic buttons to reduce sexual assault and other crimes.[19]

The restaurant industry, long known for being sexist and for its rampant sexual-harassment culture, is paying attention to #MeToo, especially women in management. A few high-profile chefs have had to resign because of sexual harassment claims, a small but significant step that seems to be taking off in New York City. Restaurateur and writer Karen Leibowitz, with help from designer Kelli Anderson, created an anti-harassment poster similar to the "Choking Victim" poster from the eighties often seen in New York City restaurants. With simple, direct graphics, it highlights an employee's rights regarding workplace harassment. The title line says, "In Case of Sexual Harassment You Are Not Powerless" and tells employees who are being harassed to "Keep a Record, Tell Your Employer, Make It Official, and Find Allies," giving instructions for each point.[20]

#MeToo is encouraging leaders to make changes, industry by industry. The demand is up for training on workplace sexual harassment as harassment claims have increased. Convercent Inc., a compliance and ethics firm that handles harassment hotlines for over 600 companies, reported that harassment claims in 2018 were up 72 percent over the prior year.[21] The Time's Up Legal Defense Fund for entertainment workers received over 3,500 requests for claim assistance in 2018, most from low-income workers.

Board members in the US and Canada have started taking action after #MeToo to make sure employees are trained on and aware of sexual harassment policies. Cycling Canada board member Robin Porter said,

"It is a very different movement than anything that's happened in the past. . . . And I believe it has staying power; I don't think we're ever going to go back."[22]

According to a survey by research and insights provider Qualtrics and TheBoardlist (a board seat marketplace), 43 percent of American board members and 53 percent of Canadian board members had discussed sexually inappropriate behavior in the workplace, a major jump from the 23 percent that had addressed the issue prior to the rise of the #MeToo movement in October 2017 (according to a previous survey by TheBoardlist). Venture capital members responded even higher, with 66 percent having discussed re-evaluating harassment policies in direct response to the #MeToo movement.[23]

Venture capitalists, the majority of whom are males, meet with female entrepreneurs seeking investors for their companies, and some have used the power to create havoc for the women looking for funding to start their businesses. The significant power differential is similar to a CEO meeting with a department head asking for a major budget increase. Without the structural accountability of a corporate human resources department, sexual harassment stories about venture capitalists have been reported with little fanfare and little results.

One group of venture capitalists is proposing that big investors fine companies with sexual harassment scandals because they believe sexual harassment problems create a financial threat to shareholders. In addition, this group is working to draft a clause to include in investors/private equity manager agreements and between private equity management companies and the enterprises using their investment capital. The group believes a threat of a fine is enough to keep startups motivated to maintain a safe, harassment-free working culture.[24]

The movement is definitely impacting businesses, and the changes are just beginning.

Political Waves

Politics has seen measurable effects in the United States at the state level. In California, a letter released in October 2017 by women who worked in or with the state legislature exposed a California political culture riddled by sexual misconduct. As a result, powerful men lost their jobs, and there was pressure to adopt new laws and policies to protect employees who report harassment. Investigations were conducted on both sides. Legislators proposed more than two dozen bills addressing sexual harassment in this legislative year,[25] and more than a dozen made it to Governor Jerry Brown, who signed laws that banned retaliation against legislative employees reporting harassment and outlawed secret settlements between lawmakers and victims of harassment.[26]

New York passed a law that requires all state contractors and all public and private organizations to have a sexual harassment policy that meets minimum standards and to train all employees on sexual harassment. Other state legislatures have proposed that public companies report to shareholders the number of sexual harassment settlements made in the previous twelve months and how much they paid, in hopes that the minimum standards and reporting will be enough to stop harassment in the workplace.

By August 2018, half of state legislative chambers had made a change to their sexual harassment policies by boosting their own training, according to a fifty-state analysis by the Associated Press.[27] In an August 2018 article, the Associated Press listed twelve states that were passing laws with #MeToo themes: requirement for sexual harassment training, external investigations of misconduct, documentation/records and public disclosure, discontinuing use of public funds for hush money, outlawing secret settlements, and new requirements for private employers.[28]

In 2018 a record was set for the number of female nominees for governors (eleven), according to data collected by the Center for American Women and Politics (CAWP).[29]

#MeToo is starting to impact politics nationally in the US. On January 21, 2017, the day after President Trump's inauguration, the Women's March brought millions of people, mostly women, across America (and the world) to the streets in solidarity for women. After the march, more than 42,000 women contacted Emily's List, a liberal PAC dedicated to engaging women to run for office. (Compare this to the previous election cycle, during which 920 women contacted Emily's List.) #MeToo got women motivated to step up and run. Women comprised half of the Democrats' 2018 first-time candidates, up from 27 percent in 2016, in comparison to 20 percent of the Republicans' candidates. Polling revealed concern about the #MeToo issue from both parties.[30]

Since the hashtag went viral, nine members of Congress facing credible charges of sexual misconduct either resigned or declined to run for re-election, and two White House officials resigned after accusations of abuse. Claims of sexual harassment or misconduct ended the bids of twelve Republicans and thirteen Democrats during the 2018 election cycle.

The rise of solidarity around empowering women defined the midterm elections. An unprecedented number of women ran for office, the majority as Democrats. A record 235 women were nominated for the US House of Representatives, beating the previous record of 167. The women nominees for Senate (22) and for governors (16) also set records. @RonBrownstein from the CNN Newsroom tweeted on November 7, 2018: "This was the first election ever where white men were not a majority of the Democratic candidates for the House," adding that "white men were still three-fourths of the Republican candidates."[31]

Solidarity after #MeToo led to six women candidates for the presidency in the US in 2019, and in Democratic debates, women candidates questioned their male opponents on their records of women's issues.

Governmental Changes

Some legislation and policies are moving toward New Normal, while some are reversing human rights advancements. The US government cut funding for the UN Population Fund, which provides lifesaving maternal care for women, because of a false rumor that the agency promoted forced abortions. President Trump's Mexico City policy, "the global gag rule," also impacts healthcare organizations receiving US aid. Under the policy, NGOs must certify they don't provide abortions (except in cases of rape, incest, or to save a woman's life), or provide information about or referrals for abortions, or fund any organization (even for nonrelated services for women or child health) if they provide abortion services. Otherwise, they lose all US funding. Affected health programs are reducing family planning offerings as well as services linked to child health, vaccinations, and services treating and preventing HIV/AIDS, malaria, and tuberculosis.[32] At the state level in the US, at least eleven states, from California to Vermont, passed new protections addressing workplace harassment in 2018, and many of them have gone into effect in 2019. Washington state passed a law requiring that any person making a discrimination claim has the right to file their claim in a public setting, as in civil court. California also passed a new law that requires women representation on corporate boards by the end of 2019.[33]

#MeToo Ripples around the Globe

The 2011 earthquake and tsunami in Japan sent big waves to Hawaii. On a trip to the Washington coast, my sister and I spent an afternoon clearing debris from the tsunami that had washed ashore. Likewise, #MeToo is bringing people across oceans together to address the universal problem of sexual violence.

For example, nine women from across the United States and France united together in speaking out against a thirty-year track record of sexual harassment and assault by the playwright Israel Horovitz. They've kept in contact, but their solidarity is merely a tiny ripple effect of #MeToo around world.[34]

Sexual harassment and violence against women remain a global problem, and even the world's largest peacekeeping organization is not immune from it. The United Nations has allowed sexual harassment to continue even as UN Secretary-General Antonio Guterres has publicly acknowledged the need for the global body to deal with sexual harassment. The UN is attempting to change its culture by instituting a strategy to increase the number of female executives. It has also increased protection for employees who report harassment. The UN also plans to initiate an electronic database to prevent those employees guilty of perpetrating harassment from finding new jobs in other UN agencies.[35]

International Women's Day has brought women together in protest marches around the world, many carrying signs with #MeToo. But the global impact is mixed, depending on a country's culture. Oppressive cultures and political systems strip girls and women of basic rights to life, education, employment, and social and economic freedom. Women's education and employment support women's ability to speak up about discrimination, harassment, and sexual violence. The imbalance of power across the globe in favor of men is a hindrance to the staying power of #MeToo. The effectiveness and longevity of #MeToo will require ongoing, long-term solidarity and unity among women and men from a variety of situations. The unfortunate truth is that in every country on the earth, women and girls are being subjected to harassment and violence. The structures supporting Old Normal remain standing. There's a culture war going on and women are losing. It's up to you, to me, to each of us individually and collectively to engage in creating the changes in our cultures that would make the world a just, safe place.

Questions to Thoughtfully Consider and Discuss

1. Is it fair to say that whoever owns the power controls the conversation?

2. How are conversations around #MeToo challenging power bases where you live or around the world?

3. How far do we think we've come versus where we actually are when it comes to sexism, professionalism, and our ability to navigate our own sexual impulses with maturity?

4. What's changed for you since #MeToo broke out?

5. What changes have you seen in your community and workplace?

6. What has changed in your country? What needs to change?

7. What changes have you seen in your friends and family?

8. What impact do you think social media is having toward conversations about sexual harassment, abuse, and violence against women?

9. What else needs to happen?

10. What do you believe are the root causes of sexual harassment and violence?

SEVEN

Part One:
Old Normal

My grandson, who is very inquisitive and smart, was playing with his grandfather's computer. He came to me and told me that there were several pictures of a naked girl on the computer that bothered him. Of course, my grandson gave up playing on the computer, and I had to investigate the extent of the damage. These weren't sweet, innocent photos of a baby in the bathtub. It turns out the photos' angles, tones, colors, and intent had been carefully curated to make them more subjective.

My granddaughter was the subject, and she had been posed.

We learned that her grandfather had been taking these kinds of pictures of her for her entire life and that he also had frequented at least one porn site. Needless to say, our world was turned upside down. The deception was very difficult because her grandfather, my husband, blamed me for turning him in to the authorities, which I'd had to do because what he did was against the law.

It was especially challenging because he did not accept any responsibility for the injury he caused our family, our grandchildren, and their parents, and he blamed me for all the pain the family dealt with because of his actions. The financial and practical results of criminal charges and psychological counseling and recovery work also weighed very heavily on the family. Things will never be the same, and honestly, in spite of all this time, it is still devastating to me and to everyone in the family.

#UsToo, Belinda

I don't know about you, but I can't read Belinda's story without feeling deeply saddened by a culture that allows such things to happen. What influences led the grandfather to act without thought about how he might be impacting his granddaughter, grandson, wife, or family? The culture that promulgates this kind of behavior is what I call Old Normal. We'll look at some of the elements of Old Normal in this chapter.

In *The Innovator's Way*, Peter J. Deming and Robert Dunham offer a perspective on change management that I find useful for looking at the issues brought up in the #MeToo movement. They define a scenario that calls for change or innovation in an organization as the "Mess." They say that "Messes are intransigent social situations that people want to exit but feel stuck in."[1] The Mess is typically viewed from the perspective of "old common sense" or an "old rule set." Deming and Dunham suggest that often there is a "transformational event (TE)" that facilitates innovation and change in a group. After the TE, a new perspective is possible that allows people to see the transformation to a post-Mess reality, defined by a "new common sense" and a "new rule set." In their diagram titled "Figure 14.1 The Mess and Its Observers," the timeline from Mess to transformational event to settlement and integration in a new rule set may be viewed from the "Before TE" or "After TE" positions, or from above, looking outside the Mess and over the transformational event timeline.[2]

If all the reality of sexual discrimination, harassment, abuse, and assault are the Mess, and if the social media firestorm was the transformational event, one can look at this from any of those perspectives: before #MeToo, which I call Old Normal; the TE that has been described by many as a turning point in relationships between men and women, and after #MeToo, which I call New Normal. This is a business model, and obviously the timeline's not quite so cut-and-dried in real life. Generations of people who have stood up for women's bodily integrity would say Old Normal started to end long before #MeToo. For the sake of moving forward, can we ask if #MeToo was actually a part of a transformational event? If so, what does Old Normal look like?

If we define the group as the world, and if we can agree that we'd like a New Normal that creates a world free from sexual discrimination, harassment, abuse, and assault, it would make sense to start coaching transformation by looking at Old Normal. Does Old Normal, a rule set or common sense, describe a cultural and institutional bath that supports by default sexual discrimination, harassment, abuse, and assault against women? Some have argued that this is the case, naming that bath *rape culture*.

The words we use to describe and define things are powerful, and I believe the Mess merits a different name. *Rape culture* has been defined as a society or environment whose prevailing social attitudes have the effect of normalizing or trivializing sexual assault and abuse. Many have hotly debated whether a *rape culture* can actually exist, such as those who said it was impossible for a husband to rape his spouse (she consented at marriage) or for a man to rape his date (she agreed to go out with him). Another problem with *rape culture* is the ease of dismissing oneself from culpability for participating in it. If you don't see yourself as a rapist, it's hard to see *rape culture*. Another problem is that it focuses on what's wrong without suggesting there is some right to be found. If we call this culture Old Normal, might those who feel disenfranchised by *rape culture* be willing to engage in this conversation and even to accept an invitation to examine how Old Normal is in fact a breeding ground for an unending stream of #MeToo stories?

Not That Bad: Dispatches from Rape Culture, edited by Roxanne Gay, is an anthology of thirty essays that illuminate the shame of this culture and how it warps our humanity. The title and stories use verbiage that victims, perpetrators, and observers alike use in experiencing and dealing with the ugliness of sexual objectification and violence.

Like many, I believe that #MeToo created such awareness of the cost of the Mess that the status quo is no longer acceptable. Old Normal began to end when people recognized the enormity of the Mess. Consider the various changes over the past two years and the momentum that's picked up since the first #MeToo tweet.

Choosing New Normal

If we choose to pursue a new set of protective practices, a new common sense, a New Normal, we will choose to no longer contribute to or pay Old Normal's heavy costs to communities around the globe. Looking at Old Normal can help us choose to move the timeline past the transformative event and work as a community in New Normal.

As a coach, I help individuals move from where they are to where they want to be. This requires honesty on their part and a willingness to engage in self-reflection in order to have clarity about where they're starting, what they hope to gain, what they need to do, obstacles they may face, how they'll overcome them to attain their goals, and how they will hold themselves accountable to act to create the future they envision. One of the wins my clients celebrate is the peace that comes with decisions and actions made in integrity and in alignment with their core values. But to achieve this requires self-reflection.

Self-reflection is challenging enough for individuals, and it's an even greater challenge to bring groups to a common understanding through self-reflection and honest sharing. An individual does not always need to look to others to create internal change, but a group absolutely must at least be in agreement; otherwise, progress toward a unified end is practically impossible.

One person can contribute but cannot by himself or herself completely create New Normal for a group. This requires group or community for New Normal to work. As a starting place to create New Normal, a group or community can agree to engage in self-reflection, to courageously and honestly look at some of the contributors and pillars of Old Normal.

I invite you to join in imagining the possibilities of New Normal. Start with self-reflection about where we are now. You might start by thinking about and discussing the questions at the end of each chapter (if you haven't already), joining the Life Beyond Me Too Facebook page, or starting book conversation groups in your neighborhood, church, school, or community organization. Your group might consider what end goals it could adopt and what steps you might implement in your community.

Let's envision where we'd like to be and how we might facilitate a global transformation from our Old Normal that makes #MeToo stories possible and creates our Mess, to our New Normal for us and for future generations that would create freedom from fear of sexual harassment, abuse, and violence. Will you be part of this movement? Will you join the conversation about how we as people who share a world might turn this dream into reality?

If you, however, don't want a world free from sexual discrimination, harassment, abuse, and violence, may I suggest you put this book down and figure out what kind of world you do want and what part you will play in creating it? Please come back if you decide you wish to join this effort in creating a global transformation that will lead to New Normal.

While there is ample room for people to contribute additional suggestions about what contributes to Old Normal, I suggest we begin with objectification, sex trafficking and prostitution, pornography, patriarchy, and patriarchal religions.

Objectification

Of the three abusers who lived in my house, one never admitted fault. One apologized insincerely with a warning not to tell. The third spoke to me once about his misconduct, less than two hours before his death, offering a heartfelt apology and seeking forgiveness for his abusive behaviors. He was the only one who gave me an opportunity to truly accept his apology and offer forgiveness.

All of them objectified me. Objectification means treating a person as a commodity or an object without regard to their humanity or dignity. Even though I gained freedom by forgiving, it doesn't change the fact that whether or not they admitted it, each abuser used me as an object rather than honoring me as a person.

Sexual objectification is the reduction of people to physical objects of sexual desire. The grandfather in this chapter's story sexualized and objectified his granddaughter. Sexual objectification, however mild or extreme the behavior it fuels, is one aspect all of the #MeToo stories have in common. In order to treat a person as an object, the offender must think solely about themselves and what they want. This precludes all thoughts of the victim and their innate worth as a fellow human on the planet, except to the degree that it benefits the offender.

Sexual Objectification (SO) theory is explained in the research article "Sexual Objectification of Women: Advances to Theory and Research" by Dawn M. Szymanski, Lauren B. Moffitt, and Erika R. Carr, and says in part:

> Many women are sexually objectified [SO] and treated as an object
> to be valued for its use by others. SO occurs when a woman's body or

body parts are singled out and separated from her as a person and she is viewed primarily as a physical object of sexual desire . . . and is likely to contribute to mental health problems that disproportionately affect women (i.e., eating disorders, depression, and sexual dysfunction) via two main paths. The first path is direct and overt and involves SO experiences. The second path is indirect and subtle and involves women's internalization of SO experiences or self-objectification.[3]

According to SO theory, the objectification happens at the time of the offense and also as the woman internalizes the experience. Sexual objectification often leads to self-objectification, which is treating oneself as an object whose value is primarily based on appearance or attractiveness to others. Instead of evaluating herself on her competence, intelligence, curiosity, leadership, emotional intelligence, or other behavioral attributes, a woman focuses on how she looks and how her body looks. Sexual objectification and self-objectification can lead to greater anxiety about appearance. When you're focused on your appearance, it can distract you from life and work and from how your body feels internally. A woman who experiences sexual objectification or self-objectifies may fail to notice when she's cold, hungry, or needs to use the bathroom until her discomfort level is severe.

Have you ever heard a baby just learning to speak say they think their butt's too big or they don't like their crooked smile? If this is something you've heard out of the mouth of a girl or woman, it's self-objectification. If a teenage daughter asks for breast augmentation surgery, you can bet she's picked up this idea from a culture steeped in sexual objectification and she's self-objectifying. Addictions and compulsive disorders (bulimia or cutting) may reveal self-contempt and objectification (therefore resulting in self-objectification).

Who perpetrates sexual objectification? Any person who speaks or acts in a way that indicates they view any other person's value primarily based on appearance or attractiveness as an object of his or her desire is a perpetrator. The person who objectifies might not feel negative consequences, especially if they are silent, but the negative consequences multiply, and they also poison the culture.

Sexual objectification can cause body shame, leading to internalized fears that are the breeding ground for depression, addiction, and compulsive behaviors including eating disorders and problems with normal sexual experiences. Dr. Brené Brown, PhD, LMSW, author and researcher on shame, found that body image is the number-one shame trigger for women.[4]

Women are subject to impossible standards for appearance: weight, hair, skin, makeup, clothing and shoes, accessories. A friend who's observed me get ready for a meeting told me once that comparison and shame sent her into self-judgment because, she said, "I can't keep up with the nineteen upgrades you do before I leave my house." How can anyone reach the nearly impossible standards that society sets for women?

Sexual objectification of women, however slight or extreme, contributes to the damage women incur as they experience or internalize self-objectification. Sexual objectification feeds the Mess of Old Normal. Whether as slight as asking a makeup-free co-worker if they're feeling well or as severe as buying sex from a trafficked girl, objectification is dangerous to a healthy culture.

Sex Trafficking and Prostitution

Objectification at its extreme is slavery, also known as human trafficking. Slavery traces its roots back to around 6800 BC in Mesopotamia and has been part of Old Normal for millennia. There are an estimated 21 million to 32 million slaves in the world today.[5] Trafficking involves recruitment of, harboring, or transporting people, sometimes across borders, into a situation where they have no way out and are exploited. Traffickers use deception, coercion, or violence to force a trafficked victim to work, robbing them of their free will. Trafficked people may be forced into prostitution or other crimes, porn production, forced labor, begging, domestic work, organ removal, forced marriage, child-soldier duties, and worse.

While the United Nations Trafficking in Persons Protocol introduced in 2003 has dramatically increased the number of countries with legislation criminalizing trafficking, from thirty-three in 2003 to 158 in 2016, the ability to enforce the laws and prosecute criminals is limited in effectiveness. The United States did not join the UN effort; rather, it passed its own law in 2000: the Victims of Trafficking and Violence Protection Act (VTVPA). Several later additions have modified the law, but the VTVPA is the basis for programs throughout federal agencies and for the US report on trafficked persons and diplomatic efforts to end trafficking. Reporting required under the act started in 2001.[6] The VTVPA defines sex trafficking as a situation in which "a commercial sex act is induced by force, fraud, or coercion, or in which the person induced to perform such act has not attained 18 years of age."[7]

Between 14,500 and 17,500 people are trafficked into the US each year.[8] Human trafficking is the third-largest international crime industry (behind illegal drugs and arms trafficking). It reportedly generates a profit of $32 billion each year. Of that number, $15.5 billion is made in industrialized countries.[9] According to the United Nations Office on Drugs and Crimes' *2016 Global Report on Trafficking in Persons*, this is worldwide and not a single country is immune.

Some of the details from this report include:

- Traffickers target any vulnerable person in any country.
- Seventy-nine percent of trafficking victims are women and children. The average age a teen enters the sex trade in the US is twelve to fourteen years old. Many victims are runaway girls who were sexually abused as children.[10]
- Forty-two percent of victims are trafficked within the borders of their own country.

- In the Americas, 55 to 57 percent of victims are trafficked for sexual exploitation, and that number is 65 to 66 percent in Western, Central, Southern, and Southeastern Europe.
- In Africa, the Middle East, and Eastern Europe, a greater share of victims is trafficked for forced labor.
- Roughly six in ten offenders are male. A qualitative analysis suggested that women in organized criminal networks participated more in lower-ranking activities—the recruitment of victims, in particular—while men tended to engage in organizational or exploitation roles.
- In conflict situations, women and girls are kidnapped and forced to marry or serve as sexual slaves in many conflict-affected countries around the world.[11]

According to the United States Department of Justice's *2018 TIP Report* (of trafficking information for all nations), the US federal government meets the minimum standards required for anti-trafficking law enforcement. Advocates reported that

> victim services were not always provided equitably, urging an increase in resources for, and equitable access to, comprehensive services across the country. . . . Advocates also reported continued instances of state and local officials detaining or prosecuting trafficking victims for criminal activity related to their trafficking victimization.[12]

Federal law enforcement agencies responsible for investigating, prosecuting, and preventing human trafficking include the Department of Homeland Security, Department of Justice, Department of State, Department of Defense, and Department of Justice. In 2017, these agencies collectively opened 962 human trafficking-related cases worldwide, down from 1,144 the prior year. The Justice Department initiated 282 prosecutions for federal human trafficking (266 for sex trafficking, 16 for labor trafficking), up from 241 the prior year. Also in 2017, 553 defendants were charged, compared to 531 in 2016.[13] That same year, US federal authorities charged a municipal corrections officer with sex trafficking that involved a sixteen-year-old, charged a municipal law enforcement officer with sex trafficking, charged a US Navy seaman with sex trafficking, and initiated an investigation against a US Navy petty officer for conspiring to bring two victims from Thailand to Bahrain to subject them to sex trafficking.[14]

War increases trafficking. Denis Mukwege and Nadia Murad were awarded the 2018 Nobel Peace Prize because both had placed themselves at risk to combat war crimes and help victims. The Nobel Prize website, www.nobelprize.org, reported in March of 2018, "Dr. Mukwege, founder and operator of a hospital in the Democratic Republic of the Congo, treated thousands of sexual assault victims in the Congolese civil war. Ms. Murad, a victim of systematic rape by ISIS forces (as a war strategy against the Yazidi people), was the UN Goodwill Ambassador for the Dignity of Survivors of Human Trafficking in 2014."[15]

In a January 2017 online article entitled *Human Trafficking by the Numbers*, nonprofit humanitarian agency Human Rights First, citing the International Labor Organization, reported,

> Sexual exploitation earns 66 percent of the global profits of human trafficking. The average annual profits generated by each woman in forced sexual servitude (over $100,000) is estimated to be six times more than the average profits generated by each trafficking victim worldwide ($21,800), according to the Organization for Security and Cooperation in Europe (OSCE). OSCE studies show that sexual exploitation can yield a return on investment ranging from 100% to 1,000%.[16]

The demand for trafficked persons fuels the business. If there were no demand, there would be no trafficking. People are willing to pay for using people, even children.

Taking Children

Traffickers are looking for and taking children. According to the National Center for Missing & Exploited Children, the number of child sexual abuse files reviewed by 2004 was 450,000. In 2015, that increased to 25 million files. Thorn, a not-for-profit co-founded by Ashton Kucher and Demi Moore that uses technology to help child victims of sexual abuse, reported that 63 percent of victimized kids Thorn encountered had been advertised online. As many as one of every seven runaways reported to the National Center for Missing & Exploited Children likely became victims of sex trafficking.[17]

Furthermore, there is support for the legalization of prostitution in the US and other countries. A 2013 article in *Business Insider* advocated the legalization of prostitution by saying,

> As Cornell law professor Sherry Colb has written, Prostitution should not be a crime. Prostitutes are not committing an inherently harmful act. While the spread of disease and other detriments are possible in the practice of prostitution, criminalization is a sure way of exacerbating rather than addressing such effects.[18]

In another article, "7 Reasons Why America Should Legalize Prostitution" from *Business Insider*, Erin Fuchs wrote,

> There will always be lonely or kinky men in America who will pay for sex, and there will always be women willing to rent out their bodies. As the anthropologist Patty Kelly has written in the *Los Angeles Times*, prostitution has become a "part of our culture" in the United States.[19]

Sex trafficking and prostitution are evidence that women and girls are objectified as sex objects around the world. Sex trafficking is part of Old Normal. Trafficking only happens because of a demand from the consumer who makes the sex trafficking industry possible. Without consumers, there is no incentive to sell humans.

Is it a victimless crime? Is it harmless to the voluntary sex worker? Anyone who pays for sex is objectifying, and therefore dehumanizing, another human being. Anyone who receives payment for sex is allowing themselves to be objectified and dehumanized.

On the rare occasion that a sex worker isn't being trafficked (with coercion as a standard, most are), the buyer is still engaging in the practice of sexual objectification. It would be hard to argue otherwise, since prostitution is engaging in sexual activity with someone for the buyer's gratification in exchange for payment to the seller. Sexual objectification and self-objectification of sex workers is part of Old Normal for which there are consequences beyond legal ones.

A porn industry secret is that thousands of trafficked girls and women are filmed in captivity, and the films are sold to porn distributors. In fact, much of the demand and financial incentive for sex trafficking is fueled by the porn industry, another major contributor to Old Normal.

Pornography

Someone I had cared for used to argue with me about whether pornography was harmless for those being filmed and harmless for the consumer. My opponent was pro-porn, and I was opposed. During one debate I asked him, "If pornography is harmless, would this be an industry you would be honored to have your wife, daughters and granddaughters, mother, and cousins excel at and rise to the top in?" He had no answer.

Porn powerfully and negatively impacts the brains of the viewer. I know children who were accidentally exposed to online porn in middle school. It took years for them to get the images out of their heads and to re-establish healthy neural pathways in their brains.

An article about the serial killer Ted Bundy, who clearly told the interviewer that he was addicted to porn, said his addiction grew, and as he got deeper into porn, he felt compelled to try what he saw. He said pornography contributed to his obsession, which led to his abducting and murdering at least thirty, and possibly up to seventy, women. In the interview, Bundy said,

> I'm no social scientist, and I don't pretend to believe what John Q. Citizen thinks about this, but I've lived in prison for a long time now, and I've met a lot of men who were motivated to commit violence. Without exception, every one of them was deeply involved in pornography—deeply consumed by the addiction. The FBI's own study on serial homicide shows that the most common interest among serial killers is pornographers. It's true.[20]

While #MeToo activity online seems like a big deal, compared to pornography, it seems insignificant. The nonprofit Fight the New Drug (fightthenewdrug.org) shares some shocking stats on its website.

- Porn is a global, estimated $97 billion industry (three times the size of the sex trafficking industry), with at least $12 billion of that coming from the US.
- At least 30 percent of all data transferred across the internet is porn related.
- In 2016, more than 4,599,000,000 hours (525,000 years) of porn were consumed on the world's largest porn site.
- Porn sites receive more regular traffic than Netflix, Amazon, and Twitter combined each month.
- Thirty-five percent of all internet downloads are porn related.

- Thirty-four percent of internet users have been exposed to unwanted porn via ads, pop-ups, etc. Porn sites lure countless unintentional viewers who stumble upon them by searching for words that porn sites co-opt, such as muffins or peaches.
- Recorded child sexual exploitation is one of the fastest-growing online businesses; more than 624,000 child porn traders have been discovered online in the US; child porn has been found on servers in all 50 states; and the number-one porn role stated in porn titles is for twentysomething actresses pretending to be teenage girls.[21]

Federal law prohibits the possession with intent to sell or distribute obscenity, to send, ship, or receive obscenity, to import obscenity, and to transport obscenity across state borders for purposes of distribution. Although the law does not criminalize the private possession of obscene matter, the act of receiving such matter could violate the statutes prohibiting the use of the US mail, common carriers, or interactive computer services for the purpose of transportation.[22]

Convicted offenders face fines and imprisonment. It is also illegal to aid or abet in the commission of these crimes, and individuals who commit such acts are also punishable under federal obscenity laws. In addition, both the production of obscene matter with the intent to sell or distribute it, and engaging in a business of selling or transferring obscene matter using affecting means (ways of transfer) or by interstate or foreign commerce, including the use of interactive computer services, are illegal. For example, it is illegal to sell and distribute obscene material on the internet.[23]

The Plague of Kiddie Porn

According to the Department of Justice, child pornography is a federal offense. If you really want to know what the law in the United States says about sharing subjective photographs (when the subject is posed) of children or how to identify illegal child porn if you stumble upon it online, you won't want to skip over this section. Here are some details of the law.

It is a federal crime to knowingly possess, manufacture, distribute or access with intent to view child pornography. In addition, all fifty states and the District of Columbia have laws criminalizing the possession, manufacture, and distribution of child pornography. As a result, a person who violates these laws may face federal and/or state charges.[24]

Federal law also criminalizes knowingly producing, distributing, receiving, or possessing with intent to distribute, a visual depiction of any kind, including a drawing, cartoon, sculpture, or painting, depicting

a minor engaging in sexually explicit conduct that is obscene, or an image that is, or appears to be, of a minor engaging in graphic bestiality, sadistic or masochistic abuse or sexual intercourse, including genital-genital, oral-genital, anal-genital or oral-anal, whether between people of the same or opposite sex that lacks serious literary, artistic, political or scientific value.[25]

Sexually explicit conduct is defined under federal law as actual or simulated sexual intercourse, including genital-genital, oral-genital, anal-genital, or oral-anal, whether between people of the same or opposite sex; bestiality; masturbation; sadistic or masochistic abuse; or lascivious exhibition of the genitals or pubic area of any person.[26]

Lascivious isn't a word you read often. It describes "(of a person, manner, or gesture) feeling or revealing an overt and often offensive sexual desire."[27] Child pornography creates deep, lasting harm to the children involved, and "images of child pornography are crime scene photos—they are a permanent record of the abuse of a child."[28]

According to the National Center for Missing & Exploited Children,

> Studies indicate that child victims endure depression, withdrawal, anger, and other psychological disorders. Victims also experience feelings of guilt and responsibility for the sexual abuse as well as feelings of betrayal, powerlessness, worthlessness and low self-esteem. It is impossible to calculate how many times a child's pornographic image may be possessed and distributed online. Each and every time such an image is viewed, traded, printed or downloaded, the child in that image is victimized again.[29]

Think about your own friends and relatives. Is human trafficking what you want for them? If not, why is it in the least bit acceptable to overlook the damage being done to others' unwilling friends and relatives who are victims in this industry?

Willing Participants?

It's not just the production of porn that harms children and women who are trafficked to produce it. Traffickers often use porn not only to make a profit off their victims' images but also to break them so they can sell them for sex and then make them participate in making more porn.

Some women unknowingly become porn stars and learn about it later, such as in cases of revenge porn, in which a person agreed to be filmed with their partner for personal use, only to discover later it was broadcast over the internet without their permission. There is also filming of individuals without their knowledge, which is easier than ever with technological advancements. Many women have had their privacy violated without knowledge or consent and have unknowingly become someone's porn. These violations impact a victim as does any sexual objectification. Thousands of South Korean women gathered in Seoul, South Korea, in July 2018 to protest the epidemic of people using hidden cameras to take intimate photos, and to seek government action.[30]

Consenting to What?

Pornography can also be harmful to the consenting adults who get caught up in its production. There is no way of knowing whether actors in porn films actually give consent, but even when they do, they may be consenting without knowledge of what they're getting into, because the industry produces increasingly violent images. One porn actor recounted having her hide whipped and caned for thirty-five minutes without having had full awareness of what would take place in that scene. She said, "I have permanent scars up and down the backs of my thighs. It was all things that I had consented to, but I didn't know quite the brutality of what was about to happen to me until I was in it."[31] This all occurs because of the demand from predominantly male consumers. Actors suffer in real life because of the consumer's desire to sexually objectify people. Actors who are required to act as if they are enjoying everything in the story on film are harmed in real life. Add to this damage the negative effects of SO and self-objectification, which were discussed earlier in this chapter.

Brain Damage

For those who don't believe Ted Bundy (he was, after all, a serial rapist and murderer), today's neuroscience would persuade them that porn is highly detrimental not only for those involved in its production but also for viewers because porn negatively impacts their brains, their relationships, and their communities.

Pornography rewires the viewer's brain. Porn is a dopamine stimulator and creates an addictive response in viewers that escalates like any drug. Dopamine triggers the creation of neural pathways between pleasure and porn viewing. The neurons that fire together wire together. Unlike natural highs such as sex with a loving partner, the dopamine let-down cycle doesn't work with porn. Viewers find they can't get the pleasure without the porn, so they get addicted and then turn to increasingly violent porn as the pleasure plateaus. This is why porn use escalates.

Pornography can cause boys and men to be unable to have an erection with a real partner, if the partner is not simulating the pornography they've viewed. Porn viewers often want to experience in real life what they see in porn, and they ask their partners to engage in sexual behaviors they have already viewed with porn. This is called sexual objectification toward the partner and removes personal creativity and agency from sex and damages the relationship and the partner.

Pornography consumes more than the currency going into the industry from buyers. It consumes the irreplaceable time, life energy, and humanity (by SO) of all who are involved in the industry and all the people who engage in viewing it, whether or not they pay for it.

Porn programs sexual objectification and violence against females into the brains of its viewers. With the availability of smartphones, this is happening at an increasingly early age. By age eighteen, 90 percent of males and 60 percent of females report having viewed porn.[32] According to NOVUS.org,

> For the majority of our nation's youth, they will not reach eleven years old before being exposed to explicit hardcore and often violent imagery while on the internet, something many of them carry in their back pocket. With the average American teenager spending nine hours a day on various forms of media, this exposure is often a daily occurrence.[33]

With such early programming of still-developing brains, porn fuels the sexual objectification of women and the resulting self-objectification, and it becomes primary and normalized. This is increasing, even accelerating, and there are consequences to society.

Old Normal is deeply ingrained not only into Western culture but into cultures around the world. Patriarchy and religion are replete with Old Normal conditioning worth examining as we continue to look at reasons for the proliferation of #MeToo stories.

Questions to Thoughtfully Consider and Discuss

1. What are your thoughts about #MeToo being a transformational event?
2. What is an individual's responsibility for Old Normal?
3. What do you believe contributes to the ongoing objectification of, harassment of, abuse of, and violence toward women and children?
4. What is your view of the implementing of New Normal?
5. What is your experience with objectification?
6. What is your experience with self-objectification?
7. What responsibility do people who are not involved in sex trafficking have for the lives and well-being of fellow and sister humans who are being trafficked?
8. What are your thoughts about legalizing prostitution?
9. How harmless is pornography?
10. What is one thing you can do to stop accepting Old Normal behaviors?

EIGHT

Part Two:
Old Normal

In the house I grew up in, only the bathrooms and exterior doors had locks. One night, after everyone else had gone to bed, I heard a soft knock on my door. I continued to breathe deeply, as I had been in my nearly successful effort to fall asleep, turned my back to the door, and snuggled under the covers, thinking whoever it was would go away when I didn't answer.

The door slid open, and light from the hallway hit the wall. I opened my eyes to my dad's shadow slipping into the room and turning to shut the door. I closed my eyes and breathed in the same rhythm as he sat on the bed, put his hand on my shoulder, and ran it down my side to my waist before returning to my shoulder to travel down my side again and again. I smelled alcohol. His hand grew heavy and hot as it rested on my waist, then he stood up and slid out the door.

A few nights later it happened again—the knock, the slide, the sit, the touch, the retreat—and many more times after that.

Then came the night that, despite my efforts to stay awake and aware, I fell asleep flat on my back and woke to a weight on my body, my father lying on top of me over the bed covers, holding my face in his hands as he kissed my eyes, forehead, cheeks, and mouth. His alcohol breath turned my stomach and tasted sour on my lips.

I breathed lightly, hardly at all. I made myself cold and stiff like a statue. I kept my mouth shut and clenched my hands to my sides and my legs tightly together.

"So beautiful," he whispered. "So beautiful." His hands moved to my breasts, and he started to grind against me, whispering, "So beautiful, so beautiful."

I pretended I was dead, like the people in caskets I had seen at funerals.

My father stopped moving in the dark. He cradled my head between his hands and kissed my lips, then rolled off me to kneel beside the bed. He stood up, slipped out the door, and closed it with a quiet click.

The next evening as my mother passed my bedroom on her way to bed, I said, "Dad has been coming to my room at night."

She turned and looked at me. "He what?"

"He's been coming to my room at night when everyone is asleep. Last night he laid on me and kissed me and put his hands on me." My voice came out in a squeaky rush. I felt embarrassed and hot, but it was true.

Her face blanched. "Did he get under the covers with you?"

"No," I said, backing up against the door.

"I'll take care of it," she said and walked down the hallway to my parents' bedroom.

Neither of my parents talked to me for a week. When my mother finally did find me in the hallway alone, she said in passing, "I told him if he ever laid hands on you again, I would kill him."

#MeToo, Raisha

Raisha's life never returned to the normal she'd known before she became a victim of sexual abuse. She was too young to understand why her father would do such things. He blamed it on alcohol. The truth is, there have been countless alcohol consumers who have never violated their families' trust by stepping over the line from honest love and appreciation to objectification and abuse. In spite of the courage she exercised by telling the truth to her mother, Raisha's experience became part of her story and part of her filter in how she took in information and how she viewed the opposite sex.

So much has been written about what causes gender-based discrimination and sexual abuse and violence. What are your thoughts about what contributes to and constitutes Old Normal? I'm pretty sure these chapters on Old Normal only tell part of the story. Let's look at a few more elements of Old Normal I hope will disappear as we create New Normal.

Patriarchy

One of the roots of sexual harassment and violence is the dynamic of unequal power relations between men and women. The cultural imbalance of power in patriarchy is fertile ground for abuse, and the target of the vulnerable victim and their vulnerability is the shield that the powerful use to keep the victim silent. Patriarchy is a society or community organized on patriarchal (the father's) blood lines and is a system of society or government in which the father or eldest male is head of the family where descent is traced through the male line. In patriarchy, men hold the power, and women for the most part are excluded from or limited in holding positions of power. The patriarchal objectification of women used as sexual objects, for creating heirs, and for labor contributes to Old Normal.

In her book *The Creation of Patriarchy*, Gilda Lerner argues that patriarchal society developed in the Near East and was fully established by 500 BC. Having traced Western history since then, she notes "the record of the past has been written and interpreted by men and has primarily focused on the activities and intentions of males. Women have always, as have men, been agents and actors in history, but they have been excluded from recorded history."[1] What this means is that in patriarchy, women are not people, but objects to be used or ignored as needed by those in power.

Most countries have governments that rarely include women as leaders, legislators, judges, or active participants in creating and managing the common resources of a country. Because women are not represented, concerns that have traditionally fallen under their purview are not addressed in law and policy. A female head of state is still rare. In 2019, twenty-three women were head of government or state worldwide,[2] and women legislators worldwide averaged 24 percent of legislative bodies.[3] Despite gains in the 2018 midterm election, the US ranks seventy-fifth globally in terms of women's representation in government.[4]

According to the 2018 Women in Congress Study, a new record was set in 2018 for the most women ever serving in the US legislative branch with twenty-two in the Senate (seventeen Democrat, five Republican) and eighty-eight in the House of Representatives (sixty-six Democrat, twenty-four Republican). The US national legislature has a significantly smaller percentage of women in legislative seats compared to the state legislatures.

Mary Hawkesworth, Kathleen Casey, Krista Jenkins, and Katherine Kleeman documented women's effectiveness in government in *Legislating by and for Women: A Comparison of the 103rd and 104th Congresses, Center for American Women and Politics, 2001*. The authors examine legislative case studies in the policy areas of crime, women's health, healthcare, health insurance reform, reproductive rights, and welfare reform. The findings were compiled from interviews with female members who served in those two Congresses. The researchers found that women legislators introduced more bills and delivered 9 percent more federal funds to their districts on average than men. Research showed that women work in a bipartisan way and are more effective when in the minority than men, and that they work behind the scenes and on committees to advance policy issues related to women, family, and the elderly. Women legislators work more for social and women's issues and speak more often on the house floor about women's issues. According to the research, women also retire earlier when they self-assess that they're not increasing in effectiveness.

Another example of how patriarchal society views females as objects is the way laws have dealt with crimes against women. Susan Brownmiller traced the laws regarding rape in Europe and found them to treat sexual assault as an assault not against the woman but against the male relatives or family of the victim. The earliest definition of rape as an attack on a person happened in England in 1285. Until then, offenses of "lying with" against the "will" of a woman was a crime not against the woman but against her family or community.[5]

Patriarchies use rape against the females of the enemy as a military strategy. The use of rape during wars has been extensively documented. Susan Brownmiller tracked millions of rapes against the occupied territory's female population over the last 2,000 years.[6] Rape during wartime is now outlawed in both US military code and international law, yet the practice continues to this day, along with sex trafficking victims of war.

In 1998, UN nations including the US made the Rome Statute, creating and governing the work of the International Criminal Court. The statute established sexual violence in war and armed conflict as a grave violation of international law and a means of undermining international peace. The UN Security Council further adopted Resolution 1325 (2000) and 1820 (2008), which determined that the use of sexual violence as a weapon of war and armed conflict constitutes both a war crime and a threat to international peace and security. The United States has since withdrawn from the Rome Statute and International Criminal Court. As a member of the UN Security Council, it was one of the countries unanimously passing Resolution 1820.[7]

Another way patriarchy objectifies women is by viewing them only as sexual and labor sources in the home, limiting their access to education and employment. Education and work (economic independence) both affect political participation. Women's access to education in the US improved through federal student loans and grants and through the 1972 Title IX laws outlawing gender discrimination in public colleges and in university admissions. As a result of increased secondary education, women have prepared for and increased their political participation around the world.

Citizenship is considered the *standing* which provides a sense of one's place in a hierarchical society.[8] People are more likely to participate as citizens when they have resources, including higher levels of education, income, and effective engagement in the political process that garners results.[9] Two of the things that give *standing* are the right to vote and the right to work.

Increased gender parity in socioeconomic status (earned income and breadwinner/co-breadwinner status) and in political engagement in the United States have resulted from women's greater access to education, thanks to access to student aid funds as a result of the National Defense Education Act of 1958, the 1965 Higher Education Act, and growing admissions to public schools under Title IX of the 1972 Education Amendments. The 1965 Act passed after the Democrats won congressional seats in 1964 and opposing Republicans were unseated. It included the Powell Amendment, which used the same language as the 1964 Civil Rights Act. President Lyndon Baines Johnson supported the 1965 Act as an anti-poverty measure. After the 1972 passage of

Title IX, the percentage of women graduates increased until in 1981 more women than men earned bachelors of arts degrees.[10]

As a result, political involvement of women in the US is increasing. More women than men voted in presidential elections after 1980 through 2004. According to Deondra Rose, author of *Citizens by Degree: Higher Education Policy and the Changing Gender Dynamics of American Citizenship*, "experts attribute this shift to a change in social climate—educational attainment and labor force participation increased among women in the second half of the twentieth century; both factors are strong correlates of voting." Any aspect of patriarchy that objectifies women and results in the self-objectification of women is part of Old Normal that leads to more of the Mess. Let's take a look at one of the big offenders, organized religion.

Religion

As a believer in Jesus, my understanding of the world includes a belief in the fallen state of humanity and our propensity to fall short of the divine pattern or plan that is ideal human behavior. Sin is falling short of perfection. To me, people's sin is part and parcel of Old Normal. The Scriptures call people to "act justly, love mercy, and walk humbly."[11] It also says, "All have sinned and fall short of the glory of God."[12] Sin will happen in New Normal too, but my hope is that people will adopt changes when we address our shortcomings as they occur, and work to minimize the damage to others.

I believe if we take an honest look at ourselves, no matter what religious beliefs we hold, we can see that humans are imperfect. We may see failures from which we can rise and learn, because every major religious group is rife with discrimination, harassment, abuse, and violence.

Nonreligious belief systems fare no better. Does the fact that we all fall short of perfection justify overlooking or perpetuating injustice, lack of mercy, and pride that fuels the abuse of our fellow and sister human beings?

In the Old Testament, in the book of Genesis, it says,

> So God created mankind in his own image, in the image of God he created them; male and female he created them. God blessed them and said to them, "Be fruitful and increase in number; fill the earth and subdue it. Rule over the fish in the sea and the birds in the sky and over every living creature that moves on the ground." . . .
>
> And it was so. God saw all that he had made, and it was very good.[13]

Judeo-Christian religions were founded on a document that calls for co-rule. Unfortunately, people had their own idea to concentrate power in the males and subjugate females and followed that idea instead. In his book *A Call to Action: Women, Religion, Violence, and Power*, Jimmy Carter asserts, "The relegation of women to an inferior or circumscribed status by many religious leaders is one of the primary reasons for the promotion and perpetuation of sexual abuse. . . . It is crucial that devout believers abandon the premise that their faith mandates sexual discrimination."[14] Take a look at Old Normal in religions around the world and imagine that the victims are people you know and love. Is sexual discrimination and abuse tolerable for them? Why are we tolerating harm done to others' loved ones?

Buddhism

Buddhist gurus and teachers are not immune to credible accusations of abuse. Journalist Ephrat Livni reported in a September 2018 article in *Quartz*, www.qz.com:

> A petition by victims of sexual abuse by prominent Buddhist teachers signed by more than 1,850 people and promoted with the hashtag

#MeTooGuru—urged the Dalai Lama to take a stand against sexual abuse.[15]

A former Shambhala teacher released a report alleging that the Sakyong had sexually abused and exploited some of his most devoted female followers for years. Women quoted in the report wrote of drunken groping and forcefully extracted sexual favors. The report said that senior leaders at Shambhala—an organization whose motto is "Making Enlightened Society Possible"—knew of the Sakyong's misconduct and covered it up.[16]

Christianity

In the New Testament of the Bible, Galatians 3:28 of the New International Version (NIV), the apostle Paul is quoted as writing regarding the equal status of all Christians in their faith: "There is neither Jew nor Gentile, neither slave nor free, nor is there male and female, for you are all one in Christ Jesus."[17] However, the Christian church has fueled discrimination and objectification of females and males, adding to the Mess. Women have never held the highest positions of authority in the structure of the Christian church. Leadership in the church is a factor in the rampant sexual abuse scandals that have plagued the church for centuries.

According to Veronica Yates, the director of Child Rights International Network,

> Child sexual abuse in religious institutions is one of the worst crimes ever committed against children. Our research shows that allegations of child sexual abuse in the Catholic Church have been made in every corner of the world, yet the Holy See continues to harbor perpetrators of abuse, obstruct justice for victims and deny accountability.[18]

In an August 2018 article in the *Guardian*, reporter Harriet Sherman in Dublin reported the Pope asking for forgiveness for the cover-ups of hundreds of priests in Ireland accused of sexually abusing children since the 1950s as part of a global crisis in the Catholic Church.[19]

According to a June 2019 story in the *Washington Post* by Sarah Stankorb, Protestant and independent Christian bloggers have uncovered and reported on a slew of #MeToo scandals.[20] And Christianity is not the only religion worldwide with a long history of sexual discrimination and abuse of children and women.

Hinduism

In the Hindu culture, children have no voice, and to report sexual abuse generates shame for the victim, so families are pressured to keep secrets. In August 2018, Thomas Mackintosh of BBC News, London, reported the story of a Hindu woman who was sexually abused by a family friend from age four to fourteen and the conviction of her abuser thirty years later. The article quoted Fay Maxted OBE, CEO of the Survivor's Trust, who said,

> [Some cultures have] particular beliefs about female purity and family honor that create additional barriers to seeking help for child sexual abuse victims . . . In some Asian communities women and girls may be held responsible for the sexual abuse they have suffered and will suffer loss of family honor as a result of the shame and stigma . . . There can be a total lack of awareness of what constitutes sexual abuse, and even discussing being a victim can be seen as dishonorable.[21]

Deepa Narayan, social scientist and author of *Chup: Breaking the Silence about India's Women*, wrote about the predominantly Hindu country India:

> Sexual abuse in India remains widespread despite tightening of rape laws in 2013. According to the National Crimes Records Bureau,

in 2016 the rape of minor girls increased by 82% compared with the previous year . . . 95% of rapists were not strangers but family, friends and neighbours.

The culturally sanctioned degradation of women is so complete that the prime minister of India, Narendra Modi, launched a national programme called Beti Bachao (Save Our Girls). India can arguably be accused of the largest-scale human rights violation on Earth: the persistent degradation of the vast majority of its 650 million girls and women."[22]

Islam

In an article by an anonymous Muslim woman posted in the *Independent*, a UK online news site, she shared her story about being sexually assaulted at age thirteen by a director of a Muslim charity. She urged other Muslim women to bravely tell the world their stories, noting that sexual assault is not limited to the Catholic Church. The author stated,

> We have talked about the abuse in the Roman Catholic Church for decades, now we Muslims need to talk about this on our own doorsteps. These men can't hide behind their beards anymore. . . . I am not alone, and I urge every survivor to speak. . . . We no longer feel shame; we will no longer keep the dirty secrets of men. I urge Muslims to stand up and speak out against those in positions of power. You have done nothing wrong. This everyday occurrence needs to be in our everyday conversations.[23]

The legality of child marriages and the unwillingness of authorities to take legal action regarding child slavery are also indicators of the damage patriarchal religion can inflict. In Afghanistan and Pakistan, sexual abuse and slavery of boys is common. Child sexual abuse and rape are also frequent in Muslim communities in Britain, according to Shaista Gohir, chair of Muslim Women's Network UK, a national charity that works to improve social justice and equality for Muslim women and girls and operates a national helpline. In an April 2010 article in the *Guardian,* she wrote,

> In Yemen, more than a quarter of girls are married before the age of 15. Cases of girls dying during childbirth are not unusual, and recently, one 12-year-old child bride even died from internal bleeding following sexual intercourse. In another case, a 12-year-old girl was married to an 80-year-old man in Saudi Arabia. . . .
>
> A too-passive attitude in dealing with child abuse has rubbed off on Muslim communities in Britain, too. I have heard many stories at first hand of child sexual abuse and rape, which show that the issue is not being addressed at all.[24]

Judaism

The Jewish #GamAni (Hebrew for #MeToo) movement started up right after Harvey Weinstein was reported as a sexual abuser. As of February 27, 2019, the #GamAni Facebook page had over 1,100 members, who were invited to share "personal experiences of the interaction of gender and culture at Jewish communal organizations."[25]

On July 26, 2018, Haaretz.com published an editorial letter by Clare Hedwat describing the Jewish world's "#MeToo Crisis." Ms. Hedwat wrote, "Working in Jewish organizations worldwide, I internalized a gender hierarchy that took years to disassemble. The Jewish institutional world suffers a sickness of ingrained, unethical gender and power relations, and sexual aggression is just one of its consequences."[26]

Other Religions

Religions can lay foundations for abuse by their teachings on male and parental authority, limiting the basic human rights of women and children. In *A Call to Action: Women, Religion, Violence and Power,* President Jimmy Carter asserts that the relegation of women to an inferior or circumscribed status by many religious leaders is one of the primary reasons for the promotion and perpetuation of sexual abuse.[27]

Organized Atheism has had its own share of abuse scandals, from atheist author and speaker Lawrence Krauss to the termination of past president of American Atheists David Silverman after sexual assault allegations. Whether religious or atheistic, any belief system that justifies the devaluation, objectification, harassment, abuse, or any sexual violence against any person is part of Old Normal. They fuel the culture war on women and on those who are considered weak.

Questions to Thoughtfully Consider and Discuss

1. How does patriarchy objectify women and children?
2. How has religion impacted your views about gender?
3. What do you believe about the value of a human being?
4. What basic rights do humans share?
5. How does country of origin or gender or religion impact someone's basic human rights?
6. What is the cost of keeping secrets about sexual harassment, abuse, and violence?
7. Whose responsibility is it to protect children from people who would violate their basic human rights?
8. What else contributes to Old Normal?
9. How willing are you to dream of and engage in conversations about a global transformation to New Normal?
10. What is one step you can take to help create New Normal?

NINE

Part One: The Culture War on Women

College is a time to find your way on your own. A time of growth and discovery. Being a lover of all things that involve creativity, I signed up for an after-hours woodworking class. I admire beautiful woodwork and wanted to be able to make my own furniture one day. In the class, I designed a box about the size of a shoebox. The lid had a glass insert framed in wood. Between the glass and wood was black sand from Hawaii and small shells that I had collected on the beach there. The base had dovetail corners and had been sanded smooth. All I had left to do was attach the brackets of the lid to the base. There was one more class, so I was right on time with my project. I was so close, yet that box is just a memory. I never did finish it.

At the end of the second-to-last class, the instructor invited me to his house to watch a movie and eat popcorn with him and his girlfriend. This is an offer I would never have agreed to had there not been a girlfriend mentioned. I arrived at his house, and it was quiet. There was no girlfriend. No movie and no popcorn. He wasted no time in raping me and then let me go.

I can still remember blaming myself. I was stunned, confused, betrayed. I didn't even think to report it to the college or police. This was 1975, and I doubt it would have made a difference, since it still doesn't today (more often than not). It took me decades to realize there is no shame or blame on my part. This person whose class I paid to take groomed me, just as, I am sure now, he had done to other young women.

It took witnessing the courage of Christine Blasey Ford to finally let my secret out. I had never told my husband, children, friends, or family. I held it inside for forty-three years. Ms. Ford did not win her case, but she is forever a winner to me and thousands of other women whose stories flowed forth as a result. #Metoo is #NeverAgain. And I will always #believesurvivors.

#MeToo, Crystal

Crystal's story took place in a culture of silence. In her culture, problems were swept under the rug and rarely addressed. It was an act of tremendous courage to tell her story decades later. *Culture* is defined as "the customary beliefs, social forms, and material traits of a racial, religious, or social group; the characteristic features of everyday existence (such as diversions or a way of life) shared by people in a place or time." War is defined as "a state of hostility, conflict, or antagonism; a struggle or competition between opposing forces or for a particular end."[1] After seeing the response of women around the world to Alyssa Milano's tweet, or after reading about the history of other women's movements around the globe, it would not be a stretch to call women a social group. And it wouldn't be a stretch to say that there's been a war against them. The struggle is real, and females as a group have been the losers. This is at the epicenter of Old Normal.

It Starts before Birth

With today's diagnostic tools for pregnancy, one can detect a child's sex in the earliest phase. Parents are using this information to terminate pregnancies of girls. In Asia, birth histories and census data show an extraordinarily high proportion of male births and male children under five, especially in China, India, Pakistan, Vietnam, the South Caucasus, and in parts of Indonesia. Researchers believe this is because of selective abortions and infanticide because the parent does not want to hear "It's a girl."[2]

In China and Korea, familial and public patriarchy combine to produce a system that places women in a subordinate position and where sons are preferred. Confucianism also leads to the preference for male descendants, as the traditional gender division makes women economically dependent on men. The strong need for economic support in old age, and discrimination against girls in education, make rural people favor sons. China's fertility control policies contribute to son preference. Because of these policies, some people turn to sex-selective abortion to ensure at least one son. And parents who strongly desire a son often abandon female children or neglect daughters.[3] In China, son preference and sex-selective abortion have led to 32 million excess males under the age of twenty years.[4]

In India, the expense of the dowry is the main cultural reason for sex-selective abortions, infanticide, and neglect of girl children. Jonathan Abbamonte, research analyst at the Population Research Institute (PRI), reported on February 13, 2018:

> Millions of women have gone missing from India's population due to persistent, deep-seated male bias and extreme son preference. According to a recent report from the Government of India, a

staggering 63 million women are now missing from India's population. The report estimates that nearly 2 million women are lost every year. The report further estimates that an additional 21 million girls are "unwanted" by their parents. . . . The figures were released by the Indian Ministry of Finance in its Economic Survey 2017–2018 this January.[5]

This fact relates to the more recent development in India, which is to eliminate girls even before birth. PRI President Steven Mosher wrote, "Sex-selective abortion is, after all, the worst form of discrimination imaginable. It is a discrimination that kills."[6]

Researchers suggest that in India, approximately 400,000 people per year decide against girls by having sex-selective abortions.[7] Pregnancy can also increase risk of intimate partner violence, whether or not the baby's sex is known. According to the World Health Organization (WHO),

One potential risk factor significantly associated with intimate partner violence during pregnancy is having an unwanted or unplanned pregnancy, as numerous population-based studies in Bangladesh, Plurinational State of Bolivia, the Dominican Republic, Kenya, Malawi, Moldova, New Zealand, Rwanda, and Zimbabwe show (16, 25). A US population-based survey also showed that women who had mistimed or unwanted pregnancies reported significantly higher levels of abuse during pregnancy compared with those with intended pregnancies (15% versus 5%).[8]

Among sixteen states in the US reporting to the National Violent Death Reporting System from 2003 to 2007, the rate of pregnancy-associated homicide was 2.9 per 100,000 live births, a higher rate than for specific direct obstetric causes (hemorrhage, hypertensive disorders, or amniotic fluid embolism).[9]

Pregnancy still leads to job loss and lower pay for women in the US, which can create stress and impact the health of the baby. The number of pregnancy discrimination charges filed with the US Equal Employment Opportunity Commission (EEOC) between 1997 and 2011 increased by 50 percent. According to the ACLU,

> Research shows that mothers' wages decrease by 4 percent per child. In contrast, fathers' pay tends to go up by 6 percent when a child is born.
>
> Since nearly half of all working mothers—and 70 percent of Black mothers—are the sole or primary breadwinners in their households, pregnancy discrimination can spell economic disaster for the whole family, as well.[10]

Lack of prenatal and early childhood healthcare can lead to long-term effects such as childhood mortality, delayed education, lower earnings, and others. Even absent abortion, sex discrimination begins in the womb in male-dominated societies. Women in India are less likely to get prenatal care when pregnant with girls, according to a study by Leah Lakdawala of Michigan State University and Prashant Bharadwaj of the University of California, San Diego:

> In India, while it's illegal for a doctor to reveal the sex of an unborn baby or for a woman to have an abortion based on the baby's sex, both practices are common. . . . But knowing the sex of the baby through an ultrasound also can lead to discrimination for those pregnancies that go full-term. . . . This type of discrimination we're seeing, while not as severe as sex-selective abortion, is very important for children's health and well-being. . . . We know that children born at higher birth weights go to school for longer periods and have higher wages as adults, so the future implications here are pretty serious.[11]

Discrimination against Baby Girls

If the gender selection doesn't happen before birth, it can happen after the baby is born. According to Human Life International India's Milagres Pereira, a resident of India, "Even now there are places where untrained village midwives have been known to put a spoonful of un-husked rice into the [newborn's] throat, so the soaked rice expands and chokes the child to death."[12]

Infanticide is the unlawful killing of very young children. It is found in both indigenous and sophisticated cultures around the world. According to the BBC "Ethics Guide: Female Infanticide,"

> Female infanticide is the deliberate killing of girl babies. Female infanticide is more common than male infanticide, and in some countries, particularly India and China, is likely to have serious consequences on the balance of the sexes in the population. The reasons behind it are almost always cultural, rather than directly religious.[13]

Gender-Based Violence

In the *United Nations 2017 Report of the Secretary-General on Conflict-Related Sexual Violence*, gender-based violence is defined as rape, sexual slavery, forced prostitution, forced pregnancy, forced abortion, enforced sterilization, forced marriage, and any other form of sexual violence of comparable gravity perpetrated against women, men, girls, or boys that is directly or indirectly linked to a conflict. International law is cast aside, and women and children pay the costs. Despite the UN Convention on Elimination of Discrimination Against Women signed by many member countries, despite the International Convention on Sex Trafficking, despite its own policy that UN peacekeepers may not assault women and children, despite its own (internal) sexual harassment policy, United Nations staff and peacekeepers have been accused of sexual assault on local populations, sex trafficking, and sexual harassment.[14]

Gender-based violence can have lifelong or lethal repercussions because it drives the forced displacement of people groups and inhibits their safe return home. Gender-based violence is used to attack and alter the ethnic or religious identity of persecuted groups. Oppressors integrate gender-based violence into their strategies to seize or occupy land, displaying women as trophies of war. Gender-based violence is often the result of a collapse of a state or nation. The economic destabilization or interruption of commerce can lead to sex trafficking. Because of this, the United Nations is putting women protection advisors where they install peacekeeping forces.[15]

The UN established the Gender-Based Violence Information System to help the international community track ongoing events. The UN also gives grants for the prevention of gender-based violence or for work to directly alleviate gender-based violence. The UN is also working with deployed UN staff to stop their abuse of civilians.[16]

UN resolutions changed the classic security paradigm by recognizing that conflict-related sexual violence is "not random or isolated, but integral to the operations, ideology and economic strategy of a range of State . . . and non-State [groups]."[17] Wars are still being fought on and over the bodies of women, to control their production and reproduction by force. Across regions, sexual violence has been perpetrated in public or witnessed by loved ones, to terrorize communities and fracture families through the violation of taboos, signifying that nothing is sacred and no one is safe.[18]

These strategies have always been predated by human rights violations against gender and group identity, with the preponderance of victims who are politically and economically marginalized being women and girls. Historically and in the present, combatants are allowed to rape with impunity, to take women's resources, and to steal women and girls for trafficking, all to help soldier income.[19]

According to the United Nations,

> South Sudan's armed opposition abducted women and girls as young as twelve and lined them up so commanders could choose "wives," and those not selected were left to be raped repeatedly by other fighters. One survivor said she was "tied to a tree and raped by two fighters until she passed out because of pain and bleeding." When she regained consciousness, she was threatened with rape again.[20]

Research shows that self-reliance, economic empowerment, and having a political voice are the most effective forms of protection from sexual violence, but in aftermath of war, occupiers' protection leads to spikes in child marriage. Results of gender-based violence include social stigma (if captured and raped in prison, released men are heroes, but women are significantly more likely to be honor killing victims because of the disgrace their rape brings on the family), lack of reparations, and the cultural rejection of children of rape victims.[21]

Dr. Peggy Reeves Sanday is an anthropologist and researcher from the University of Pennsylvania. She was awarded the 2015 American Anthropological Association's Committee on Gender Equity in Anthropology Award for her numerous contributions to the fight for gender equality.[22] Dr. Sanday is the author of a number of groundbreaking scholarly works, including "The Socio-Cultural Context of Rape," which established the paradigm for explaining the occurrence and context of rape cross culturally. Dr. Sanday's books *Fraternity Gang Rape: Sex, Brotherhood and Privilege on Campus* and *A Woman Scorned: Acquaintance Rape on Trial* have also been highly influential in the field of public interest anthropology.

In her book *Women at the Center: Life in a Modern Matriarchy,* Dr. Sanday reported about her studies of the Minangkabau, one of the largest ethnic groups in Indonesia. This society, numbering about 4 million in West Sumatra, is a highly literate, productive, creative, and peaceful society with strong egalitarian and democratic relationships between genders and a powerful respect for women.[23] An abstract published in the *Journal of Social Issues* regarding her research about the cultural forces impacting sexual violence reported:

> This research departs from the familiar assumption that rape is an inherent tendency of male nature, and begins with the assumption that human sexual behavior, though based in a biological need, is an expression of cultural forces. The incidence, meaning, and function of rape in a cross-cultural sample of tribal societies are presented. Two general hypotheses guide the research: first, the incidence of rape varies cross-culturally; second, a high incidence of rape is embedded in a distinguishably different cultural configuration than a low incidence of rape.
>
> The data suggest that rape is part of a cultural configuration which includes interpersonal violence, male dominance, and sexual separation. Rape is interpreted as the sexual expression of these forces in societies where the harmony between men and their environment has been severely disrupted."[24]

Sexual violence is a cultural phenomenon. In her article "Rape-Prone Versus Rape-Free Campus Cultures," Dr. Sanday writes,

> Rape in tribal societies is part of a cultural configuration that includes interpersonal violence, male dominance, and sexual separation. Phallocentrism is a dominant psycho-sexual symbol in these societies and men "use the penis to dominate their women" as Yolanda and Robert Murphy say about the Mundurucu. Rape-prone behavior is associated with environmental insecurity and females are turned into objects to be controlled as men struggle to retain or to gain control of their environment. Behaviors and attitudes prevail that separate the sexes and force men into a posture of proving their manhood. Sexual violence is one of the ways in which men remind themselves that they are superior. As such, rape is part of a broader struggle

for control in the face of difficult circumstances. Where men are in harmony with their environment, rape is usually absent.[25]

One of the ways males start to dominate in a society is by sexualization.

Sexualizing Girls

Sexualization is not a healthy form of sexuality. According to the American Psychological Association (APA), sexualization happens when a person's worth is assumed to only come from his or her sexiness, when a child is expected or encouraged to act or dress sexually, when a person is treated as a sex object rather than as a whole person, and when physical characteristics are considered to be the only indicator of sexiness. The term sexualization is also used to refer to a type of psychological defense mechanism in which people use sexual behavior as a means of managing their anxiety."[26] If you see a person in a T-shirt that reads "Future Porn Star" (or an infant onesie—they're available online), you're reading sexualization. Western culture is becoming increasingly sexualized, girls are the preeminent target, and it's gone global.

Studies say the sexualization of girls is happening at a younger and younger age as parents allow their girls from toddlerhood to preteen to be bombarded with adult influences and perceptions. To sexualize is to make something sexual. This is a role meant for an age where sexual consent is possible, adulthood. Researchers at Knox College found that choice of dolls indicated the prevalence of self-sexualization in girls as young as six to nine. In the study,

> the researchers showed girls two different paper dolls, one in tight, revealing clothing, the other in a modest popular looking outfit. When asked to choose which doll looked most like themselves, which represented how they would like to look, and which looked like the popular girls at school, and which doll they would rather play with, 68 percent of the girls said the sexy doll looked most like how they

want to look, and 72 percent reported that the sexy doll looked more popular than the non-sexy doll.[27]

A study at the University of Kent School of Psychology found there is a direct link between sexual objectification of females and aggression toward them:

> The study found that higher levels of objectification were significant predictors of aggression towards girls, consistent with the claim that, among other negative outcomes, the perception of females as nothing but sexual objects also evokes aggression against them. The study featured 273 participants aged 12 to 16 years old from a secondary school in London (in an area experiencing problems with gangs and delinquency). The findings showed that the objectification-aggression link manifests itself at least as early as the teenage years, suggesting that the detrimental effects of perceiving females as objects begin at an early stage of development.[28]

As a result of sexual objectification, self-objectification is also rampant in Western culture. Eighty percent of ten-year-old girls in the US report they have been on a diet, according to a recent study, "Eating Disorders Today—Not Just a Girl Thing." The study also reported the number-one wish for girls from the ages eleven through seventeen is to be thinner. Self-objectification also shows up in selfies girls post on social media. Sexy clothes, sexy poses, even nude photos are common.

A study based on interviews with more than 200 adolescent girls shows that social media and access to cell phones often reinforces sexualization of girls. Whether it's getting bullied or harassed about appearance or sex by text (sexting) or receiving unsolicited photos of boys' private parts or getting blackmailed to send nude pictures (which mostly happens to girls) that are forwarded through social networks, social media can bring out the worst in adolescents. The pressure to get "likes" on Instagram or Facebook is intense, and girls will self-objectify and display sexually suggestive or explicit photos in an effort to get group approval.

Stephanie V. Ng, MD, writes in her article "Social Media and the Sexualization of Adolescent Girls" in the *American Journal of Psychiatry Residents' Journal*:

> Emerging empirical research also corroborates the notion that while sexualization of females is rewarded online (usually by males), females are also punished for these same displays and are quick to be labeled by other female peers as "sluts" or "skanks." This perpetuates sexual double standards that reinforce gender stereotypes. A review of research on media and sexualization notes that the effects of social media on females is still in its infancy, but it is hypothesized that because social media features peers (rather than celebrities), exposure may generate even more social comparison and body shame than traditional media.[29]

Change in the Perception of Girls

If you ask her what it means to "throw like a girl" at age four or five, she'll take a ball and throw it. By the time she's six, she'll tell you that's an insult. If you ask four- or five-year-old children who they believe is smarter, boys or girls, most boys will side with boys, and usually girls will side with girls. By the time they're six, both will side with boys being smarter, though research shows no significant difference in cognitive abilities.

In studies about girls' self-perception, by age six or seven, girls start lacking confidence in their ability to learn and solve mathematical and scientific problems. Their beliefs become self-fulfilling prophecies, lowering the number of girls who study in the STEM fields. Changes in self-perception are exacerbated and influenced by educational systems that perpetuate old cultural norms in a variety of ways that diminish the capacity of females to see themselves objectively and refrain from self-objectification.

Hair and Cosmetics

Women who choose long hair get to pay extra for care. When they choose to go short, they get negative reviews from men and women alike. In a January 2014 article in the *New Statesman*, contributing editor and author Laurie Penny wrote,

> The "manosphere" . . . hates short-haired girls. On "game" forums and in personal dating manifestos, the wickedness of short-haired women pops up time and time again as theme and warning—stay away from girls [with short hair]. They're crazy, they're deliberately destroying their femininity to "punish" men. . . . Wearing your hair short, or making any other personal life choice that works against the imperative to be as conventionally attractive and appealing to patriarchy as possible, is a political statement. And the threat that if . . . we don't play the game we will end up alone and unloved is still a strategy of control.[30]

The US military standards do not permit women to shave their heads, even though this look is popular and easy to maintain for civilians, especially black women. Female servicemembers are not permitted to wear their hair in any of the short styles that men can wear their hair. The priority in the military is that women fit some male's version of what a woman should look like.

Any decision or action made on the basis of a person's gender is sexism. Sexism continues in the promulgation of cosmetics. Modern cosmetics are used to create false impressions of youthfulness and health, two keys to a woman's fertility.[31] Men, whose fertility window is longer, don't generally wear cosmetics, which are costly (it's a $60 billion dollar a year industry[32]) and time consuming (twenty minutes or more per application once or twice a day) and increase the objectification and self-objectification of females.

The use of cosmetics is so deeply ingrained in Western culture that it's an unspoken requirement to wear makeup in order to look acceptable. A 2003 study found that women pictured wearing cosmetics were evaluated as healthier, more confident, and even having greater earning potential than the same women wearing no makeup.[33] In another study participants were more likely to award "prestigious jobs" to women who were made up than to the same women makeup-free. Makeup earns female servers more tips from male (not female) patrons. The unfortunate truth that makeup is applied on the skin and absorbed directly from pores into the bloodstream, and that some ingredients used by cosmetics manufacturers are known carcinogens and are linked to other diseases, compounds the problem.

More children are using cosmetics. According to CosmeticBusiness. com,

> In Japan, one child in six uses cosmetics. On a global scale, children aged nine and younger account for 9.5% of beauty and skincare purchases, while the age group of 10 to 15 accounts for 7.1%. In 2013, consumers between nine and fifteen years of age made purchases worth $13.8 billion in total. By 2018, this figure is expected to rise to $18.1 billion. This data by Canadian, an international market research company, shows that children as a consumer group are in fact a force to be reckoned with when it comes to the beauty and cosmetics market.[34]

Cosmetics use also increases risk for sexual harassment. A 1991 study put a model in no makeup, moderate makeup, and heavy cosmetics and asked study participants to rate the model on likelihood of "provoking sexual harassment." When the model wore heavy cosmetics, she was rated as more likely to provoke sexual harassment than when she wore moderate cosmetics. Similarly, when the model wore moderate cosmetics, she was rated as significantly more likely to provoke sexual harassment than when she was not wearing cosmetics. When the model wore either heavy or moderate cosmetics, she was also rated as more likely to be sexually harassed than when she did not wear cosmetics.

In addition, male subjects rated the (female) model as more likely to provoke and to be sexually harassed than did female subjects. [35]

The word choice in this study is unfortunate, because it fails to address a cultural standard of beauty that makes it an unspoken (and sometimes spoken) requirement for many Western women to wear makeup in social and professional settings.

A culturally neutral description (of someone's likelihood of harassing someone based on how much makeup they wore) might put the onus on the harasser. Increasing the likelihood of a person harassing them is not the intention of women who wear cosmetics. As a rule, women adhere to the custom of wearing makeup to create favorable living and working conditions for themselves, however costly and uncomfortable it might be to observe this cultural norm.

The culture war has put women in a double bind, saying women are inciting violence against themselves if they do wear makeup, and they're showing up as unprofessional and less successful if they go without cosmetics.[36] How would you address the double bind?

Education

Research in the United States has proven that sex differences in learning are insignificant or nonexistent, and if there are any differences, they are not cognitive but originate from culture. An article by the American Psychological Association entitled "Think Again: Men and Women Share Cognitive Skills: Psychologists Have Gathered Solid Evidence That Boys and Girls or Men and Women Differ in Very Few Significant Ways" reported that research debunks myths about cognitive differences:

In a 2005 report, Janet Shibley Hyde, PhD, a psychologist at the University of Wisconsin, reviewed 46 different meta-analyses on sex differences, not only in cognition but also communication style, social and personality variables, motor behaviors and moral reasoning. In half the studies, sex differences were small; in another third they were virtually nonexistent.

Also in 2005, Elizabeth Spelke, PhD, a psychologist at Harvard University, and colleagues reviewed 111 studies (which) suggested that men and women on the whole possess an equal aptitude for math and science.[37]

Joseph Cimpian, Associate Professor of Economics and Education Policy—New York University, has researched gender differences in learning in the US education system with his colleague Sarah Lubienski, a professor of math education at Indiana University–Bloomington for over a decade. Research data and analysis showed that about half of the gender gap in math achievement was caused by teachers' low estimation of girls' abilities. Based on the results of their research, Professor Cimpian wrote,

> The obstacles that women face are largely societal and cultural. They act against women from the time they enter kindergarten—instilling in very young girls a belief they are less innately talented than their male peers—and persist into their work lives. Educational institutions—with undoubtedly many well-intentioned educators—are themselves complicit in reinforcing the hurdles. In order to dismantle these barriers, we likely need educators at all levels of education to examine their own biases and stereotypes.[38]

Globally, girls are shortchanged on education generally by lack of access to schools.

UNESCO is tracking education around the globe and confirms that

> despite progress, more girls than boys still remain out of school—16 million girls will never set foot in a classroom (UNESCO Institute for Statistics)—and women account for two thirds of the 750 million adults without basic literacy skills.

Poverty, geographical isolation, minority status, disability, early marriage and pregnancy, gender-based violence, and traditional attitudes about the status and role of women, are among the many obstacles that stand in the way of women and girls fully exercising their right to participate in, complete and benefit from education.[39]

If they do get into school, they're likely to experience implicit biases against girls and in favor of boys and socialization that uses boys as the measure or focus for girls. Biases include omission of and unequal space to women in the curriculum in most textbooks and examples, unequal time given to students to answer or expound on answers to questions (boys getting more time and encouragement from teachers), and social stereotyping.[40]

Fewer programs are available, and the funding for girls' and women's sports is significantly lower than for males at most schools. It took a movement to get athletics for girls, resulting in movement toward gender equity in sports for girls, but the playing field isn't level yet. The US Department of Education's Office for Civil Rights (OCR) enforces, among other statutes, Title IX of the Education Amendments of 1972. Title IX protects people from discrimination based on sex in education programs or activities that receive federal financial assistance. Title IX states,

> No person in the United States shall, on the basis of sex, be excluded from participation in, be denied the benefits of, or be subjected to discrimination under any education program or activity receiving Federal financial assistance.
>
> Title IX applies to institutions that receive federal financial assistance from ED, including state and local educational agencies.[41]

In spite of the fact that Title IX is over forty years old, many university athletic programs are still not in compliance. Fifty-nine percent of college students receiving athletic scholarships in 2017 were male. If there aren't strong enough team programs or enough female athletes applying, colleges don't spend all of the athletic scholarship money allocated to them, and there is an imbalance between male and female athletes. Even when scholarships are equitable for female college student athletes, oftentimes the females involved in intercollegiate sports are denied opportunities or are treated like second-class citizens, with much private funding going into the men's sports programs.[42] Professional sports see a huge pay gap between men's and women's sports. Separate but equal is not always equal.

Educational opportunities for girls and women rise (and often fall) with the women's movement. In general, it is women who advocate for women's education; however, some of the male leadership in some religions, including the Quakers, insist on equal education for all. For example, Maria Mitchell, astronomer who was awarded a medal from the King of Denmark for discovering a comet, was educated and served as a teacher's aide to her father, a Quaker living in Nantucket.

Upon her discovery, Mitchell earned respect and recognition among the scientific community as the first woman to be named to the American Academy of Arts and Sciences (in 1848). In 1849, Mitchell made computations for the American Ephemeris and Nautical Almanac. In 1850, she was elected to the American Association for the Advancement of Science. After nine years of travel, she accepted a position as professor of astronomy at Vassar College, where Mitchell and her students tracked and photographed sunspots and documented Venus traversing the sun—one of the rarest planetary alignments known to man, occurring only eight times between 1608 and 2012.[43]

The first academies and universities for girls were private, as public secondary schools did not serve girls. Education offered to girls did not include history of women except as a sidebar to the "real history" of war and politics, which was dominated by males. In terms of educational achievement, single-sex high schools and colleges graduated more women of achievement. In all-female environments, women faced no pressure to dampen or hide skills, and no gendered expectation limiting achievement.

Women had no professional role models of their gender beyond female staff of female academies and universities. Up until World War II, society expected women to end their education (or teaching position) with marriage. The culture dictated the terms of your education. Males had the privilege of graduating at a higher rate than women. During WWII the US military required educated and skilled women in the workforce, opening some doors to higher education, and since the second wave of the women's movement, more women started attending college. And as a result of increasing participation in higher education, more women started voting. Education and working outside the home led to increased participation in politics. According to the World Economic Forum (WEF), education equalization means women are educated and equipped to perform in good-paying jobs and careers of their choosing.

Social Conditioning Influencing Work

In India, as in the US, there is a shortage of women professionals working in STEM fields. Major barriers to women entering and keeping careers in STEM include subconscious bias about gender roles and capabilities, teacher prejudice similar to the US, limited grassroots efforts of employers to recruit and hire women, and limiting beliefs women have been conditioned by Indian culture to hold that diminish self-confidence.[44]

It's not just STEM that is failing to reach out to women employees in India. Except for India, the proportion of women who work worldwide is 50 percent. But in India, it has declined from 35 percent in 2005 to 26 percent in 2018. Indian women are not expected to have a job, and the culture has a strong influence on a woman's decision about whether to work.[45]

Forty-one percent of young Indians believe married women should not work outside the home. The median age of marriage for women is nineteen, and the majority of women do 90 percent of the family's unpaid housework, the highest proportion among families globally.[46]

In most cultures, women are expected to do domestic labor for free so that male relatives can earn the money. The burden of unpaid care work rests primarily on women all around the world, limiting their choices of occupations based on cultural, social conditioning. According to Our World India Data:

> Social norms across the world have long dictated that women should perform unpaid care work—taking care of children and elderly parents, making meals, doing laundry, maintaining family relations—while men engage in market work. . . . [T]he factors that have given married women the option to enter the labor force are foreseeably those that have lowered the time-cost of unpaid care work or made employment more compatible with it. . . . [T]his is not to say that unpaid care work is unimportant: it is a crucial, albeit unrecorded, aspect of economic development and well-being.[47]

Social conditioning to do unpaid work shows up in the workplace, where women are more frequently asked to do unpaid work. Female senior employees are asked to plan the office birthday party. Women are asked to clean up the conference room after a meeting, never seeing in the history of their employment a single male colleague asked to do this work. A new client comes to the company for a meeting. When he sees the senior vice president for the first time, he winks at her and orders, "Bring me a cup of coffee, honey." Women contributing the majority of work on a report find their names are left off the report when the male co-workers present it to the executive committee. These are all-too-common scenarios of unequal, unpaid work, which often goes unnoticed if they happen in a company culture accepting of this discrimination.

Opportunity Gaps

In 1963, women were paid on the average 60 percent of what men were paid to do the same work. The difference is called the pay gap. In 2019, the pay rates for women on average are 79 percent of what the average male earns. For black and Hispanic women, the pay gap is even larger—they earn only 74 percent of what the average white male earns.[48]

In the US, Equal Pay Day symbolizes how far into the year women must work to earn what men earned in the previous year. According to the National Committee on Pay Equity:

Equal Pay Day was originated by the National Committee on Pay Equity (NCPE) in 1996 as a public awareness event to illustrate the gap between men's and women's wages.

Since Census statistics showing the latest wage figures will not be available until late August or September, NCPE leadership decided years ago to select a Tuesday in April as Equal Pay Day. (Tuesday was selected to represent how far into the next work week women must work to earn what men earned the previous week.)[49]

In the UK, Equal Pay Day is observed in November, to call awareness to the 14 percent pay gap between men and women. According to the British NGO Where Women Work, which connects women to prime employers who are committed to closing the gender pay gap,

the UK's Office for National Statistics has published data showing the gender pay gap is not closing. The average for full-time workers stands at 14.1%, a figure that hasn't changed in the last three years. The gender pay gap is persisting, and so must we because woman must not be discriminated against at work for having a child.[50]

According to the World Economic Forum, women earn 23 percent less than men, and that pay gap is widening. Men earn and take home significantly more money than women, and men's earnings are increasing at a faster rate. The WEF measures and publicizes global performance of nations with its Gender Gap Index. Even Iceland, the country with the lowest Gender Gap Index score, deals with gender-based assumptions causing discrimination against women. For example, the WEF states that

> occupations predominantly held by women, such as nursing, are valued less than men's occupations, such as construction. There is a gender pay gap for work of equal value despite the existence of a law on equal pay since 1961. Icelandic women have been protesting against this imbalance by going on general strike since 1975.[51]

A November 2018 editorial in the *Wall Street Journal* presented a study suggesting "choices, not sexism, explain wage disparities." According to the WSJ Editorial Board, the study "offers compelling evidence that the choices and priorities of women account for much of the disparity in the pay differences between men and women."[52]

[53]The data from the Massachusetts Bay Transportation Authority evidenced that males worked 83 percent more overtime (which pays time and a half), were able to accept overtime shifts with less notice, and took 48 percent less unpaid leave, and that fathers took more overtime while mothers took more time off. Single mothers especially took less last-minute overtime. Harvard economists Valentin Bolotnyy and Natalia Emanuel concluded that women, especially single mothers, "value both time and the ability to avoid unplanned work much more than men" and that "these differences in choices" are "at the core of the gender earnings gap we observe."

The study does not look at motivations for these value choices. To understand and close the gender pay gap, it is essential to examine the motivations for choosing to forego additional income and the motivations for doing unpaid work.

The members of the *Wall Street Journal* editorial board believe that the best way to accommodate the differences in pay between men and women is "through the marketplace, not the untender mercies of government."[54] If the marketplace is going to succeed in remediating the pay gap, it will need to review historical marketplace conditions that have narrowed the gender pay gap, such as corporate responsibility for childcare as was common in World War II, when women filled roles abandoned by men. Such a review could shine a light for leaders to create future marketplace initiatives to bring fair compensation opportunity to women.[55]

In his book *Temp: How American Work, American Business, and the American Dream Became Temporary*, Louis Hyman makes the point that in the 1930s, new laws passed for Social Security, minimum wage, and labor unions were the result of 100 years of labor activity and the basis for the economic stability of the 1950s. Hyman also asserts that temporary (temp) workers define the labor force for everyone because the ability to hire temps makes it possible for employers not to offer full-time, permanent benefits and living-wage-paying jobs.

Hyman devotes a chapter to "Temporary Women," showing the development of office temp services (Kelly Girl and Manpower Inc.). Women were recruited to work in "interchangeable" roles for less money, and being mostly younger, they received less training and less pay. Theoretically these women only wanted temporary work that would allow time for child-rearing. Statistically, studies found that white women were more likely to do temp work when they lived in areas with a large African American population and could get domestic help.[56]

Manpower provided many reasons why temp work for women should be acceptable: to supplement household income, for luxuries, for savings. "All these ideas justified a kind of work that provided no career path, no true stability, and less money than a regular job."[57]

As temp work has increased, it has also become the only way many hardworking men and women are able to provide a living for their families while working "side hustles." For example, Uber (87% male) and Etsy (87% female) are platforms for people who are suffering job insecurity. Fifty-five percent of average American households in 2014 had month-to-month fluctuations in their income of 30 percent. Seventy-five percent of households in the lowest 20 percent of earnings had these fluctuations, not from changing jobs, but from working different amounts every month. They pull in more income by driving for Uber or selling stuff over the internet. Twenty-two percent of Etsy earners combined revenue sources.

Most workers cannot expect regular hours within service industries. Scheduling uncertainty pairs with digital on-demand jobs. Many employers are using scheduling software to assure they don't work their employees more than twenty-nine hours per week (in order to minimize paying benefits). As a result, employees face ever-changing, uncertain schedules.

Sara Sanford, executive director of Gender Equity Now (GEN), a not-for-profit research and policy organization and creator of GEN Certification, the first standardized certification for gender equity for US businesses, wrote,

> Experts had identified 2059 as the year the pay gap would close. In September 2018, the same experts announced that we'll need to adjust our expectations—to the year 2119.
>
> Looking beyond the wage gap, we've researched hidden opportunity gaps, which are just as significant:
> - Men are twice as likely to state they've been offered the opportunity to shadow someone in a senior role.
> - Men are 50% more likely to state that their manager has asked them about their career goals in the last 12 months. Women aren't asked as often what they want to do with their careers.[58]

In their book *How Women Rise: Break the 12 Habits Holding You Back from Your Next Raise, Promotion, or Job*, women's leadership expert

Sally Helgesen and executive coach and author Marshall Goldsmith discuss the way women and men see things and are treated differently at work. Opportunity gaps are real. On top of obstacles that women encounter from subconscious (or conscious) bias in the workplace, women have internalized cultural messages that also hold them back, such as placing a higher value on experiences they have working, as opposed to men, who place a higher value on position and salary. Men like competing and view winning as more important, and while women also like to win, they want the whole team to win, so they keep score by the results of the team and are willing to pick up the slack to make sure the team succeeds.

Helgeson and Goldsmith identify twelve habits women have that hold them back from success: Women don't toot their own horns. Women expect others to "spontaneously" notice and reward their contributions. Women place too high a value on expertise. Women don't leverage relationships. Women don't enlist allies from the very start of a job. Women tend not to seek to advance their careers when they place too much value on their current role. Women can become perfectionistic. Women get tripped up by people-pleasing. Women minimize themselves to fit in. They can overshare, use too many words, or express too much emotion for a work situation and alienate team members. Women dwell on what they can't change rather than moving on. And women can get distracted by things they intuit or pick up from others, without exercising discipline over those distractions.[59]

Where do women learn these habits? If cultural conditioning is involved, they are part of Old Normal's gender war.

Gender-Based Poverty

Around the globe, cultural conditions prevent females from gaining education, employment, and economic security. As a result, women bear the greater burden of poverty.

According to Oxfam International, a global nonprofit that works to end the injustice of poverty,

> gender inequality is one of the oldest and most pervasive forms of inequality in the world. It denies women their voices, devalues their work and makes women's position unequal to men's, from the household to the national and global levels.
>
> Despite some important progress to change this in recent years, in no country have women achieved economic equality with men, and women are still more likely than men to live in poverty.[60]

Worldwide, women earn the lowest wages and hold jobs that pay the least. In developing countries and areas, the vast majority of women work in the informal economy, without legal or social protection from exploitation.

Even if they worked and brought in enough money to qualify to use credit, it wasn't until 1972 in the United States that married women were legally permitted by the Equal Credit Opportunity Act to apply for credit in their own names without a spouse cosigning the application.

In a 2012 discussion paper for the Consumer Finance Institute, Dubravka Ritter, a senior industry specialist at the Federal Reserve Bank of Philadelphia, wrote,

> "[D]isparate treatment of protected classes in credit markets is certainly less common than it was 40 years ago. Disparate impact, however, may persist so long as credit qualifications that lenders consider are affected by markets where discrimination continues to occur." Thus, "[i]t is for this reason that the ECOA continues to be relevant today. . . . Nevertheless, statistically significant differences between [protected classes and base groups] remain even after accounting for a variety of factors and using a range of econometric techniques."[61]

Discrimination still exists in lending practices. Protections offered by the Equal Credit Opportunity Act (and Regulation B regarding spousal guarantors) should not be scaled back but increased to protect those most at risk of credit discrimination.

Caregiving Expectations

When it comes to societal expectations for childcare and home care, women bear the burden. Women do anywhere from twice as much to ten times as much unpaid work as men, whether they work outside the home or not. "The global value of this work each year is estimated at $10 trillion—which is equivalent to one-eighth of the world's entire GDP,"[62] Oxfam reports. Unpaid work for populations without access to modern clean water sources includes spending hours each day carrying water. For example, according to Oxfam,

> Nine percent of the global population (about 663 million people) are still without access to improved water sources. A recent study by Graham, Hirai, and Kim (2016) looked at water-collection in Sub-Saharan Africa—where it is estimated that more than two-thirds of the population must leave their home to collect water—and found that this time-consuming and physically grueling chore falls primarily to women.[63]

And when that home care work is added to employment, women work longer hours each day. Or they give up opportunities to work overtime at their jobs in order to tend to unpaid home care and childcare work. This means that globally, on average, women work about four years longer than men.[64]

Healthcare

Funding for women's healthcare is significantly lower than for men's healthcare. In an article in *Forbes*, Reneeta Das, partner and senior vice president of Healthcare and Life Sciences at Frost & Sullivan, a global growth consulting and research firm, wrote about the funding gap for research and development for women's health:

> Women's health accounts for only 4 percent of the overall funding for research and development for healthcare products and services. The majority of spending on other diseases has a male-specific research focus and this is separate from the research spending on male-specific conditions such as prostate cancer, which accounts for 2 percent of overall funding. Yet women today make up 49.6% of the total population and the economic burden for women's diseases is currently more than $500 billion.[65]

The United Nations Population Fund (UNFPA) is a United Nations agency operating in more than 150 countries around the world. The UNFPA supports programs to end female genital mutilation (FGM) and child marriage. The fund also works to reduce preventable deaths during childbirth, through technical support and training of skilled birth attendants. The UNFPA helps women who want family planning services. In humanitarian emergencies, the UNFPA is there to support sexual and reproductive health services and to prevent and respond to violence against women in these crisis situations. In April 2017, the US Department of State blocked funding to the UNFPA, removing $69 million each year, limiting its ability to serve the health needs of women in crisis around the world.[66]

In general, the wage gap in the healthcare industry highly favors men over women. According to a 2016 study published in *JAMA Internal Medicine* of 10,000 physicians from two dozen medical schools, women earned $20,000 less than men. Only full-time female professors earned the same as male professors. Health eCareers reported that in its annual salary survey, in every support role—pharmacists, nurse practitioners, physical assistants, medical imaging specialists, and other support positions (except occupational therapy)—men earned significantly more than women.[67]

Harassment is common and often unreported in the healthcare industry. A 2017 study published in the journal *Physical Therapy* found that over 80 percent of almost 900 physical therapists surveyed had experienced harassment in the form of sexual suggestions, inappropriate touches, sexual assault, and indecent exposure in the workplace. Almost 50 percent claimed they had been harassed or assaulted in the past year.[68]

In December 2017, nine former faculty members and students sued the University of Rochester for sex discrimination for failing to curtail Professor Florian Jaeger's ongoing pattern of abusing his position to coerce students into sexual relationships.[69] Ani Chopourian, a former cardiac-surgery physician's assistant at Mercy General Hospital in Sacramento, CA, was awarded nearly $168 million in 2012 after suing for ongoing sexual harassment.[70]

We've looked at a few strategies that have been used to discriminate against women. The culture war rages on. Let's move ahead and consider how music and entertainment, media, and sports are also adding fuel to the fire that is Old Normal.

Coaching Questions for Thoughtful Consideration and Discussion

1. How does culture make it possible for stories like Ellen's to perpetuate?
2. What cultural allowances increase risks for child sexual abuse?
3. What difference is there in the value of a baby boy and a baby girl?
4. How does gender impact cognitive ability?
5. How are girls objectified?
6. What is the result of sexualizing someone against their will?
7. What are the costs or results of self-objectification?
8. How does lack of women's history and women role models impact girls and women?
9. What are the causes of a gender pay gap, and why is it widening?
10. What can be changed to equalize economic opportunity and wealth?
11. What changes to healthcare research will level the playing field for women?
12. What can you do to help end the culture war against women?

TEN

Part Two:
The Culture War
on Women

It was the '80s, and we were twenty-one. *Footloose,* dancing and fun. I lived with a roommate, another female, on a ground-floor, ungated apartment in a middle-class neighborhood. We were both working as nursing assistants, dating, and throwing a few parties in our apartment for friends and their friends.

I began dating one man steadily. When I was out of the apartment, my roommate reported that she received prank phone calls (on the landline) and heard someone in and around our apartment (we sometimes forgot to lock the back door; it was a small town). I wrote this off to paranoia.

One evening, my roommate and I prepared for a girls' night out. There were no cell phones or text messaging, and sticky notes were high tech. As we locked the apartment, we left a sticky note on our front door for our friends and boyfriends who might stop by: "We are at the

Club. Back after 2." We went out and danced until 2:00 a.m., returned home, and noticed on the way in that our sticky note was gone. We had a snack and noticed it was very cold in the kitchen but didn't think much about it. We went to our separate rooms to go to bed.

I woke up a short time later with a man on top of me. He was dressed in all black and wore a ski mask. He ordered me to stay still and be quiet, and everything would be okay. I screamed my roommate's name, praying that my voice would work, and he fled out the back door.

We called 911 and sat in my bedroom. When the police arrived, they found a perfect circle cut out of the dining room window, next to the kitchen table where we normally ate, but the curtains had covered the hole. That was how the masked man originally entered. He had made the hole sometime while we were out. We don't know if he had been in the apartment the whole time or outside waiting for us to go to bed. When the police asked for the details of the attack, we recounted everything about the evening with them and gave them the names of our friends.

They did not comment much, but at the end of the interview, the police officer asked me, "When you are out until 2:00 in the morning partying, what do you expect to happen?"

The phone calls stopped. The noises in the apartment stopped.

I broke up with the man I was seeing. My roommate and I moved to another state, but I no longer felt safe. Every time I looked out a dark window, I thought I saw someone. I did not know which friends to trust. I felt unprotected, guilty, and ashamed. I did not move back to my home state for fifteen years.

What I now know is that I have every right to do what I want when I want, as long as I am not hurting another person. No one has the right to follow me, enter my home, or touch me without my permission. To this day, however, I still only give my address to female friends. I still meet male friends elsewhere and do not hold events or parties at my home. I remain hyperaware of anyone following me and of my surroundings, especially in the hours after sunset. In short, I am stronger, but I still carry a deep scar.

#MeToo, Janet

Who is at fault in Janet's story? Why would a police officer infer that fault is the victim's after hearing an incident like Janet's? What does culture say about rights and responsibilities around the issue of personal safety?

Patriarchal cultures have promulgated the objectification, sexualization, marginalization, and acceptance (and neglect of consequences) of male violence against women. The culture war against women brings pain, which has been normalized. This is called normalization of pain, it showed up in Janet's experience, and it shows up in countless ways in advertising and marketing, music, films, television, videogames, sports, and cultural preference for males in leadership roles.

Advertising

In media and advertising workplaces, sexual harassment remains woefully prolific. A 2018 survey of 3,500 workers in the media and advertising industries in the UK commissioned by Women in Advertising and Communications London, the Advertising Association, and the media and advertising industry charity NABs (formerly called the National Advertising Benefit Society), found that in the UK, 20 percent of women between eighteen and twenty-four years old have been sexually harassed within the first few years of working in the media and advertising industries (and 5 percent of men in the same age group).

Twenty-six percent of respondents said they have been harassed while working in the media and marketing industries, with a high volume of female employees citing either single or multiple experiences of sexual harassment. Of the respondents who have been sexually harassed, 72 percent said it occurred more than once, and 25 percent said it had happened six times or more. Most refrain from reporting issues, for fear of being fired or demoted. Just over 80 percent of the respondents who said they had been harassed experienced it from people who were in a more senior level than them.[1]

In the US, a yearlong research initiative reported in 2016 by the American Association of Advertising Agencies (4A's) confirmed the prevalence of sexual harassment and discrimination in advertising. Of the 549 4A's members surveyed, more than half reported having experienced sexual harassment. Over half of female respondents also said they have felt vulnerable in the workplace because of gender. Thirty-three percent of the women said that gender caused them to miss out on key assignments or promotions (more than once), and 42 percent claimed to have been excluded from key decision-making processes because of gender-based discrimination.[2]

The *New York Times'* award-winning "The Truth Is Hard" campaign in March 2018 "elevating women's voices and exposing those who would otherwise silence them" was created by an agency that let go of its chief creative officer in order to provide employees with a "safe and inclusive work environment."[3]

When it comes to leadership, only 11 percent of industry creative directors are female,[4] and female founders are even more rare.

Plenty has been written about the sexist nature of many of the advertisements we're exposed to that body shame women, demean their intelligence, sexualize them, role stereotype them, and patronize them by use of images and copy. Ads in fashion magazines show half-naked women lying down, women with vacuous stares, and women as part of a happy couple. Ads not only reflect the disparity between how genders are perceived, they perpetuate it. Women's bodies are used to sell things that have absolutely nothing to do with sex.

Music

The music industry is an old boys' club. A study by Stacy L. Smith, associate professor at the University of Southern California Annenberg, found that women are underrepresented in popular music in the US. She says,

> Among artists on Billboard's Hot Chart top 600 songs from 2012–2017, women comprised 22.4 percent. Among songwriters, only 12.3 percent were women. Only 2 percent of the producers of a subset of 300 songs were women.[5] Of Grammy nominees from 2012 to 2017, 90.7 percent were men and 9.3 percent were women, usually in the best new artist category.[6]

Canada's music industry also discriminates against women. In an August 2018 *Forbes* article, Pauleanna Reid, senior contributor at *Forbes* and co-founder of New Girl on the Block, a mentorship platform for millennials, listed the stats of discrimination against women within the music industry:

> In 2016, more than 200 artists and music industry professionals were nominated for Juno Awards, Canada's most prestigious music accolade. Only 32% of them were women. This glaring underrepresentation was a mere reflection of a much larger problem: women have been pushed into the background of Canada's music landscape. A survey of 455 female industry professionals found that only 10% held executive positions, just 6% worked in music production, and these women earned, on average, 27% less than the typical salary for their roles.[7]

In Australia, according to a report of University of Sydney, sex discrimination is rife in their music industry as well, both in male domination on the air, in the studios, and on boards of Australian music organizations.[8]

In the UK, over two-thirds of the music acts performing in the UK are male only. Of 2017 summer music-festival headliners in the UK, 80 percent were male. Of senior executive roles, 70 percent are occupied by men.[9] A report conducted in the UK by PRS Foundation found that 78 percent of women interviewed had experienced some form of sexism in the music industry. The study reported that of UK songwriters and composers, only 16 percent are female.[10]

In China, while women are advancing in promoter and offstage roles, men dominate the headlines and programs at most shows and music festivals. There, "female DJ" is code for sexualized, objectified woman. Women DJs in low-end venues wear bikinis and reveal skin rather than focus on providing quality music wearing whatever they're most comfortable in, because skin is what's expected.[11]

Sexual discrimination and harassment are also prevalent in the music industry in India. For centuries, women who did not come from musical families were not permitted to study music. While in today's society women are growing in the ranks of performers, the opportunities for composers, producers, and behind-the-scenes work is dominated by men.

In classical music, to eliminate gender discrimination, many orchestras are holding blind auditions. As a result, women are 50 percent more likely to be called back for second or more auditions.

It's not just sexual harassment and gender bias in hiring, production, and funding that create problems for women in the music industry. The escalating sexualization in the marketing of women in music is the norm, with barely-there costumes, sky-high heels, and sexy makeup. Artist photos are increasingly provocative, with more and more skin showing across the music industry from country and pop to rhythm and blues (R & B). Even in the traditional classical-music industry, Chinese classical pianist Yuja Wang performs in bare feet with several dress changes.

With most writers and composers being male, across the music industry compositions reflect a patriarchal view with themes and lyrics full of the objectification of women. For example, the classical opera *Madame Butterfly* tells the story of the rape and purchase of "exotic" women. Popular music videos and lyrics demean and objectify women, placing them in roles such as strippers, whores, pole dancers, and sex toys.

According to a study from Brigham Young University, lyrics that push sexualization have skyrocketed, and the acceleration is exponential. The study analyzed Billboard Top 100 hits stretching back a half century, showing an overall increase of sexualization from 1959 to 2009, with the most dramatic increase from 1999 to 2009.[12] It may be time to check this again because there are numerous songs available on streaming media such as Pandora and Spotify that carry the *Explicit* notification label and encourage the use of women as willing sex objects.

Though sexualization is widespread in the music industry, rap and hip-hop music in particular push the sexualization of women. The endless list of songs that objectify women include Drake's "No Lie" (by 2 Chainz), which boldly proclaims the abuse of women in a grudge war.

Jay-Z's "Big Pimpin" video is full of women whose value is all based on their appearance in bikinis and other skimpy costumes; the "She on My Dick" music video by rapper Rick Ross is of numerous naked or almost naked women in a strip club. When he was called out for rape lyrics in his song about drugging someone and taking her home and using her, Ross said, "U.O.E.N.O. Apologize for the lyric interpreted as rape."[13] After losing an advertising deal with Reebok, Ross made another statement:

> To every woman that has felt the sting of abuse, I apologize. I recognize that as an artist I have a voice and with that, the power of influence. To the young men who listen to my music, please know

that using a substance to rob a woman of her right to make a choice is not only a crime, it's wrong and I do not encourage it.[14]

In a middle school classroom, as Rese Knickerbocker, a representative from Rebuilding Hope!, the Sexual Assault Resource Center of Pierce County, spoke to students about ways to help contribute to the safety of their peers and community, one boy held up a handwritten sign that read, "FREE R KELLY." Ms. Knickerbocker took time out from the normal presentation to address the sign and to discuss decades-long, credible child-abuse accusations.

She asked him, "Why do you feel the need to hold this sign up?"

He answered, "He's my favorite musician, and these women made a choice to be with him."

She addressed the age of the girls, the issues of power, control, and manipulation, and how these issues impact a minor's choice. Consent was discussed and what true, authentic consent looks like. "The students really were processing the idea of consent and the thought that people they look up to and admire might actually be in positions of abusing others," Ms. Knickerbocker said.[15]

While Kelly has been charged, the multiplatinum R & B musician hasn't been convicted as of November 2019, though there is a movement to limit his cultural influence. Time's Up joined the #MuteRKelly hashtag when it issued a statement addressed to women of color: "The scars of history make certain that we are not interested in persecuting anyone without just cause. With that said, we demand appropriate investigations and inquiries into the allegations of R. Kelly's abuse made by women of color and their families for over two decades now."[16]

Rap and R & B aren't the only music genres with lyrics and videos full of sexualization and objectification. Country music is following suit, drawing a protest in "A Girl in a Country Song" by Maddie & Tae, which calls out sexualization of women in popular country music songs and videos.[17] Rednecks or rubbernecking, country music videos are filled with scantily dressed girls and cowboys looking for a ride.

How easily can Old Normal be overcome when it's perpetuated by the images and tunes that run through people's minds and the idols they look up to? The fact is, we are choosing Old Normal when we choose to put into our minds the lyrics of songs that objectify and sexualize.

Film

The culture war against women flickers on screens around the globe and bleeds through the film industry, as #MeToo clearly pointed out. In addition to female actors facing sexual harassment, discrimination shows up in the exclusion of women from filmmakers, directors, studio owners, and major artists, and through meager funding of female-produced films such as *The Color Purple*. The "casting couch" is symbolic of innumerable women who have been denied access to jobs with no regard to their skill or talent because they refused to give into sexual pressure from casting agents.

Limited female influencers in filmmaking impact the content and messages films send to society. In the first-ever global study of popular films across the most profitable countries and territories, speaking characters in film are predominantly male, with under 33 percent women, only 23 percent in the action/adventure genre. Less than a quarter of films feature a female heroine. Under 23 percent of the fictional on-screen workforce is made up of women employees. Under 15 percent of business executives, political figures, or STEM employees represented on film are women. Male characters outnumber female characters as attorneys and judges (thirteen to one), professors (sixteen to one), and doctors (five to one).

It's no surprise to anyone who watches films that they exploit women by sexualizing them on screen. When it came to hyper sexualization, "females were over twice as likely as males to be shown in sexualized attire, nude or partially nude, or thin."[18] Female characters are referenced for physical characteristics five times as much as male characters. The hyper-sexualization of females isn't just the adult characters. It's just as likely to be a teenage character. From its institution to today, the popular film industry has sent a message through its discrimination and representation of females that is the epitome of Old Normal.

The sexualization and objectification of women in film in the US goes all the way back to the early films in which women played the role of an Egyptian or exotic symbol or were victims, tied to train tracks needing rescue. In the 1930s, Jean Harlow (nicknamed Baby) was the on-screen image of a sexually loose woman. The 1940s film industry cast Rita Hayworth and Betty Grable in sexualized roles, where they set the standard for women objectified as pinups for male soldiers. The '40s also stereotyped female roles, as in films like *Woman of the Year,* starring Spencer Tracy and Kathryn Hepburn.

In the 1950s and 1960s, the term *sex symbol* came into being with Elizabeth Taylor, Marilyn Monroe, Jayne Mansfield, Lana Turner, Raquel Welch, French actress Brigitte Bardot, and Italian actresses Gina Lollobrigida and Sophia Loren appearing in increasingly scanty clothing, not only on-screen but also on film posters such as the poster for *Myra Breckenridge*, a movie that was controversial for its sexually explicit story. The 1960s brought us Honey Ryder, the "Bond Girl" in a white bikini with a huge hunting knife, and Jacqueline Bissett swimming in only a T-shirt in *The Deep.*

Sexualization of women in films since the 1980s has become less suggestive and more graphic. As a result, critics of mainstream films generated the term *soft-pornification* to describe the gratuitous hypersexualized female roles in films.

Not only that, but the film industry also presents sexual objectification and rape as normal behavior, and consent as meaningless. In *Asking for It*, Kate Harding says, "Reframing consent as a gray area that's always open to interpretation affords plausible deniability to pop culture makers who present criminal assaults as normal sexual behavior."[19] Ms.

Harding gives an example from *Observe and Report* (2009), a film in which a male character rapes a passed out drunk female character who wakes up to say, "Did I say stop?"[20]

The film industry is rife with sexualization of women. All pornography films, all involved in porn production, and all consumers of pornography objectify and sexualize girls and women.

Television

Throughout my childhood I saw the objectification and sexualization of girls whenever the television was on in my house. In one local children's show, a sock puppet donkey tried to kiss all the Girl Scouts who visited the show, but never the Boy Scouts. One savvy Brownie Girl Scout, however, turned and slugged Crazy Donkey in the kisser when it passed by her in the line, sending the shocked puppeteer's arm flying.

The popular *I Dream of Jeannie* kept a woman in a bottle at her master's beck and call. *The Benny Hill Show* featured an old, lecherous male harassing females in every episode. Sexualization and stereotyping of genders continued in popular 1970s shows, including soap operas from noon to five each afternoon focused on the woman getting the man or getting unwanted attention from them.

A study investigated viewer perceptions of female and male characters in 1980s television shows based on the viewer's gender and sex role orientation. Young adult viewers rated four television characters (two male and two female work-partners-in-crime dramas) and themselves based on a personal attributes questionnaire (PAQ). Instrumental and expressive (I/E) traits represent stereotypical masculine and feminine personality characteristics that are exhibited at varying levels in both genders, with instrumentality representing masculine traits and expressiveness representing feminine traits.[21] Viewers rated all four male characters as stereotypical masculine instrumental but only one female character as stereotypical feminine expressive. The female viewers saw the female characters as possessing typical masculine traits while still being feminine expressive, but male viewers didn't. Viewer gender had a greater impact on the ratings of female characters than on the ratings of male characters.[22] Young males couldn't see the feminine character traits in female characters that also exhibited developed "masculine instrumental" traits. This study demonstrates cultural bias.

Gender stereotyping and sexualization of women continue on shows like *Two and a Half Men,* in which the protagonist is a womanizer and commitment-phobe and *Game of Thrones,* which uses rape as a common plot twist.

Gender discrimination shows up in unequal industry opportunities for women. Women speaking out about Hollywood may have led #MeToo headlines, but gender discrimination didn't leave with all the people who've been shown the door. The television industry has perpetuated Old Normal since it launched from radio, where there were no female announcers. You may have read about the former *Fox and Friends* co-host Gretchen Carlson and the sexual harassment claim she filed against Fox. Her book, *Be Fierce,* gives solid advice for other women who have sexual harassment claims.

The women's movement in the 1970s brought some female announcers to the screens, but the ratios still favor males, as do ratios of funding awarded and number of creative and camera roles. There are fewer female directors, producers, writers, and showrunners in television than men. This holds across national borders around the world except in Sweden. In the US in 2014, according to the Center for Study of Women in Television and Film, women made up 42 percent of all characters on TV, but only 27 percent of behind-the-scenes roles were filled by women.[23] In 2014, only twelve out of ninety-seven one-hour dramas on the five biggest prestige networks (HBO, Showtime, FX, AMC, Netflix) were created by women.[24] The movement toward diversity seems slow or nonexistent.

In an online article in the *Guardian* entitled "Despite Reckoning on Hollywood Diversity, TV Industry Has Gotten Worse," writer Sam

Levin quoted Darnell Hunt, a sociology professor at UCLA who co-authored the *Annual Hollywood Diversity Report*. Hunt said, "Of the 45 newly scripted television shows approved for 2017–18 across broadcast, cable, and digital platforms, there were only four creators of color, all of whom were Black. There were also only seven female creators. With women behind only 16 percent of new shows and minorities behind just 9 percent, the outlook was worse than overall representation in the previous season, which was marginally better in both categories. All new broadcast shows had white creators."[25]

Sweden's film industry has set the bar for New Normal. Anna Serner, the CEO of the Swedish Film Institute, successfully implemented a 50/50 gender mandate for all Swedish productions. Swedish TV depends on government funding. Reflecting on Hollywood's slowness to diversify creative roles, Ms. Serner said,

> I really feel sorry for everyone in the Hollywood industry because it's so money-driven, and the [financiers], unfortunately . . . don't [realize] that half the population looks at films in a new way. They just stick to what they've always done. Eventually, they'll be forced to find new consumer groups. They can't keep on pretending. . . . The only thing that will change the system in the US is for the rest of the world to change first and show that it's an old-fashioned way of doing things. Then let the American consciousness wake.[26]

Video Gaming

Watching television is positively correlated with sexual objectification and aggression toward girls, and research shows that these correlations extend to the video game industry. Most games show hypersexualized girls and women. War games depict women as captured spoils and not as valued humans with rights: they're princesses that you keep as prizes once you (the male character) have rescued them, and whether good or evil, they're sexualized, wearing little or impossibly tight clothes. Women characters generally are depicted as secondary or weaker, and female protagonists are in the minority.

Female online video game players are being stalked and harassed with threats of rape and worse. In the male-dominated world of multiplayer online games like *Grand Theft Auto*, *Halo*, and *Call of Duty*, many women say they've had to take drastic steps to escape harassment, stalking, and violent threats from male players. Some quit playing games, and others change screen names or play only with friends.

The "Gamergate" campaign of harassment, started in 2014, targeted women working in the video game industry by men who were supposedly focusing in on ethics in the industry. Gamers launched Twitter attacks, using vile language, rape threats, and death threats. The threat of danger was severe enough to make women leave their homes, which had been identified and located by address in hate communications, and cancel speaking engagements in order to stay safe.[27] Industry press did nothing or added to the harassment. Many women attempting to make changes in the industry have been harassed until they finally decided it wasn't worth the trouble and left the industry to move into some other (usually less lucrative) line of work.

Women are excluded industry wide, like television and film, or at least underrepresented in creative roles and funding. The industry is made up of 79 percent male employees.[28] With males making up the lion's share of both creators and viewers, it's not too difficult to see why the industry is turning to soft-core, and now more graphic, porn to add to the addictive, sexualized content. For years, pornified games have been available online and found by young children who were looking for games, with soft-porn images leaving an indelible imprint in their developing brains. Now sexual content is being added to mainstream games, training game players to view a sexual partner as a conquest you earn by following the rules of a game. The graphics are more realistic than one might expect. Game producer Fabrice Condominas told an interviewer about the latest version of a widely popular game, "You can have sex with a lot of people. I won't tell if it is everyone (in the game) or not, but it's a whole lot of people. Plus, you can even have one-night stands."[29]

Sports

In 2016, five of the team members on the US Women's Professional Soccer team submitted a workplace discrimination case to the EEOC, claiming unfair and unequal pay, including bonuses, appearance fees, and per diems.[30]

The 2015 women soccer players across all teams were paid forty times less than male players in 2014 ($15 million for women's teams, $576 million for men's teams). In addition, women were required to play on artificial turf, which wouldn't happen to male teams. Basketball and tennis also have significant gaps between male and female athletes.

Coverage on television is also deeply skewed in favor of men. The Tucker Center for Research on Girls and Women in Sport reported in 2014 that 40 percent of sports participants are female, yet women's sports receive only 4 percent of all sports media coverage. As I often watch ESPN's *SportsCenter* when I'm on the treadmill in the morning, I wasn't surprised to learn that they gave only 1 percent of on-air time to women's sports in 2014 (if the Olympics was not included). Women also are shortchanged off the fields and courts, as only 10 percent of sports journalists are women.[31]

Sexualization and stereotyping of women athletes are common. In a 2015 article in *Mic*, columnist Julie Zeilinger wrote,

> Websites like The Athletic Build, Men's Fitness, The Richest, and others have created entire lists devoted to ranking the comparative sexiness of female athletes overall. Media coverage of female athletes often revolves around their bodies over their skills. The public still fails to see female athletes as just that—athletes—rather than sexualized objects to be ogled.[32]

Sexual harassment in sports is prevalent. Women aren't the only victims, as the Jerry Sandusky scandal clearly showed; however, males are more likely to harass both male and female athletes. According to the International Olympic Committee,

> [S]exual harassment and abuse happen in all sports at all levels. Prevalence appears to be higher in elite sport. Members of the athlete's entourage in positions of power and authority appear to be the primary perpetrators. Peer athletes have also been identified as perpetrators. Males are more often reported as perpetrators. . . . Research demonstrates that sexual harassment and abuse in sport seriously and negatively impact on athletes' physical and psychological health. It can result in impaired performance and lead to athlete drop-out. Clinical data indicate that psychosomatic illnesses, anxiety, depression, substance abuse, self-harm, and suicide are some of the serious health consequences.[33]

Dozens of current and former NFL, NBA, and NHL cheerleaders described systematic exploitation because they are required to mingle with fans, who get unruly and handsy when intoxicated. "When you have on a push-up bra and a fringed skirt, it can sometimes, unfortunately, feel like it comes with the territory," said Labriah Lee Holt, a former cheerleader for the Tennessee Titans in the NFL. "I never experienced anything where someone on the professional staff or the team said something or made me feel that way. But you definitely experience that when you encounter people who have been drinking beer."

Team officials are aware of the situation, the cheerleaders said, but do little to prevent harassment.[34]

The average cheerleader earns $10 or less per hour over the course of a season.[35] The average football player earns $2.5 million[36] per season. Consider the difference in earnings and the prevalence of harassment, and ask yourself if the differences in earnings and in how these athletes and entertainers are treated are just.

Over 130 women gymnastics athletes, including Olympians, suffered abuse and assault at the hands of Larry Nassar, former physician for the US Olympic women's gymnastics team. Nasser was sentenced in December 2017 to sixty years in prison on child pornography charges, with ten additional molestation charges.[37] Interestingly enough, on a Ranker.com list accessed September 19, 2019, of twenty-six professional athletes who went into politics, all were male.[38] But Olympic pro figure skater Michelle Kwan, named a public diplomacy ambassador in 2006, was overlooked.

Politics and Leadership Roles

Historically around the world, women have been excluded from political participation. The women who participated in founding the US counted for representation but had no vote, except property owners in New Jersey who were female or African American, until their voting rights were abolished in 1807. Citizenship followed the husband's or father's status until 1924. Women won the right to vote in Wyoming Territory in 1869 and kept the right when Wyoming entered the Union in 1890. Wyoming, Colorado, Utah, and Idaho were the first four states to give women the vote.

The constitutional amendment giving all women the right to vote in the US wasn't passed until 1920, after nearly a century of effort across the nation by women protesters. On November 2, 1920, over eight million women across the US voted in elections for the first time. Wyoming, the first state to grant voting rights to women, also elected the first female governor, Nellie Tayloe Ross (1876–1977), who was elected governor in 1924. From 1933 to 1953, she served as the first woman director of the US Mint.

Even now, there are three men for every woman in a political office in the US. When women are active in the political spheres, they focus on issues that concern them most, which men have ignored or actively worked against in the past. Some campaigns in which women have prevailed include voting rights, labor legislation affecting women, strategic arms limitation agreements (when women went on strike for peace), civil rights, women's education, childcare, and legislation to improve healthcare and hospital systems. For this reason, there's been a gender gap in the past nine presidential elections, with women favoring the Democratic Party.

According to the UN Women.org website's *Facts and Figures on Leadership and Political Participation*, unequal representation in leadership positions in both the public sector and the private sector is reflective of rampant discrimination against women in society. In 2016 only 22.8 percent of all national parliamentarians were women. As of October 2017, eleven women are serving as head of state, and twelve are serving as head of government. Globally, there are thirty-eight states in which women account for less than 10 percent of parliamentarians in single or lower houses as of June 2016, including four chambers with no women at all. As of January 2017, only 18.3 percent of government ministers are women. The global proportion of women elected to local government is currently unknown, constituting a major knowledge gap.[39] While the Beijing platform has set a target for equal representation of women in government, the global proportion of women elected to government is severely below equal representation.[40]

Women also did not serve on juries until the 1920s. Most states exempted females from jury service until recently; therefore, women who went to trial were systematically denied the right to a jury of peers.

The marketplace also shows a dearth of women in leadership roles in the US and around the world. In spite of research proving that companies with women in leadership roles perform considerably better than companies with predominantly male boards and executives, organizations are slow to promote or hire women in leadership roles. Researchers found that among the twenty-five firms with the highest percentage of women execs and board members, "median returns on assets and equity in 2015 were at least 74 percent higher than among the overall group of 400 companies surveyed."[41]

Dr. Kathleen Buse, Director of the Women's Leadership Institute, works to increase the share of leadership roles women hold in business. She says,

> While women make up 51 percent of the population and 47 percent of the US workforce, they're underrepresented in leadership roles and other critical professions. She adds that females comprise just 5 percent of CEO positions in S&P 500 companies and 12 percent of the engineering workforce nationwide, [and significantly fewer women] elected officials compared to other countries.[42]

It's a War Out There

I recently saw a TV commercial for men's skincare products. There was a mild struggle between a male and a female over a bottle of lotion. The closing line was "Men have skin too." The ad nodded to a bigger battle for control. Looking at the bigger picture and all the "small cultural battles" and putting them together, it looks like a war out there!

It may not be the intention of some males, but it's undeniable that the culture war against women is real and longstanding. Can males declare a victory when half the world is hurting? Fortunately, the thirst for a just and fair world has engaged many on behalf of girls and women to replace Old Normal with New Normal.

Questions for Thoughtful Consideration and Discussion

1. Under what conditions should anyone have the right to cut holes in your home's window, enter your home without permission, or lie on top of you when you're sleeping?

2. What happens in the brain when a person is repeatedly exposed to sexualized, misogynistic advertising or song lyrics?

3. What are the barriers to equal pay in advertising, television, entertainment, and sports?

4. What are the costs of continued objectification and sexualization of females in media?

5. Given the studies proving that including women in leadership is better for everyone, what's holding back progress in creating parity among genders in the marketplace?

6. How can industries hold businesses accountable for tolerating harassment?

7. How can consumers hold businesses accountable for sex discrimination in marketing and in product development?

8. What is the cost of allowing the culture war on women to continue?

9. Who really "wins" the ongoing culture war against women?

10. What is one action step you can take to move the needle forward for your community?

ELEVEN

What Must Change to Create a New Normal?

I was eighteen years old when I got my first job at a large department store in California. My first day on the job, and where I was assigned for the next two months, was in the gift-wrapping department. I loved working in that department and learned from the oldest employee in the store how to wrap gifts "picture perfect." After those two months, however, I was reassigned to the shoe department, and that was where it started. My first day in the department was normal. I met the other employees and learned the ropes, but then another worker joined the team who was ten years older than me and had transferred from the men's department.

The department manager introduced Daryl to everyone, and he was well liked by both departments. After a couple of weeks, Daryl started making inappropriate comments and gestures toward me, and no one else was around.

Being very shy, I did not know what to do, so I just walked away.

But he would follow me around and tell me how he liked my sexy curves, making noises, and he always seemed to know how to corner me.

I hoped if I ignored him he would stop and leave me alone, but he didn't. I was embarrassed and scared. As time passed, he became bolder, telling me that he would love to feel his body up against mine. I didn't know where to go or what to do, so I stayed silent.

One day, I learned my day shift had changed to the closing shift, and so had Daryl's. I thought that as long as I hung around other employees during this shift and left when they did, I would be okay, but that was not the case. The harassment escalated from words, gestures, and sounds to touching. He would always wait until I was in the secluded stock room, where he'd "accidentally" rub up against me, make groaning sounds, and tell me in a quiet voice how he liked my curves.

One evening before closing, the manager needed to leave unexpectedly, and she put Daryl in charge. After closing, I was in the stockroom trying to hurry up and put the remaining boxes of shoes away so I could go home. He cornered me, and I was trapped again. As he got closer, he smiled, caressed my shoulders, and groaned. I attempted to get away, but with every move, his grip got stronger. I could feel his hands hold me in place and his knee press into my inner thigh. I felt one of his hands leave my shoulder and touch my side, then brush across my chest.

I began to cry, and as his face went into my neck, he stopped and loosened his grip enough for me to push away and run. I took a shower when I got home and cried myself to sleep.

The next day I looked in the mirror and saw the bruises on my inner thigh and shoulders. I was shocked and didn't know what to do. I felt ashamed of myself and my body as if I had done something to provoke him to hurt me. I told myself it was my fault, so I called work that day and quit. I never returned to that store.

I buried that experience deep within me and never talked about it for years. It was not until I became an advocate for survivors of domestic violence and sexual assault that I saw myself in them. I was fortunate to have people come into my life at the right time and help me heal. In the healing process, I learned through my work as an advocate that my own experience was not merely harassment, but in fact I had been sexually assaulted.

Over time I have had to learn to rebuild trust in men, because I saw them as violent, having grown up with domestic violence. Thankfully, I've had men come into my life who were not violent but were caring and kind. I had never known this type of man before. Thank you to all who have helped me along the way.

#MeToo, Julie

Criminals like Daryl are careful to make sure nobody else is around to witness their harassment, abuse, or assaults. They don't regard their victims as persons of equal worth. They see them as objects to be used. Your daughter, sister, mother, grandmother, cousin, aunt, babysitter, teacher, classmates, students, friends, dates—all your beloveds—Old Normal promulgates beliefs that say these women are unimportant, inferior objects to be used and thrown away.

If you want New Normal, you'll need to let go of those beliefs to live in integrity. The power of Old Normal has lasted millennia at an incalculably deep cost. I believe #MeToo is a transformational event that has indicated a worldwide desire to end Old Normal and create deep, lasting change. Change must happen individually, within families, groups, communities, cities, states, and countries, until the whole world embraces New Normal.

Addressing Global Change

The World Economic Forum has tracked education, economic, health, and political parity in participating countries (144 in 2017) since 2006. The *World Economic Forum Annual Gender Gap Report* measures zero parity between genders (0.00) and parity between genders (1.00). For the first time since 2006, the 2016 report found the gender gap widening.

Worldwide, gender gaps for health outcomes for women versus men are 96 percent, for educational attainment 95 percent, for economic participation 58 percent, and for political attainment only 23 percent. The average across all the gaps measures worldwide 68 percent, which leaves a 32 percent gender gap between men and women in these four categories.[1] Of 144 countries, the US was ranked number forty-nine in 2017 at 0.718 with parity for health outcomes and near parity for education but not political or economic parity.[2]

Health Rank: 1   Score: 1.000
Workplace Rank: 19   Score: 0.776
Education Rank: 82   Education Score: 0.973
Political Rank: 96   Political Score: 0.124
Rank: 49   Overall: 0.718[3]

A world that has parity between genders with zero sexual discrimination, zero sexual harassment, zero sexual abuse, and zero sexual violence won't magically appear by wishful thinking. The #MeToo movement is one of many rallying cries, but without further action, it cannot accomplish lasting change leading to New Normal.

Much Work, Multiple Approaches

Addressing global cultural change requires a great deal of work and a multiplicity of approaches. Tearing down cultural mores that allow and encourage Old Normal will take as much time as we allow. Culture change won't happen until we stop tolerating

- objectification and self-objectification,

- sex trafficking and prostitution,
- pornography,
- patriarchal, gender-based discrimination,
- religious gender discrimination and sexual abuse,
- gender-based violence,
- sexualization of people,
- unrealistic standards of physical appearance,
- discrimination in education,
- biased social structures,
- unequal unpaid work,
- opportunity, pay, and leadership gaps in the workplace,
- gender-based poverty,
- gender discrimination in caregiving and healthcare,
- and anything else of importance that you've noticed contributes to Old Normal.

It's an understatement to say there are numerous forces opposed to such changes. The widening gender gap indicates opposition to New Normal. Abusers and harassers are resistant to change. Profiteers of Old Normal are firmly opposed to change. And there's also inertia.

Momentum toward New Normal is visible in campaigns including #MeToo, #TimesUp, #BalanceTonPorc, #NiUnaMenos, #MetooIndia, #HollaBack, and others. UN women called for sixteen days of activism against gender-based violence (November 25–December 10, 2018) under the UNiTE to End Violence against Women campaign using the theme #OrangetheWorld and #HearMeToo.

Engaged and Committed

To break through opposition and inertia, each person needs to ask herself or himself, "What is my part as an influencer or a change maker?"

One step is to reframe problems into opportunities or projects. In his essay "What if There Were No Problems, Only Projects?," published in the book *Work Is Love Made Visible*, David Allen, one of the world's top thinkers on productivity and one of America's top executive coaches (rated by *Forbes* magazine), wrote,

> Are we supposed to deny the things going on in our universe that we don't like or consider terrible, unjust, immoral, or just plain stupid? Not at all. We simply need to recognize them as something we can or might do something about, or not. And those that we can or might do something about, we need to ensure that we are appropriately engaged with our commitment to doing so. Because we see it that way doesn't mean there's not another way to see it.[4]

Mr. Allen continues and shares a coaching secret that brings freedom, creativity, and energy to create solutions. Each person has the right, the power, and the responsibility to decide what their interest is or what their investment is when they are involved or engaged in any way with those things that they allow to enter their universe. The freedom comes in knowing which projects are yours and in owning the responsibility to act on a project to create a certain outcome.[5]

From a coaching perspective, when we break down a massive problem or an amalgamation of massive, unsolvable problems into a project or collection of projects, we can identify what outcomes we're looking to attain, figure out what steps we or others need to take to create those outcomes, and take action. Change is possible one project at a time for those willing to act.

Examining Assumptions

You may have heard an old story about a child asking a mom, "Why does Auntie cut both ends off the ham before she puts it in the oven?" The mom answers, "Because your grandma always did it that way, and it's the right way." So the child calls grandma to ask her, and grandma tells the grandchild, "I cut off the ends because I didn't have a pan that was big enough."

Just like assumptions have wasted ham, assumptions also lead to worldviews, perspectives, beliefs, behaviors, and habits formed generations earlier and carried down from generation to generation without examining why or whether they are true or appropriate for the current generation or situation.

There are many ways to see something. Cultural mores are based on assumptions. Assumptions are unexamined, unspoken thoughts accepted by a person or a community as true. They are hidden building blocks that make up belief systems that become the basis of arguments and undergird actions.

Creating change would require a global willingness to uncover, review, examine, and dismiss those assumptions that are no longer acceptable and true, which chain the world to Old Normal. To create New Normal free from harassment, abuse, and violence, we need to agree that some current assumptions about females, and about relationships between females and males, are not valid or useful, and we need to let them go.

That's Just the Way It Is?

A young wife was frequently critiqued, criticized, and berated with yelling and cursing by her husband. One evening, the wife quietly requested, "Will you please stop yelling profanities at me in front of our daughters? I don't want them to grow up thinking it's okay to be spoken to like this, because it's not. Instead, if you have a problem, will you please speak about it with me in private, using a calm voice?"

The husband answered, "When a car's going down a street, if someone's crossing in the middle of the crosswalk, they're going to get hit if they don't move out of the way. It's your fault if I yell at you. You're the one who made me mad."

She replied to him, "If a car's speeding down a street and someone's crossing, the driver's job is to slow down or stop so they don't hit the pedestrian."

He answered, "Yeah, well, that's just the way it is. So just get out of my way, or deal with it."

In this story, the man exhibited a fixed mindset.

Carol Dweck, the Lewis and Virginia Eaton Professor of Psychology at Stanford University and author of the book *Mindset,* revealed the power of two mindsets. One assumption people with a fixed mindset make is that nothing can change. A fixed mindset says, "That's just the way it is." Without assessing the astronomical cost of all kinds of violence to society, a person with a fixed mindset views the situation as inevitable. A person with a growth mindset examines and challenges assumptions and then risks making mistakes in order to learn and grow.

To create and promulgate nonviolent cultures, we can dispose of the assumption that there is no end to violence, because such an assumption undergirds cultures that promote violence and the use of physical force to reach some desired end.

There are several things we can do. We can ask ourselves, "What is the value of each person?" In some cultures, people assume females are inferior, less valuable, and less deserving than males. This assumption is patently false.

We can come to agreement and enact legislation to equalize power between genders, including equal access to health, education, economic participation, and political representation. For example, legislation might be introduced that mandates all children are educated equally, and makes sure their equal access to education isn't undermined by gender-based discrimination in how students are treated.

We can ask whose job it is to do society's unpaid work such as childcare, carrying water, care of clothing, obtaining or preparing food, maintaining property, etc. We can accelerate contribution toward infrastructure in impoverished communities so that women and children are free from the onerous task of carrying water. We can create new societal norms that allow men and women equal reward and recognition for work whether paid or unpaid. A father shouldn't get more kudos for caring for his children than their mother gets. Whatever gender, parents share the children; they can share the work of caring for them.

Beyond recognizing and compensating people for the value of unpaid work or sharing it more equally among all regardless of gender, we can question the assumption that parity in the workplace is unrealistic and not beneficial to society. Research shows a strong link between gender parity (women working for pay as much as men and getting paid equally for their work) and economic growth. The facts show that countries increase national gross domestic products (GDP) by increasing the number of women working.

We can ask ourselves if we will continue to tolerate harassment and if we will allow people to continue to be ignored, marginalized, and ostracized for reporting harassment.

We can ask business leadership to invest in creating nonviolent, psychologically safe workplace cultures and commit to gender balance in the marketplace across all levels from entry level to board representation. Gender diversity in the workforce increases opportunities for growth. In the World Economic Forum's Future of Jobs Survey, "42% of business leaders perceived addressing gender parity in their company as a matter of fairness and equality; yet more than a fifth of those surveyed also highlighted rationales closer to their core business: reflecting the changing gender composition of their customer base as well as enhancing corporate decision-making and innovation."[6]

We can question the assumption that because sex sells, it's the best way to sell anything. We can stop ignoring the damage we create when we sexualize people to attract buyers for products, services, or ideas. A sign reading, "SEX! Now that I've got your attention, quit f—ing with the planet" may be useful for protesting for climate change legislation, but it furthers Old Normal. Content creators in advertising, marketing, media, and entertainment can examine the opportunity to honor the value of each human without regard to gender and commit to stop paying people to objectify, sexualize, or demean any gender.

We can create a profit motive for culture change that will lead to New Normal. Globally, women control the spending of 64.5 percent of the world's income. If females consistently demand change or take their dollars elsewhere, and if allies support their requests, then companies might re-examine their assumptions about the propriety of using objectification and sexualization as marketing messages.

People with growth mindsets risk taking action to challenge the status quo. For example, nine-year-old Riley Morrison wanted a pair of Under Armour Curry 5 shoes for her new basketball season, but she found none in the girls' section on the Under Armour website. She wrote to Stephen Curry of the Golden State Warriors requesting he do something about this. In fact, Curry has spoken and written about how personal the issue of women's equality is for him as a husband and father of two daughters. Curry and Under Armour responded positively, and now Curry and Riley have been recognized as change makers.[7] Change is possible one project at a time for those willing to act.

The Cost of Lost Talent and Leadership

Looking at Old Normal, it's also important to consider what changes we can start making to level the playing field for genders, to reduce the cost of ignoring talent and undeveloped leadership. Instead of saying "That's just the way it is," we can question the cost of lost opportunities to develop business talent or leaders in companies when people avoid meeting, working, or traveling with women alone.

We can examine the fear of untrue sexual harassment claims and the risk of creating "hostile environment" types of sexual discrimination claims by discriminating against people because of gender.

We can question the assumption that nothing is lost when women are discriminated against. That assumption is robbing the world of untapped wealth. According to the World Economic Forum:

> Talent is one of the most essential factors for growth and competitiveness. To build future economies that are both dynamic and inclusive, we must ensure that everyone has equal opportunity. When (females) are not integrated—as both beneficiary and shaper—the global community loses out on skills, ideas and perspectives that are critical for addressing global challenges and harnessing new opportunities.[8]

Countries with the highest scores in the Global Human Capital Index maximize engagement of citizens in the economy by making sure there is gender parity in the marketplace. Gender parity and growth in GDP are linked, and although qualified women are coming out of the education system, many industries don't hire, retain, or promote women, thereby lowering their capacity to contribute or gain rewards from participating in the paying economy.

The World Economic Forum has concluded from the research that having females in leadership positions is a top indicator for an organization's success at hiring women at all levels from entry to C-suite. Such companies are deepening the female talent in the organization to feed future management and executive roles.[9] According to the WEF website, "Female talent remains one of the most under-utilized business resources, either squandered through lack of progression or untapped from the onset. Business leaders and governments increasingly note that tackling barriers to equality can unlock new opportunities for growth."[10]

Not only is increased parity in the labor force linked to increased earnings and participation of females, it is also linked to lowered infant, child, and maternal mortality rates and increased spending for children, especially for girls.[11] For example, according to the World Bank, when girls are educated at the same level as boys, it increases females' lifetime earnings by 54 to 68 percent of that country's gross domestic product (GDP). In addition to investments in girls' education, increased investments in health for pregnant moms and children also has a multiplier effect, increasing the GDP for that country.

We can recognize that when women are engaged economically and politically, there is positive movement toward gender equality across society. Women involve themselves in advocating, prioritizing, and investing in issues to improve family life, education, and health. When women are engaged in public life, institutions gain credibility, and democratic outcomes increase. Evidence also points to a correlation between women's political leadership and wider economic participation.[12]

Moral Disengagement

Normally, people act in alignment with their moral codes or beliefs. Those who discriminate against, harass, abuse, or violate others are morally disengaged. Morally disengaged thinking processes allow for the global subjugation of, discrimination of, and sexual violence against females to continue.

In his research paper entitled *Moral Disengagement in the Perpetration of Inhumanities* (Stanford University, 1999), Albert Bandura, professor emeritus of social science in psychology at Stanford University, identified seven strategies people use to act apart from aligning their behaviors with their morality. These are moral justification, euphemistic labeling, advantageous comparison, displacement of responsibility, diffusion of responsibility, disregard or distortion of consequences, and dehumanization.[13] In the global war against women, these strategies might show up in the following ways:

Moral Justification. Closing our minds to the immorality of a course of thought, speech, or behavior by creating a "moral framework" that allows it to be overlooked.[14] Some examples of these thought patterns include *I protect women; therefore, I have the right to control* *them. If I bear the burden of war, then I deserve the spoils. I bring home the bacon; therefore, I rule the home.*

Euphemistic Labeling. Using words to sidestep the reality of the offense. The online *Urban Dictionary* lists almost endless euphemisms to describe sexual violence. Examples of euphemisms include *train ride* or *chaining* (gang rape), *Molly in her pop to pop her bottle* (drugging a girl before raping her), *play with small balls* (child sexual abuse of boys).

Advantageous Comparison. Justifying bad behaviors by comparing grievous wrongs with things you believe are worse. For example: *We decimated that village, but I saved her life by making her my wife. Other pimps off hoes* (kill prostitutes that run away), *but mine are lucky, I just teach them a lesson* (a savage beating) *and let them get back to work* (human trafficking). *I can watch porn or whatever else I want while she's doing all the chores* (unpaid work) *because I take home $5,000 more per year.*

Displacing Responsibility. Closing your mind to the ownership of problems that are clearly in your wheelhouse. This strategy looks like: *I don't need to speak up when I see harassment because that's the Human Resources Department's concern. I would never hurt a woman myself; I'm just buying the porn; the producers are the ones who handle the actors.*

Diffusion of Responsibility. Taking the blame off yourself and putting it on the group. People are more likely to discriminate or harass when the company or group culture supports this misbehavior. People act more cruelly or are more likely to harm without conscience when they're in a group. Examples are: *The crew was just having a bit of fun* (a group of guys who stripped a girl they stopped on the street who was walking home from work, before they got distracted by an approaching car and she escaped). *We were just partying; nobody was hurt* (fraternity brothers who were sexually assaulting party guests).

Disregard or Distortion of Consequences. Closing our minds to the reality of impact or minimizing the consequences to the victim. For example, guys reviewing media reports of a political candidate's confession of groping women saying, "What's the big deal with grabbing her by the p———y? It's not like he's raping anyone." A co-worker vying for a promotion talking about another candidate, saying, "She can't handle a promotion; she's pregnant." (Because of the culture of discrimination, she loses the promotion and has to move to a lower-rent neighborhood, increasing her commute time and childcare costs.) A harasser in the workplace defending himself when accused: "Sure I teased her a little bit, but it was all in fun," while HR reviews the images of the bruises he left on her body.

A classic example of minimization is the response of Brazilian men before and after they were observed at a party putting their hands on models who gave them no invitation to touch them. As a social media experiment to create awareness of harassment behavior of men, the drink manufacturer and distributor Schweppes created a garment they called the Dress for Respect to measure unwanted groping behavior by men. The dress had sensors all over it that could detect and report to a monitor in the next room exactly where and how much pressure was used when someone touched the model's dress. Before the experiment, researchers talked to men, and they said that men in Brazil don't normally touch women at parties; within four hours at a nightclub party, however, three models were touched 157 times, over forty times per hour, by different men without permission or invitation. After the experiment, the researchers showed the men their actual behavior, and they acted surprised at the outcome.[15]

Dehumanization. Closing your mind to the humanity and value of each person. This strategy sounds like: A guy telling his friend about his disappointment in a Tinder date that didn't end up in sex: "Bitch's [female dog] not worth the money I paid for her drink." Man talking to a co-worker about a new employee: "Look, fresh meat." Guy talking about a girl at his school, "Yeah, I did her. Who didn't? . . . cumbucket [nonhuman synonym for slut]."

Victim Blaming. Fixing blame for your behavior on the victim or on external circumstances is also a way people morally disengage. Here are some examples of victim blaming: A man who has no guilt for raping an unconscious woman might say, "She was passed out drunk. If she didn't want to be used, she should have left after her first drink." A man who sexually assaulted another man might defend himself by saying, "His pants were so tight you could see his fruit basket. . . . I just gave him what he wanted." A man who beats up and rapes his girlfriend might say in justification, "She made me lose it. . . . she knows not to cross me by looking at anyone else when we leave the house." A soldier who sexually assaults a female civilian in enemy territory might say, "The military has no business putting men with needs in situations where they're at risk of being seduced by enemy civilians."

These strategies come into play when a person or organization is acting in ways that are self-centered, self-serving, judgmental, antagonistic, or intentionally disconnected from their moral center. These comments might come from years, decades, even generations of default training and reinforcement from a culture that has failed to value humans equally. This type of training has come through practice of a code of conduct that allows and encourages the kinds of behaviors that create a world that is unsafe for females.

Babies are born full of curiosity. Children start out trusting and learn to stop trusting. Old Normal has created a world that stifles the best of hopes for positive relations between people. Moral disengagement is learned behavior, and studies have shown that males begin to practice moral disengagement as young boys at a much higher rate than females.[16]

The Crux of Hope for Life Beyond #MeToo

The hope for New Normal, where there is hope for peace, cooperation, and freedom from fear between males and females that leads to deep, trusting relationships and true happiness, is personal choice.

To create New Normal, those currently supporting Old Normal need to choose what kind of world they want to be a part of and what honestly is in service to their deepest wants and dreams.

We've looked at Old Normal and seen how costly it is to individuals, groups, organizations, and society. Our choices impact the lives of unborn girls, baby girls, little girls, teen girls, young women, career women, middle-aged women, elderly women, and everyone else in our world. By our actions we choose what we want for our own and our friends' neighbors, colleagues, friends, girlfriends, wives, daughters, sisters, mothers, aunts, and grandmothers.

By your choices you are also creating a future for your sons, grandsons, brothers, fathers, uncles, and grandfathers. Consider what choices you are making and what will bring the results you most desire. Your future happiness depends on your recognizing your choices about how you relate to other people. If you choose words and actions that show contempt and disregard for others in your personal and professional relationships, you will be choosing death to healthy relationships. These choices are the antithesis of the New Normal man, who chooses to honor people and protect the relationships he values and who demonstrates equal respect for women and men. Choose what you want.

The women's movement has for generations cost the literal blood, sweat, and tears of countless people (many women, some men) who've worked tirelessly to advocate for justice and seek freedom from oppression. Women have expressed collective outrage at sexual violence and discrimination for centuries, and many have worked to change laws and effect change. But too many women have rested on the laurels of others who sacrificed to win every right they freely exercise as they are morally disengaged from the work of creating New Normal.

Females not actively supporting New Normal need to ask themselves whether disengagement, apathy, and inactivity are servicing their deepest wants and dreams. What kind of world do you want for yourself and for your family, friends, neighbors, and colleagues, female and male? New Normal is present where women speak up and act to insist females get the same respect as men. Choosing to judge and dishonor women who are seeking freedom from violence and injustice with petty, self-centered, antagonistic, or apathetic attitudes and actions puts you squarely in Old Normal.

You get to choose whether you will be a woman whose words and actions evidence self-objectification, self-centered contempt, and disregard for others in her personal life and in working and social relationships, and pride in using others for her personal agenda. Or you can be a woman who refuses to sacrifice her integrity or her soul, insists on authentic, brave, bold, loving relationships with the females and males in her life, and demonstrates respect for others based on her concern for their well-being. Apathy, fear, and judgment are antithetical to action and advocacy for women. Choose what you want.

Women have spoken for millennia about the fervent desire to end subjugation, discrimination, harassment, abuse, and assault, but the change that brings the greatest benefits requires all people to engage and become allies and everyone, male and female, to work together for global transformation.

Physically, we are a binary species with some exceptions, and every exception is as valuable as everyone else by right of being human. Some people do not identify as binary. Transsexuals may identify as binary or not. All sexual orientations have a place in this conversation. Your sexuality is expressed in relationships, and your choices in relationships will either keep you (and all whom you impact with your life) in Old

Normal or move you into New Normal. It's the choice of honoring and respecting yourself and others. Choose for yourself.

The quality of our relationships depends on every single choice we make to either respect and love another or to disrespect, objectify, or harm another. Cultural change on a global level across all spectrums (home, family, healthcare, education, workplaces, religions) will only happen if there is buy-in from each person, regardless of gender, that we will come together as a world and engage in positive, personal choices to create New Normal. One person at a time, one choice at a time, we can change the world.

Research from the Harvard Study of Adult Development shows that solid positive relationships are key to happiness, health, and well-being. The study shows that

> close relationships, more than money or fame, are what keep people happy throughout their lives. . . . Those ties protect people from life's discontents, help to delay mental and physical decline, and are better predictors of long and happy lives than social class, IQ, or even genes.[17]

New Normal provides fearless, respectful, nonviolent communities and supports social structures that will institute justice and partnership across leadership structures in all cultural and social organizations. New Normal requires every person to engage to ensure each person is valued for their humanity, not for their power, and that none are devalued because of gender.

Who Can Engage in the New Normal?

Culture is built on a foundation of values that is established in the home. Traditional cultural structures for life in the privacy of the home have been perverted, allowing widespread sexual, physical, and psychological abuse of children and women. If we want New Normal, we need to engage personally, one by one, worldwide, to gain commitment by all to create nonviolent homes. We need as a society to agree on ways to make the most of social-science research and to do what it takes to grow healthy homes. We need to engage our communities to commit to homes with zero tolerance of sexual objectification, harassment, abuse, or violence.

Families need cultural support to create internal changes to end objectification and self-objectification of all family members, especially females. How will we engage families to agree and commit to call out and eliminate gender stereotypes that subject women to lesser status?

One of the roots of Old Normal contributing to the pay gap is unequal contributions to unpaid work in the home. To create New Normal, we need to work together to equalize the burden of unpaid work among all genders, both in the home and in the workplace. Families can support unpaid work by equalizing expectations for family members to contribute unpaid work. To share unpaid work and to promote equal male and female advancement in education, employment, and leadership, family units can hold each other to higher standards guarding against discrimination, harassment, abuse, and violence.

Socially, to create New Normal, first we need to look globally, nationally, locally, and in our homes at what access to porn, sex trafficking and prostitution, and porn games and entertainment is doing to harm those who participate. How will we engage to finally count the staggering cost to the victims and to the world of violence against women? We need to come to agreement about the best ways to address the roots of Old Normal.

Economically, to create New Normal, we need to look at how we support parents, especially single parents, to care for children while earning living wages. We need to engage economies to bring nonexploitative, sustainable workplaces to New Normal. We need workplaces that honor and build up the heart of humanity by valuing all people.

The world's governments and communities must engage and agree not only on principle, but in reality, to provide equal access to education for females. Society and educators must support a New Normal, making and keeping a commitment to recognize and eliminate gender stereotyping. Parents and education systems need to educate children from a young age on emotional intelligence and moral agency to reduce the risk of moral disengagement. People supporting New Normal will educate kids beginning in K5 about the power of a growth mindset, and educators will work with families to help children understand how each of us is part of something bigger than ourselves, responsible to community.

How will we engage our middle schoolers to create awareness of the costs of harassment and help youth practice prevention of harassment and sexual violence in society? The changes must start in the homes, and parents who need help need the support of community to bring New Normal from home into the schoolroom. Crackdown on harassment in schools with strict policies and swift, clear consequences, and accountability to adhere to national and global standards of human behavior can help create change in classrooms and on campuses. Educational institutions need to enact consequences that will effectively increase offenders' knowledge of the damage of harassment and violence to society and encourage the offender to reform his or her views to change behavior.

To move into New Normal, males must agree to champion gender-equal participation in government and vote to encourage women to lead in policymaking about women. New Normal will facilitate equalization of leadership for policymaking on healthcare, funding research dollars, and access to employment.

To move into New Normal, faith communities must absolutely stop tolerating sexual abusers. No more hiding the truth or refusing to be accountable to the greater good of society at large. Broad social recognition is needed in all religions as well as nonreligious belief systems of the high cost to community of the objectification of children and women. Organized religions or belief systems cannot be exempt from the requirements of the law to enforce consequences of the perpetration of sexual harassment, abuse, or violence. To move into New Normal, people of all belief systems must understand and communicate to their communities that any tolerance of objectification or abuse of any kind will diminish and negate the positive impact of this belief system. Zero tolerance and swift, agreed-upon societal norms of consequences for perpetrators of sexual harassment, abuse, or violence must be acted upon and observed. Zero tolerance can't simply be spoken about. Zero tolerance must be lived.

Faith communities can't stop at fighting Old Normal on the issue of abuse. All organized religions supporting New Normal need to commit to attain equity of genders in leadership and in service opportunities. There are no second-class citizens in New Normal.

If there ever can be New Normal, these and many other changes need to be seen not as problems but as projects to engage in. This is not an exhaustive list of changes or projects to address, but, rather, a starting place for conversations. The tremendous cost of Old Normal to our world must be understood. Each person needs to own their responsibility and right to contribute to a world where respect for each human being is the norm.

Questions for Thoughtful Consideration and Discussion

1. What choices did Julie have after seeing the bruises? What costs did she suffer from quitting her job?

2. If you oppose culture change that could lead to a nonviolent future, what are your reasons?

3. In your opinion, can we do something about Old Normal?

4. If Old Normal is an actionable concern, what would it take for you to decide to personally invest your time and energy in projects that will do something to facilitate change?

5. How would you describe your willingness to uncover, review, examine, and dismiss assumptions that are no longer acceptable or true or certain and keep the world in Old Normal?

6. How do moral justification, minimization, dehumanization, and displacing responsibility show up in your life? Your family? Your workplace? Your circles of influence?

7. Who needs protection and help to develop new assumptions until they become full participants in society? How will that protection and development be provided?

8. How could men benefit from New Normal?

9. What will facilitate entrenchment in Old Normal?

10. What do you think it will take to create New Normal?

11. What conversations need to happen to let go of what's not working and embrace a new nonviolent culture that protects each person?

TWELVE

How Do We Enact Change?

It was a rare night out for me. I was pretty new to the college town, and I wasn't one to party, knowing from experience that alcohol made people stupid. But my friend convinced me to go out with her. We walked out of the steamy July night into a cool, dark, loud bar on Main Street, seeking relief from the heat that pulled my hair out of curls and sweated up my lacy, button-up-the-back sleeveless top, the waistband of my knee-length skirt, and my toes in their clogs.

We sat at the bar and ordered drinks. After one amaretto sour, I was feeling happy. The guy to my left said something really funny, and I laughed, slid off my barstool, gave him a hug, and hopped back up next to my friend.

A few minutes later, the guy further down said, "Let's go for a walk."

My friend and I stood up, paid for our drinks, and followed the guys back out into the heavy air. We headed up the street past other open bar doors.

As we turned a corner into a side street, the guy to my left grabbed my hand. "Come on. There's a great view of the city up there." He pulled me across the street away from his buddy and my friend and up several flights of poorly lit stairs to a waist-high wall with a railing, high above a steep drop off to the street below. He dropped my hand and stood beside me. The lights of the city and its lit monuments were spread below. A cooling breeze blew off the river.

As I took it all in, I felt a tickle at the nape of my neck. I didn't understand where it was coming from, but then he was behind me, crushing me against the railing. With one hand he pulled down my underwear and shoved my hands off the railing. His arms held me like iron as my feet lifted off the patio. He shoved into me two or three times.

A shock ran through me. "No!" I cried. "No. I don't want this!" I clutched the railing and pushed against it, twisted and dropped my weight into my knees as my feet felt the ground solid under me. I crouched beside the half wall, grabbed up my underwear, and ran away from the city lights and the shining river below.

I stumbled down the stairs to the street, my feet and ankles sliding in my clogs, and caught up to my friend and the other guy from the bar.

"We have to go," I said. "Now." She looked at me. I turned to walk away. She followed as the guy to the left came up behind her.

He shouted, "Hey, what's your number?"

I yelled, "I'm not easy."

"You're the easiest I ever had."

My friend turned to me and said, "I was going to tell you, don't hug guys in bars."

When I got home and pulled off my clothes to shower away the feel and smell of the guy to the left, the top three buttons of my blouse were unbuttoned. I never wore those clothes or hugged a guy in a bar again.

#MeToo, Sara

I can't stand that the guy in this story raped this young woman. That's what he did. He sexually assaulted her and then acted as if it were something she consented to. Why didn't asking (for a name, a phone number, permission to unbutton a button, permission to remove clothing, permission to touch her body, consent to sex) precede his actions? Wherever he learned that it's remotely okay to do what he did, he absorbed Old Normal, and he allowed it to run his life as if he were an animal and to destroy Sara's future.

I dream of a world where laughing at a stranger's joke and hugging them in joy is never interpreted as consent. I dream of a world where men are never threats that a girlfriend needs to warn another girl about. I dream of a world where #MeToo stories like those in this book never happen. I dream of a world where children are taught to respect other people from birth and not use them. I dream of New Normal, where people can go anywhere and interact with anyone and not be objectified or devalued by them.

I believe that in eternity, such behavior doesn't happen. But no matter what beliefs anyone might hold about life after death, humans do not have to wait until we're dead to start living in a safe, just world. We absolutely have the ability to choose individually and collectively to start creating New Normal so that stories like this never happen. If there's any possibility of moving past Old Normal, how can we enact change?

Start with Acknowledgment

It is important to begin any change with acknowledgment of past efforts, barriers, successes, and allies. In the search for New Normal, it is important to acknowledge

- that women and allied men have been working on this forever, made progress, and had that progress attacked and undermined so they had to start all over again,

- that there are so many changes needed that it can seem impossible, and that it is far too hard for men (and women) to break out of their conditioning without help, and
- that there are those who will consistently fight against women having any say over their reproductive capacity or any other role, other than submission and service to males, because that is what cultures worldwide are now set up to do.

Given the active opposition and worldwide cultural conditioning that exists, is New Normal free from sexual discrimination and violence the impossible dream? Anyone who has studied history knows that progress is possible, however difficult, painstakingly slow, erratic, and contrary to cultural norms. A few generations ago in the United States, women had no rights to pursue higher education, no voting rights, no property rights, and few human rights. History proves change is a possible dream and that all progress is fragile until it becomes the unspoken assumption of a thriving New Normal.

Envisioning Change

When I work with clients, I ask them to clearly define where they are now and to clearly envision where they want to be at the end of our coaching. We not only examine the desired external changes but also the internal shifts that can facilitate the changes. We look at reasons for making the changes and the deeper why behind stated reasons. We examine assumptions about the situation and possible results of not making the changes. We look at the implications of the choices they've been making already or new choices they might need to make.

Once there's clarity on the desired change, we consider the necessary pathways toward change and the obstacles to those pathways. We identify resources, strategies and goals, key performance indicators, and accountability structures—all before the client takes action. This process brings clarity on the value of the proposed changes and clarity on how the change can be facilitated. In groups, in addition to buy-in on the change, we seek input from all group members on the reasons, implications, and benefits of making the desired changes.

A coaching model to facilitate New Normal would encourage people seeking change to clarify exactly what results are being sought. A coaching model asks everyone concerned to take a long, hard look at assumptions people bring with them in their desire to make change. People are encouraged to invite other groups that are also facilitating change to open discussions and seek input and perspectives from others who might be able to add value in the change process.

Influencing for Change

If you look at what influencers have done to drastically reduce polio cases, you might gain hope that influencers can also work to bring us to New Normal. Up until the baby-boom generation, the polio virus had devastated human lives and was once considered an impossible threat, but now, according to the Rotary International's End Polio Now website, we are just three countries away from complete eradication, thanks to the work of the Rotary Foundation, the Bill & Melinda Gates Foundation, cooperation from governments around the world, and feet-on-the-ground efforts of thousands of volunteers.[1] Similarly, Old Normal devastates human lives, and we're just getting started on the efforts to eradicate it. I believe that progress toward New Normal is as possible as the progress that's been made toward the eradication of polio.

In the book *Influencer*, the team of authors, Kerry Patterson, Joseph Grenny, David Maxfield, Ron McMillan, and Al Switzler, demystify how influencers create systemic, lasting change. The first step is to recognize that we have the power to change something. We can choose to be influencers. I believe this with all my heart, and I believe that you can choose to be an influencer and that change is possible to create New Normal with no sexual discrimination, no sexual harassment, no sexual abuse, and no sexual violence.

As a coach, I work with my clients to determine what actions or behaviors must happen for them to create the results they want. The book *Influencer* explains that the steps to change require identifying key, vital behaviors that must change and focusing in on those. In order to change behaviors, people's minds need to change first, and to do this, people need two things: one, they need to believe the change is possible and will be worth it, and two, they need to believe they can do what is required for the change to be effective.[2]

#MeToo brought to light testimonies and stories that carried such a huge amount of pain from the shadows and showed the world we're ready for a different kind of future.

Creating massive, systemic cultural change to create New Normal will require more than simplistic solutions. Prolific author and strategic thinker Seth Godin wrote in his blog on December 12, 2018, "Difficult problems require emotional labor, approaches that feel risky, and methods that might not work. They reward patience, nuance, and guts, and they will fight off brute force all day long."[3]

The Mess of Old Normal is a difficult problem that will take emotional energy, multiple views, multiple strategies, and work from a variety of possible risky approaches to identify vital behaviors and create systemic changes. The difficult problem will require identifying the vital behaviors that must change and also will require connecting vital behaviors to intrinsic motives, so people of all cultures, backgrounds, ages, perspectives, and genders will want to change and be willing to internalize change. The difficult problem will take buy-in on a personal level and on a global scale.

With conflicts of beliefs, values, and cultures, creating positive change takes a willingness to examine thoughts and behaviors and a commitment to dig in together to look at the roots of conflict and to harness the creative potential in conflict. For example, according to international leadership development expert, psychologist, and author Nate Regier, "Eliminating the casualties of conflict cannot happen by repressing the conflict and just 'being nice.' It happens by stewarding the energy inherent in conflict to make something positive, even amazing."[4] Regier believes that when people embrace the process of "struggling with" others in creative conflict, they gain power to create transformation.

The question is, What do we want most? Do we want a transformed world? Are we willing to see things from other perspectives, to struggle with one another and take risky approaches, study what methods have worked, and repeat that while simultaneously trying new things to bring about New Normal?

Vital Behaviors for Change

In a coaching situation, clients are the ones who identify what must change. Coaches offer external perspectives, but the offering must be given with open hands as one possible solution. It's the client's work to search for the real keys to change, to identify vital behaviors and steps that will lead to lasting transformation, whether that's getting rid of the procrastination habit, learning to be early after a lifetime of habitual tardiness, kicking the cell phone and social-media addictions, or envisioning and planning an accelerated growth curve for a new product line.

In the case of creating a New Normal that is safe for all, I invite you to come up with your own list of vital behaviors that need to change. I offer the following six vital changes for you to consider:

1. Value individuals. Every individual deserves to grow into the fullness of who they are without another's bias warping or limiting their potential. Every person is as individual, precious, and valuable as everyone else. Stop stereotyping, dividing, and devaluing people.

2. Initiate peace. Our inalienable rights to life, liberty, and the pursuit of happiness don't give us free rein to infringe upon or devalue another's right to life, liberty, and the pursuit of happiness. If it doesn't lead to peace, don't do it. Stop acting with contempt and violence against people.

3. Demonstrate respect for people. Humans, at every point in life, are never objects to satisfy our personal needs or desires. Rather, each person is an equally valuable life force and community member, equally worthy of respect, each bearing incalculable, innate worth. Stop objectifying people.

4. Gain and clarify consent. Consent at every point in any sexual encounter with any other human being is essential. Any verbal or physical engagement with another person about any sexual matter is an unwelcome intrusion if consent has not been obtained at that time for that interaction. To obtain consent, the person we seek consent from must be capable of offering consent physically, emotionally, and cognitively or rationally, from an adult perspective. Exercising power by violating another's basic human rights is unacceptable. Stop using other people's bodies without their consent.

5. Honor people's complexity. Beyond basic human desires and needs for sexual expression, including scientifically built-in gender differences, each person brings to community the multidimensional aspects of their entire person. Stop believing or acting upon the assumption that anyone has a right to (in any slightest way) place a limit on the fullness of another's individuality by viewing them as nothing but a source of sexual gratification. People are much more than their gender or sexuality. Stop minimizing or sexualizing people.

6. Embrace accountability. Individuals must be accountable. Communities must commit to zero toleration of Old Normal behaviors (in ourselves and in others). These negative behaviors need to be called out by the community. Individuals who are harmed need to allow the community to support them, and the community needs to step up and be there to support victims and to deal with perpetrators so they stop offending. Stop tolerating, excusing, ignoring, overlooking, or failing to hold people (including self) accountable for unacceptable behaviors.

A Model for Change

The second section of the book *Influencer* identifies a change model with six sources of influence. These address motivation and ability from personal, social, and structural perspectives. The sources of influences include

- personal motivation (making the change desirable),
- personal ability (growing will by growing skill),
- social motivation (peer pressure),
- social ability (strength in numbers),
- structural motivation (designing rewards, demanding accountability), and
- structural ability (changing the environment).[5]

To create change, all six sources of influences must be applied to the change.[6] If these influences are not present, the change won't happen. I suggest the absence of a number of these sources of influences is a main reason we keep losing ground in efforts to create New Normal.

Losing Ground

In some cases we are losing ground on structural motivation. For example, Iowa State University reports showed twelve rapes in 2014, fourteen in 2015, seventeen in 2016 on campus, with over 80 percent occurring in residence halls. According to the 2017 Iowa State Police Annual Security and Safety Report, when you include off-campus crimes, those numbers are fifteen in 2014, seventeen in 2015, and twenty-five in 2016. Starting in 2018, colleges are no longer legally required to publish off-campus crime statistics.

In the US, the forward movement to enforce existing laws is not only stalled but also has been pushed back when it comes to reporting violent crimes to the public. The 1991 Clery Act, strengthened by the Violence Against Women Act, which was reauthorized in 2013 after a massive campaign and the July 2013 petition from ED Act Now,[7] brought over 100,000 signatures to ask the Office of Civil Rights of the Education Department to (1) conduct timely investigations, (2) include victims in voluntary resolution agreements between the Department of Education and Schools, and (3) issue meaningful sanctions against noncompliant schools (those receiving federal dollars for any purpose liable under 1972 Title IX). (Points 1 and 3 of the petition were already required by law.) For example, the Clery Act and Violence Against Women Act required the report of violent crimes and property crimes on and off campus of a Title IX school.

The Iowa State Police Report included off-campus crimes as a result of the White House Task Force to Protect Students from Sexual Assault 2014,[8] which was established to coordinate and strengthen the enforcement of existing laws. In addition to strengthening cooperation between local and campus law enforcement, it required local jurisdictions to track and report Clery Act crimes and make this information available to the public. Title IX schools failed to report the violence to their communities if it didn't happen on campus. The 2014 White House Task Force required the Department of Education and the Justice Department to work together. One result was a press release with a list of open sexual violence investigations against fifty-five various Title IX schools.[9]

The current US Education and Justice Departments are revamping Title IX regulations, allowing colleges to cut already limited sexual harassment investigations by 39 percent. The Education Department's new plans require schools to only look into allegations that happened on campus and were filed with the correct school officials. Off-campus violence or rapes reported to the dorm resident assistant but not campus police are not required to be investigated or reported.[10]

The US passed the Violence Against Women Act in response to the Convention on the Elimination of All Forms of Discrimination Against Women (CEDAW) as an alternative to seek to protect its citizens from violence. The US's lack of structural motivation and structural ability allows for backpedaling on progress. We need creative solutions to keep progress moving forward in the protection of human rights. One possible solution to support structural ability as a first step to continue moving toward New Normal is to change how institutions codify legislation enacted to help laws permanently create accountability to put an end to violence. The United Nations has an international agreement with most of the world to end discrimination. If we want to move to a safer world for women, New Normal will require that we look again at why the US is among the few countries that have yet to ratify this agreement.

UN Convention to End Discrimination against Women

The Convention on the Elimination of All Forms of Discrimination Against Women was adopted in 1979 by the UN General Assembly and is described as an international bill of rights for women. The UN describes CEDAW as follows:

> Consisting of a preamble and 30 articles, it defines what constitutes discrimination against women and sets up an agenda for national action to end such discrimination.
>
> The Convention defines discrimination against women as ". . . any distinction, exclusion or restriction made on the basis of sex which has the effect or purpose of impairing or nullifying the recognition, enjoyment or exercise by women, irrespective of their marital status, on a basis of equality of men and women, of human rights and fundamental freedoms in the political, economic, social, cultural, civil or any other field."[11]

As of September 2019, a total of 189 nation states have ratified the treaty. The United States signed CEDAW in 1979. In 1980, President Jimmy Carter signed CEDAW and sent it to the Senate. The Senate Foreign Relations Committee has debated the treaty five times, but it hasn't made it to the full Senate for a vote for ratification. The

League of Women Voters and AARP support CEDAW. Concerned Women for America opposes it, arguing that the treaty is unnecessary and subjects the US to the whims of the CEDAW Committee. The CEDAW Committee's advocacy of reproductive rights and enforcement of gender-neutral work rules are controversial especially to religious conservatives. Concerned Women for America also believes the CEDAW Committee concentrates power unfairly.

According to the Office of the High Commissioner of the United Nations Human Rights organization,

> the Committee on the Elimination of Discrimination against Women . . . is composed of 23 experts, elected by secret ballot by States parties. The Committee is tasked with the review of the reports of States parties. . . . The Optional Protocol to the Convention empowers the Committee to consider communications submitted by individuals or groups of individuals alleging violations of the Convention in States parties to the Convention and the Optional Protocol. The Optional Protocol also entitles the Committee of its own motion to inquire into grave or systematic violations of the Convention in those States parties where this procedure is applicable.[12]

Many of the states that ratified the treaty did so with written reservations, desiring to maintain their citizens' national sovereignty over the United Nations' laws. Implementation over the past thirty-nine years has been spotty. Compliance is hard to track and more difficult to enforce. Although the Democratic Republic of the Congo signed and ratified the treaty, since the war started in 1996, the country's failure to comply is beyond description and horrific.

Global change protecting women has happened bit by bit and has been hard won, as national and state and local changes add up, such as the right to vote and the right for a woman to make choices about her body. The work is unfinished. Those who disagree on this treaty must come together to craft laws that all can agree on and ratify. Legislation must support basic human rights for each individual.

Enacting Change Globally

For women and girls in northeastern Democratic Republic of Congo (DRC), rape is a constant threat. Sexual violence as a weapon of war to control, humiliate, and intimidate millions of women and girls has been used since the First Congo War in 1996.

Men largely go unpunished. Armed groups attack villages, kill men, rape and kill or enslave women and children, and terrorize their enemies. Most using rape as weapons of war are not brought to justice but instead are given amnesty and integrated into the national army or let into general society, where they rape again and again. Most females do not report their rapes, as those who do are blamed, even shunned by their communities.[13] The Global Fund for Women is actively helping girls and women who now can't go to school, the market, or even get water without fear of rape both by combatants and civilians, which is a daily problem because of the war-torn country's instability and violence.

The United Nations Security Council Resolution 1820, which condemned sexual violence as a tool of war and offered specific actions to address the causes and consequences of wartime sexual violence, was passed in 2008. Chairing the debate on behalf of the United States, which held the Security Council presidency during the month it was passed, former Secretary of State Condoleezza Rice noted that there had long been dispute about whether the Council was authorized to address the issue of sexual violence against women in conflict.

"I am proud that, today, we respond to that lingering question with a resounding 'yes!'" Secretary of State Rice said, "We affirm that sexual violence profoundly affects not only the health and safety of women, but the economic and social stability of their nations."[14]

Ten years later, a report by the US Institute of Peace indicated that the issue had not improved, and the data showed the cost of sexual violence is deeper than had been understood at the time Resolution 1820 passed. Ten years of programming and research have demonstrated clear connections between conflict and sexual violence that extend beyond wartime and into civilian life. Conflict-associated sexual violence in the DRC and globally

[includes] other forms of sexual violence, including sexual exploitation and abuse, domestic sexual violence, and violence targeted at women in politics, are often exacerbated by armed conflict and increase insecurity. Conflict-associated sexual violence contributes to the normalization of violence, undermines social cohesion, and worsens structural inequalities. [Its] harmful impacts threaten the security of women, communities, and states, and disrupt peace processes. The United Nations, its member states, civil society organizations, media outlets, the private sector, and academia must recognize and address the detrimental impacts of conflict-associated sexual violence. [15]

The United States also signed the UN Convention against Transnational Organized Crime, adopted by General Assembly resolution entered into force in September 2003. The convention is supplemented by three protocols, which target specific areas of organized crime: the Protocol to Prevent, Suppress and Punish Trafficking in Persons, Especially Women and Children; the Protocol against the Smuggling of Migrants by Land, Sea and Air; and the Protocol against the Illicit Manufacturing of and Trafficking in Firearms, their Parts and Components and Ammunition. Structural motivation and structural ability require investments of energy, funds, and people. The work continues.

As diverse as the populations and cultures are around the world, governments can protect their women and children and create a world free from violence. This is imperative for the creation of New Normal. Signs of change will include prioritization of governmental funding to combat sexual violence and sexual discrimination. Legislation enacted and enforced globally, nationally, and locally on a variety of fronts that holds citizens to standards that are just and fair for all concerned helps keep people free from harm and violence.

Governments including the UN and governments of each nation-state are only as good as the people who make them up, the elected and appointed and ruling authorities. And they're only as good as their willingness and ability to act justly, love mercy, walk humbly, and wisely and fairly enforce the laws that people have agreed to. Though governments have accomplished some things to propel change, they can't do everything. This is where you and I and all the people of the world come into the picture.

Social Ability, Social Motivation

We the people of this earth change things by using our influence, choices, words, and actions to create change. The vital behaviors we adopt will support the rule of law and the work of countless nongovernmental organizations (NGOs), such as the Global Fund for Women, that also participate in bringing New Normal.

We the people of earth, by our choices, either accept societal norms in each nation-state or agree to work together to change them. Old Normal currently protects and hides abusers and rapists in our families, schools, churches, mosques, synagogues, temples, and village squares. Old Normal accepts street harassment as inevitable.

We the people of earth can change norms, call out offenders, and require more from ourselves, more from our families and associates, and more from our communities.

We the people of earth can choose to sit in apathy or choose action to further global, national, and local work to give equal access to education and political and economic participation to females.

We the people of earth can choose to set up structures to support change. We the people can choose to create change at individual and local community levels. Are you one of "we the people"? If you're a person and you are on earth, you're included.

Personal and Social Motivation

What motivates personal change? Let's examine one of the six vital behaviors mentioned earlier to consider what drives this behavior, and what would motivate us to change.

Value individuals and stop stereotyping. A stereotype is "a fixed, over-generalized belief about a particular group or class of people."[16] A stereotype might enable a person to respond rapidly to situations based on similar past experiences. Prejudice and discrimination can stem from fear, a need for belonging, projection (keeping a person from having to look at weakness or negative things in themselves) or a lack of emotional competence.[17] According to Saul McLeod, researcher and author for the website Simply Psychology,

> The use of stereotypes is a major way in which we simplify our social world; since they reduce the amount of processing (i.e., thinking) we have to do when we meet a new person. One disadvantage is that it makes us ignore differences between individuals; therefore, we think things about people that might not be true (i.e., make generalizations).[18]

To value each person as an individual and choose to stop stereotyping, it may help to know that evidence shows stereotyping has lasting negative effects on those who experience this kind of prejudice.[19] Subjecting people to stereotyping increases their risks of acting aggressively; exhibiting a lack of self-control; having trouble making good, rational decisions; and overindulging in unhealthy foods.[20] When threatened by judgment based on stereotype, the victim is less likely to perform as well as they would when there is no threat. [21]

At its worst, the impact of bullying behaviors based on stereotyping and discrimination can end lives. On December 10, 2018, nine-year-old McKenzie Adams, a bright, outgoing girl who loved math and science, from Linden, Alabama, killed herself after enduring ruthless bullying from children at US Jones Elementary School who taunted her the entire school year with messages like "black bitch," "you ugly," "just die," and "kill yourself."[22] The fact that she was a black girl who was friends with a white boy contributed to the bullies' prejudice.

Stereotyping others reveals projection and the inner negativity in a person. In a psychological study led by Dustin Wood at Wake Forest University, subjects rated the personalities of several acquaintances, and Wood says,

> The more frequently people rated others as kindhearted, happy, emotionally stable, or courteous, the more likely they were to rate themselves as having these traits, and the more likely outside evaluators were to agree. The results remained stable even when the subjects were tested again a year later. "Seeing others positively reveals our own positive traits," Wood commented. The same thing worked for darker personality traits, too. "A huge suite of negative personality traits is associated with viewing others negatively," Woods added. "The simple tendency to see people negatively indicates a greater likelihood of depression and various personality disorders."

Stereotyping hurts everyone involved, has a huge negative toll personally and to our community, and offers a relatively small positive gain. Personal and social benefits are far greater for valuing individuals and seeing the whole truth about them, as are the psychological benefits of releasing fear, choosing healthy, non-discriminating groups for belonging, making honest self-assessments and releasing projection, and developing emotional competencies. The reasons for social motivation to stop stereotyping are clear.

Personal and Social Ability

Even if you buy into the personal and social motivation piece, your ability to change behaviors (in this case eliminating stereotyping) and choose instead to see each person as the individual they are requires growing will by growing skill.

Education and growing skills start at birth in every family and are reinforced at school and in community. According to the National Association for the Education of Young Children (NAEYC),

> We know from research that children between two and five start becoming aware of gender, race, ethnicity, and disabilities. They also begin to absorb both the positive attitudes and negative biases attached to these aspects of identity by family members and other significant adults in their lives. If we want children to like themselves and value diversity, we must learn how to help them resist the biases and prejudices that are still far too prevalent in our society.[23]

The NAEYC offers suggestions to parents and educators of young children to help them learn from a young age to spot bias and resist it, and to recognize that silence is complicit agreement.[24] Discovery Education is one of many organizations that offers free lesson plans on teaching older (high school age) children about stereotypes.[25] The ACLU launched their Teach Kids, Not Stereotypes campaign to gather information about single-sex education programs around the country that are rooted in outdated, nonscientific gender stereotypes. Findings demonstrate that single-sex education programs that reinforce negative, false stereotypes in coeducational public schools are widely outside of compliance with the stringent legal requirements of Title IX.[26] Like the NAEYC, every nation group is seeking the welfare of young children, and organizations like the ACLU seek freedom for each person.

Social Ability

Who is responsible for educating children from birth to adulthood regarding vital behaviors that would move us out of the Mess? How do individuals lose the training that keeps us in Old Normal and gain the training that moves us to New Normal? Once the individual has fostered the will and the skill, how do we reinforce vital behaviors with social conditioning to take action leading to group and local change?

A small group of Seattle-area women, experienced with case management and wraparound services and helping troubled youth and sexual abuse issues, met to do something about helping girls and women who want to get out of the life of sex trafficking. These women founded REST (Real Escape from the Sex Trade) in 2009 to serve and care for women caught in the sex trade and help them find a path to freedom. In its first nine years, REST has proven its effectiveness in helping women and girls leave "the life." Now it is an official part of the city of Seattle's Coordinated Effort Against Sexual Exploitation (CEASE) response network and partners with Seattle Vice Squad, SeaTac, Kent, and Burien police officers; Seattle's Union Gospel Mission; Shared Hope International; Businesses Ending Sex Trafficking (BEST); Organization for Prostitution Survivors (OPS), and several others.[27]

The organization and its partners in CEASE are role models for enacting change at a local level. It starts with caring enough to make a difference. Local Sexual Assault Resource Centers (SARCs) are also examples of community action creating a difference. #MeToo has led to an increase in the number of people talking about sexual assault. At Pierce County's SARC, Tate Bates, director of advocacy and prevention education, said, "Because of social movements that have gained traction in the last few years, such as the #MeToo movement, we are witnessing a shift in the public's awareness of sexual violence. I believe that people from every age . . . race . . . ethnic group, socioeconomic status, gender and sexual orientation and ability level are sharing their stories and creating a culture that hopes to expose the extent of sexual violence in an effort to end it."[28] It's getting more common to hear from friends and family, "This happened to me twenty years ago, thirty years ago." The King County Sexual Assault Resource Center (KSARC) reported a 47 percent increase in calls in 2018 over 2017. Director Mary Ellen Stone said they've seen "dramatic increase for services overall."

The week after the Kavanaugh hearings for Supreme Court Justice, their call volume was up 300 percent as hotline-trained counselors offered a variety of services and referrals around the clock. According to Stone, though they receive calls from a wide variety of callers, since the hearings, KSARC was getting many more calls from "people in their 50s, 60s, 70s, and 80s saying, 'This happened to me and I never told anybody. But now I want you to know that I exist, and it still impacts me.'"[29]

The same is true at the national level. For example, RAINN hotline had a 338 percent increase in calls between the start and end of Kavanaugh's hearing compared to prior years. "Friday, September 28, was the busiest day in the 24-year history of the National Sexual Assault Hotline, with more than 3,000 people receiving help."[30] In September 2018, nearly 29,000 people were served, compared to 18,000 in September 2017.

Scott Berkowitz, RAINN's president, said,

History shows us that when high-profile allegations such as these are in the news it often causes others to reach out too. This story has clearly resonated with survivors and has led thousands to reach out for help for the first time. Over this past year, following the cases of Weinstein and Cosby and the explosion of #MeToo, our numbers have been growing pretty rapidly, but we've never seen anything like this before.[31]

With funding cuts after the failure to reapprove the Violence Against Women Act, the Sexual Assault Resource Center (SARC) staffs are strained and in need of donations from the community to continue to provide the resources they offer to assault victims.

Social motivation draws forth social ability. Social motivation and ability together engage people in groups to help make change possible. Leaders in every segment of society help others to recognize the imperative to participate in dialogue and to reinforce positive behaviors that help people leave behind the Mess. With individual motivation and ability, social motivation and ability rise. And with structural motivation and ability, gains are made, and losses can be prevented.

Structural Motivation and Structural Ability

Designing rewards, demanding accountability, and changing the environment to support the desired change are keys to structural motivation and accountability. When grassroots community efforts to create local accountability align with nationally and globally acceptable standards, people will facilitate change. For example, in France, a new law requires companies to report differences in pay between men and women and to correct the differences over the next three years.[32]

The law doesn't apply to companies with fewer than fifty employees, and those with 50 to 250 have until 2020 to comply, Labor Minister Muriel Pénicaud said in an interview.

Some economists said the law doesn't do enough to address the main factors driving France's pay gap: that men get most of the high-paying jobs while women are saddled with more of the childcare.

"We shouldn't ignore what actually accounts for the biggest part of the difference in pay between men and women," said Hélène Périvier, an economist at the French economic observatory who specializes in gender issues.[33]

In his "Violence, Peace, and Peace Studies" in 1969, Johan Galtung observed, "When one husband beats his wife, there is a clear case of personal violence, but when one million husbands keep one million wives in ignorance, there is structural violence."[34] This is the antithesis of structural motivation and structural accountability.

There are many smart, good people who are already working to analyze change and what specifically must happen with personal motivation and ability, social motivation and ability, and structural motivation and ability. Together we all have an unprecedented opportunity to put changes into place for the safety of half of the people on this planet who are currently at greater risk of being victims of discrimination and violence. The result will be a safer world for everyone.

Questions for Thoughtful Consideration and Discussion

1. Who was responsible for the rape in Sara's story?
2. What does individual physical strength or weakness contribute to Old Normal?
3. What vital behaviors do you believe must be adopted to create New Normal?
4. What specific rewards need to be enacted to create accountability?
5. What specific demands for accountability must be made?
6. What specific change must be enacted to create New Normal?
7. How do we as a world come to an agreement about the behaviors that need to change?
8. How do we handle conflicts of worldviews or values to gain creative positive momentum?
9. How can you be part of the conversation so that the vision of New Normal flourishes?
10. How would you suggest we the people all contribute to creating New Normal?
11. How do we do this as communities of people?
12. How do we do this as families?
13. What has to happen to support individual motivation and ability?
14. What has to happen to support social motivation and social ability?
15. What has to happen to support structural motivation and structural ability?

THIRTEEN

Taking Ownership of Responsibility to Change

I was on contract as director of food service for a K–12 school district. I will never forget that day.

My food service team at the middle school was short staffed. I told them I would come help cashier for the three lunches. As I stood at the cashier station on the far right, I verified if students had the right nutritional components on their plate to count as a state and federal reimbursable meal, if they punched in their PIN number correctly, and if they had enough money in their account.

A male teacher approached the front of the line. I'd known him for decades. He had taught at my high school, and his daughter was two years older than me.

I rang in his lunch. "Mr. Jones, you owe $3.50 for lunch today."

"How long have we known each other?" he replied. "When are you going to call me by my first name?"

"Oh, since high school. It would be weird to call you anything else."

He put his wallet back in his pocket, picked up his plate with one hand, slipped his other hand onto the curve of my lower back, leaned into my ear, and whispered, "Well, you better just get used to it." He then walked out of the cafeteria as if this had been normal interaction.

I could feel my face getting hot. I felt violated and embarrassed and quickly looked around to see if anyone had seen what had just happened. I got through the next hour and a half, but after my shift, I went to the principal to report the incident and to express my concern for students who might be subject to such harassment.

The principal was blown away and told me to call the school district Human Resource office.

The director of HR was out, but her assistant asked if I was okay. I assured her I was and told her what had happened. After I left the school, I called my boss from the contract management company.

"Hi, Stan. . . . I was sexually harassed by a teacher." I explained what had happened and that I had reported the incident to the school district HR.

"Kathleen," Stan replied, "I wish you'd have called me and our HR team first. Are you sure this really happened, and he wasn't just helping usher you out a door or something like that? Our contract is out for bid, and we need to make sure we aren't causing waves in the district. Do you think this is a popular teacher and if the community finds out we might have a bigger issue on our hands?"

"He is a popular teacher for both middle school and high school. My bigger concern is that he might be inappropriate with a student. I think we need to be concerned not only about my safety, but the safety of every student, regardless of our contract."

"I understand, Kathleen, but we don't want to cause any waves if we don't have to. If we can get our contract renewed without bringing attention to this, it would be a win-win for everyone involved."

I told Stan that I would just call HR myself. I did and called the district HR again too.

Later that day and evening, I started having flashbacks of the other inappropriate comments this teacher had said to me. I was working sixty-plus hours a week and had forgotten about them within a few minutes of him having said them. "Has anyone ever told you how beautiful you are?" "How are you not married yet? Guys your age have no clue what they are missing out on." And worse, "You know I had a dream about you last night that you changed the employee uniforms to the Playboy Bunny costumes. It was really gross to think about on your employees, but not with you."

My co-worker and mentor, Mike, encouraged me to call HR and let them know how Stan had been responding to me. I was stunned with the HR staffer's response: "Sometimes men just aren't as sensitive as women are in these kinds of situations. I wouldn't take it personally or worry about it."

However, the school district did ask the teacher not to have contact with me. He stayed away, but one day he showed up at the middle school kitchen and wanted to talk.

"I'm not sure what I said or did that made you feel so uncomfortable, but it wasn't on purpose."

I remember nodding my head and trying to get the teacher out of the tiny, soundproof kitchen office where the door was shut. It was almost more uncomfortable than the actual incident.

I left the company a few months later, and it was one of the best decisions I ever made.

#MeToo, Kathleen

Kathleen's story illustrates how people and organizations either accept responsibility or fail to accept responsibility for fostering safe work cultures. Kathleen experienced additional discrimination as her employer put the profitability of the organization ahead of the safety of its employees and ahead of the safety of its client, the students, and teachers.

As a coach, I witness those powerful *Aha!* moments my clients have as they recognize the element of choice in their situation. At this moment, the excuses fall away, obstacles crumble, the clouds part, the sun comes out, and alternative realities show themselves, sometimes after lifetimes of being hidden in shadows.

Prior to that moment of recognition, my clients seem stuck in what they've grown accustomed to or have tolerated. They have plateaued for a number of reasons, and multiple influences have factored into their current state of being. But when they come to me, they have reached a point where they have decided they no longer wish to be in their current situation, or they've decided to pursue a new future with new goals that will require a choice to move out of their comfort zones and take new actions to attain new results.

As the client envisions their future, they clarify a new, positive vision for their future that will motivate them to pursue the change they want. They look at what's under their control and what is not under their control. They own the consequences of the choices they've made up to this moment. Then they look at options they can pursue to create the lasting change they would like to see.

They outline an action plan and how they'll handle any obstacles. Finally, they choose to take specific actions to create changes they want to see. As they make the choice to act, they take ownership of their responsibility to make the changes happen. Ownership is key to change.

What We Choose

What we choose chooses us, except when it doesn't. Women and girls do not choose to be harassed, abused, or assaulted. Nobody does. At age five, I chose to visit a friend after school. I didn't choose to have two big boys stop me at a schoolyard and start trying to corner me with their pants down at their knees. I instinctively chose flight over fight or freeze. I chose not to walk that way alone again.

As a school-age child, I didn't choose to be sexually abused by relatives. I did choose, as soon as the option was open, to delay my return home after school and to stay at the library or other safer places until there were more people in the house besides just my abusive relatives.

I chose to forgive those who harmed me and release bitterness. I've taken my experiences, gained wisdom from them, and now use them for my growth and others' benefit when possible.

When I decided to write a book, I chose to ponder the possibility of New Normal. When I contacted a publisher and wrote them a check, I solidified my commitment to speak out against violence and speak up for the vision of a violence-free world. To exercise your power of choice is to freely engage in co-designing and co-creating your future. Responsibility and choice go hand in hand. We all have choices to make.

When you're proactively choosing and responsibly aligning your values and actions with your choices for the future you want, there's no room for victimization or for pointing fingers. Those who fail to take responsibility for their choices keep choosing Old Normal for themselves and for the rest of us, as long as we allow them to.

Now that we've identified the situation and looked at information showing us how things have been, we can move ahead by asking and pondering tough questions. Questions can illuminate choice.

We also need to take a second look at a very common way that people choose Old Normal by refusing to take responsibility for their behavior. One strategy of moral disengagement, blaming the victim, stands out as an impediment to New Normal.

Victim Blaming

Victim blaming is common and compounds the massive shame that a woman already feels because of the crimes against her spirit and body. When a woman experiences sexual discrimination, harassment, or violence, she's frequently asked questions that place the onus of the perpetrator's behaviors squarely on the wrong shoulders—hers.

Questions about her choices, such as: What were you wearing? Why were you out after dark? Why were you alone? Why did you have headphones on? What were you doing on this bus? In this neighborhood? On this road? Why didn't you bring someone with you? Why didn't you have your cell phone? Why don't you carry a gun? Why didn't you take a self-defense class? Why didn't you do something different than what you did? The unspoken judgment here is that the victim is to blame: "If you didn't [fill in the blank here], you wouldn't need to fear men's violence."

As a result, women (and all victims) take extra precautions every day that men don't even think about. Old Normal heaps responsibility on the victims when it's not their fault or responsibility, which places victims in a no-win situation. When they're going to be judged for being victimized, some remain silent.

Who Is Actually Responsible?

Is the person carrying a wallet responsible for it getting stolen, or is the pickpocket responsible? Is the car owner responsible for their car being stolen, or the thief? Is the homeowner responsible for the break-in, or is the burglar? Is the girl or a woman walking down the street minding her own business responsible for harassment and violence perpetrated against her, or is the harasser or rapist responsible?

The victims are not at fault. People take extra steps to avoid being a victim, but there's no guarantee of safety or freedom from harm. Predators still do bad things even when their prey has taken every known precaution to avoid being victimized. Whether victims take those precautions or not, the problem with victim blaming is that it keeps the perpetrator from owning their agency and their power to choose to act in ways that will not harm others. The perpetrator actively chooses to harm another person.

Although victims are not responsible for the crimes committed against them, as a result of victim blaming and shaming, generations of people, most often men (sorry, guys, the numbers tell the truth) continue to fail to own their responsibility to treat other human beings with respect. Whose fault is that?

From a coach's perspective, I offer a thought to consider: it's not the victim's fault, no matter what body parts they were born with, what they were wearing, what they had to drink, or where they were. It's not the fault of the alcohol, or the drugs, or whatever the offender ingested into his body or brain. Violence against another person is always the responsibility of the perpetrator. Responsible people take responsibility for their actions.

Systemic Responsibility

It's extremely common for male-dominated systems and structures (and the resulting poverty and violence) to dehumanize and harm females. This statement may have been a bit controversial before #MeToo, but now it's simply acknowledged truth. The struggle is magnified for poor women and children who are vulnerable to objectification and have little or no support to prevent it. According to Christy Abraham, who is international coordinator for women's human rights for the NGO ActiveAid,

> In Kenya, women and children live off what they can find in Bamburi (a waste dump) in Mombasa. One child interviewed as part of our research said: "No one knows us here. We are just children of the dumpsite; we work here and eat here; there are no services that we know of, we just survive. . . . It is very normal to have men demand sex in exchange for goods or waste. Rape happens many times—sometimes girls choose to accept it, after all who can help?

Is it possible for any girl in this dumpsite to be 10 years before they have sex?"[1]

Old Normal shirks responsibility for ten-year-old girls in Mombasa.

In Ferguson, Missouri, Colette Green, an adult daughter of an eighty-four-year-old mother, visited her mom in a Christian care home and bathed and dressed her, as was her normal practice. She found injuries and evidence of sexual abuse. Her mother, who suffers with dementia, doesn't speak or feed herself and has the cognitive capacity of an infant. The daughter spoke with the management, who said they would investigate. The next day, the injuries were worse.[2]

Saturday when I saw my mother there (was) no doubt about what was going on," said (the daughter). "This was a total violation of an 84-year-old lady that's contracted dementia . . . that could not speak. Equal to a newborn baby." She said there's no way her mother can defend herself. "She cannot holler, scream," she said. Her mother was taken to the hospital where she said doctors performed a rape kit and, according to paperwork from the family, doctors determined the woman's elderly mother was sexually assaulted.[3]

She's not even the oldest reported rape victim. In October 2018, a twenty-year-old man confessed to the rape of a 100-year-old woman who died from the injuries. He blamed being under the influence of alcohol.[4]

Another 100-year-old Kansas woman died as a result of injuries sustained when she was raped in September 2014.[5] Old Normal shirks responsibility for the safety of centenarians in India and Kansas, and octogenarians in Missouri. As a result, those weakest in our society are victimized.

A man in Texas was arrested in 2016 and sentenced to life without parole in 2018, after investigators found homemade child pornography on his laptop. Police compared the images to family photos on the computer and learned the baby was a relative. The man had filmed himself raping a three-month-old and took photos of himself sexually assaulting her for the entire first year of her life.[6]

"This baby was raped before she could roll over," said Mary Nan Huffman, Chief Prosecutor of the Internet Crimes Against Children Division in Montgomery County. "For the sake of our county and our children, I hope we never have another [name intentionally omitted] in my entire career as a prosecutor." [During his trial] other child victims testified including two female relatives who claimed he raped them—one at age five and the other from age three to eleven. He had spent time in a juvenile detention center for rapes when he was fourteen years old.[7]

The perpetrator was a repeat offender who was not rehabilitated. Old Normal shirks the responsibility of the safety of three-month-old babies in Texas. The shame settles on the weakest in society. But whether the victim is a baby, a grandmother, a four-year-old, a nineteen-year-old, or a one-hundred-year old, the responsibility belongs to the offenders *and the cultures that allow the offenses to continue.*

Across the world, countless Rohingya women have given birth to children conceived by the rapes of Myanmar soldiers who are using rape as a weapon of ethnic cleansing. If the women tell their communities the child was conceived by rape, they will be shunned.[8] Old Normal unfairly places the responsibility for these children, and for the rapes that conceived them, on the mothers. Women and girls are disproportionately bearing the responsibility and the costs, as do all the victims of sexual violence. Victim blaming and shaming simply must stop, and the blame and shame must be placed correctly on the offenders.

Whether it's a catcall, a grope, cornering, stalking, abusing, assault, or any kind of sexual objectification, *the fault lies on the perpetrator.* Old Normal is full of people who encourage violence and people who look the other way, reducing consequences for offenders. People in New Normal begin to share the blame as soon as they know about the offender and about the offense and fail to act for the common good. If New Normal is to be, communities must start owning responsibility for what is ours and stop letting others off the hook.

The Offenders in Our Midst

Offenders continue to harm others without accountability that will change their minds, hearts, and especially their actions. Old Normal continues to harbor the offenders in our midst, and most of them are people who know the victim. Chances are if you know someone who is a victim of discrimination, harassment, abuse, or assault, you may also know the perpetrator. According to the United Nations Entity for Gender Equality and for the Empowerment of Women,

> between 15 and 76 percent of women are targeted for physical and/ or sexual violence in their lifetime, according to the available country data. Most of this violence takes place within intimate relationships, with many women (ranging from 9 to 70 percent) reporting their husbands or partners as the perpetrator. Across the twenty-eight States of the European Union, a little over one in five women has experienced physical and/or sexual violence from a partner (European Union Agency for Fundamental Rights, 2014).[9]

In the US, the National Sexual Violence Resource Center started an annual campaign in 2011 called Sexual Assault Awareness Month. The campaign is an effort to educate people about the prevalence of sexual violence in the United States and bust the myths that usually the perpetrator is a stranger; that the victim is to blame; that there is no recourse for the victim who reports, because they will suffer even more (one possible reason why of every 1,000 rapes, only 310 are reported to the police);[10] or the big myth that somehow the victim should have been able to prevent the trauma from happening.

In November 2018, a Washington-state man was sentenced to two years and ten months in prison after drugging and raping an eighteen-year-old girl and texting explicit photos of her as she died of an overdose. The victim's mother said she felt anything but a sense of justice after the man responsible for her daughter's death was sentenced to spend less time in prison than a car thief.[11]

This eighteen-year-old woman thought she knew this twenty-year-old man well enough to decide to be in his room with him. She didn't intentionally mix two drugs that would be a lethal combination. In this case, the man was found guilty of rape, manslaughter, and unlawful disposal of remains.

Old Normal taught him to make light of someone overdosing from drugs, to not seek any help, to rape someone who is passed out, to text photos of him using her unresponsive body, to use her dead thumb to open her phone and make posts in her name to make it look like she was still alive, to handle a corpse by putting it in a crate and planning to bury it. Old Normal decreed that by spending time with this man, she invited her rape and early death. His actions and abject failure to consider her best interests were not her fault, but she elected to be there and to accept what he gave her. Who owned the responsibility for this young woman's death?

We live with offenders in our midst. Offenders are our neighbors, co-workers, friends, community members, schoolmates, and even leaders. Most of the time, the offender is someone we know, and most of the time, the victim is wearing sweats, pajamas, or casual clothes they wear at home.[12] When we allow the offenders to continue to harm others without the level of accountability that will change their minds, hearts, and especially their actions, we share in the responsibility for perpetuating Old Normal.

What Should Be?

I encourage you to take a look at the words *should* and *shouldn't* to determine where the message comes from, where it leads, and what authority or agency is related to or behind the use of this word. Upon examination, clients decide that some *shoulds* and *shouldn'ts* don't deserve to remain in the brain, but there are some that I believe are reasonable to consider and to keep:

- An infant should never have to fear sexual assault.
- A child should never have to fear abuse or rape.
- People should never have to fear being groped or molested.
- People should never have to worry about getting attacked or being stalked.
- No one should ever have to worry about getting assaulted, ever. Not even while they are drunk, high, or unconscious.
- A worker should never have to fear harassment at their place of employment.
- Freedom from fear of sexual harassment and violence shouldn't be kept from someone based on their age, gender, race, religion, sexual preferences, or any other status.
- Freedom from sexual harassment and violence should not belong only to the wealthy or famous or people from a certain geographic region, but to all people.

What might you add to this list? As a society there are parts of Old Normal that we must stop tolerating.

Collective Responsibility

Responsibility = Response + Ability. We all own the responsibility for one another as humans sharing this planet. We own our agency, and each one of us owns the responsibility for the hurt we cause others. People show responsibility for others in a variety of ways: stopping at traffic lights, taking down dead trees along the fence line so the neighbors' house doesn't get damaged in the wind, or not robbing someone who happens to be crossing our path. When it comes to sexual harassment and tolerating a culture that condones violence, we need to define collective responsibilities to stop the endless flow of #MeToo stories.

A few suggestions include:

- We all can become champions of New Normal.
- We all can call out behaviors that contribute to Old Normal.
- We can all insist that offenders learn that they can't continue harmful behaviors.
- We can all understand the negative impacts of sexual discrimination including harassment and violence and refuse to tolerate it.

We talked about this as part of social motivation in chapter 12. If social motivation and ability is not there, change will not happen. It's up to all of us and each of us but starts with every individual.

Change can be challenging. The social and psychological rewards of Old Normal to those in power have kept us in this place that is deeply damaging to billions of people in the world. It can be hard to see the truth of the damage through our biases and hard to see discrimination if I'm the perpetrator rather than the victim. It may be hard to see privilege if I'm the person who enjoys it rather than the one who's been excluded. It can seem counterproductive to desire change if I believe I benefit more from the status quo. Some change requires considering community as well as self.

Solitary confinement is deemed severe punishment. Though we are individuals, without others we would die. We depend on others, even when we don't believe we are dependent. As long as community tolerates Old Normal behaviors in one person, others will be victimized.

To change community, change must start with each individual. One option might be to adopt the six key change behaviors mentioned in the previous chapter. We can examine what types of accountability and positive reinforcement we create for ourselves. What does a person need in order to act in line with positive behaviors that will make the change happen?

If each person must take responsibility for change, starting with themselves, who has the right to exclude themselves from adopting changes leading to New Normal with no more sexual harassment, abuse, or violence?

If you believe you are part of a community that is about change so we can move from Old Normal to New Normal, you'll agree to make an individual commitment to change, perhaps starting with adopting the key vital behaviors listed in chapter 12. Each person has the right and responsibility to choose the vital behaviors that will usher in New Normal. Each of us is responsible to know how our community will respond to individuals who act outside of New Normal norms. We can all be allies (those who stand with others) and activists.

For example, Yasmeen Hassan, a lawyer and executive director of Equality Now, has dedicated her career to helping women and girls who struggle from gender-based injustices. Ms. Hassan encourages all, even youth, to engage as allies and activists in the fight for gender equality. "Never forget that no voice is too small to make a difference. Young people today have an activist spirit," Hassan says. "If they understand feminism, they will understand how we all are affected when women and girls are not treated equally next to men and boys."[13]

Families' Responsibilities

You didn't get here alone. Even those abandoned as infants can call family those who supported their life and growth to help them get where they are today. We all can create family by our commitments to love and care for others. Families have a tremendous opportunity to recognize and use their power to impact children and grandchildren for good. Families instill worldviews and filters in each family member as they pass along often unspoken and unexamined culture, values, norms, traditions, and either tolerance or intolerance for diversity.

Sometimes family members, by simply being present and involved with children, can create positive change. At the University of Oxford, Department of Social Policy and Intervention, research by Professor Ann Buchanan showed that a high level of grandparental involvement increases the well-being of children. A study of more than 1,500 children showed that those with a high level of grandparental involvement had fewer emotional and behavioral problems. Professor Buchanan's study has demonstrated that their involvement is strongly associated with reduced adjustment difficulties in all family types, but particularly so among adolescents from divorced or separated families.[14]

Families contribute both risk factors and protective factors that influence children for good or for ill. Families at risk may have parents who are ineffective at parenting; who tolerate sexual harassment, criminal behaviors, conflict, or substance abuse; or who may have suffered many adverse childhood experiences. Single parenting is also a risk factor, as is having parents with mental illness, young parents who are not prepared for the demands of parenting, a high number of children, and a lack of supervision and stability. Additionally, families may face the extra challenge of living in disadvantaged neighborhoods where crime and illegal substances or guns are prevalent.[15] Risk factors do not always contribute to sexual discrimination or violence. Positive factors can counteract risks.

Families can protect children from risk by having close, positive, healthy, and affectionate relationships, consistent parental supervision and discipline, higher education levels, financial stability, family stability, and the support and involvement of community, such as participation in extracurricular activities and positive relationships with neighbors and community organizations.[16] Families can educate children better about their responsibility to respect others and the need to report should they encounter a predator.

Families can choose to be conscious to minimize cultural impacts that increase likelihood of harassment and violence against females. Given the increased risk to child brides of sexual violence and death during childbirth, families can mitigate the risk by delaying marriage until the age of consent. Families can mitigate the increased risk of sexual violence against girl children of divorced women by reaching out for support, and communities can help. Parents can choose to educate children from birth to have zero tolerance for sexual violence and discrimination.

Intergenerational culture, values, traditions, stories, habits, and mores are being passed down through families that are allowing Old Normal to grow into a new generation.

Richard Weissbourd, a senior lecturer and director of the Human Development and Psychology Program at the Harvard Graduate School of Education and faculty director of Making Caring Common, and Alison Cashin, the director of Making Caring Common at the Harvard Graduate School of Education, along with

> the team at Making Caring Common conducted a national survey of 18- to 25-year-olds in which 87 percent of respondents reported they had been the victim of at least one form of sexual harassment . . . yet the same survey indicates that most parents have failed to address and prevent misogyny and sexual harassment in their children's lives: 76 percent of survey respondents—72 percent of men and 80 percent of women—reported that they never had a conversation with parents about how to avoid sexually harassing others. Similar majorities had never had conversations with their parents about various forms of misogyny.[17]

Weissbourd recommends families (parents first) follow these strategies:

1. Define the problem.
2. When you hear a sexist or sexually degrading comment from your child or their peers, step in—and continue to intervene until this behavior stops.
3. Teach your child to be a critical consumer of media and culture.
4. Talk to your child about what they should do if they're sexually harassed or degraded or victimized in any way.
5. Encourage and expect upstanding (intervening when the child sees or hears another being harassed).
6. Provide multiple sources of recognition and self-worth.[18]

If women and men are of equal value and girls and boys are of equal value, your family has the responsibility to live this out. First steps might include having a conversation among family leaders to agree on how you will put these strategies into practice.

What is your family's responsibility to stop the discrimination, harassment, and violence of Old Normal? What are your family's responsibilities for making sure there is equitable opportunity for the greatest contribution of all members without regard to gender? What are your family's responsibilities for education of children to eliminate discrimination?

The community supports change with systems and structures to uphold families who are working to create change. We can also study and learn from those who are already supporting family change that could lead to New Normal.

Education

Discrimination prevents girls and women, especially in poorer parts of the world, from getting educations that help build their futures and their communities. Gender discrimination is part of Old Normal that is undermining girls and their communities.

Educating girls saves lives and builds stronger families, communities, and economies. Some countries lose more than $1 billion a year by failing to educate girls to the same level as boys. Sixty-one million girls are out of school, according to UNICEF in 2016, thirty-two million girls of primary school age and twenty-nine million of lower secondary school age. Often, this is simply because they are girls, and it is not the cultural norm. Poor girls are four times more likely to be out of school than boys from the same background. The poorest girls are least likely to complete primary school.[19]

Old Normal cultures are keeping girls from getting primary educations and secondary educations. Communities and families own the responsibility for making sure all children receive access to education.

Central Asia Institute (CAI) has focused on educating girls in remote regions of Pakistan, Afghanistan, and Tajikistan for over twenty years. Why focus on girls' education? CAI co-founder Greg Mortenson sums it up this way:

> Once you educate the boys, they often leave the villages and search for work in the cities, but the girls stay home, become leaders in the community, and pass their knowledge onto their own children. If you really want to empower societies, reduce poverty, improve basic hygiene and healthcare, reduce the population explosion, and fight high rates of infant and maternal mortality, the answer is to educate girls.[20]

Safer Schools

Discrimination in the form of sexual harassment and violence harms students who do make it to school, even in wealthier communities. Once in school, students deserve to be safe from harassment or violence.

According to a 2011 study by the American Association of University Women, 48 percent of US students experienced sexual harassment during the school year; 87 percent said it had a negative effect on them. Most were harassed verbally, but physical harassment was far too common. Sexual harassment by text, email, social media, or other electronic means affected 30 percent of students. Many students who were sexually harassed through cyberspace were also sexually harassed in person. Fifty-six percent of girls were harassed versus 40 percent of boys surveyed. Girls were harassed more both in person and via text, email, Facebook, or other electronic means.[21]

Whatever nation you live in, chances are pretty high that sexual harassment and violence are happening right where you are too. It's a global problem.

In England, Scotland, and Wales, more than 5,500 allegations of sexual offenses in schools were reported from 2011 to 2014, including 600 rapes. Lucy Russell, a representative from the NPO Plan International, said cases involving very young children were rare. Many girls may be underreporting sexual offenses. "There is an indication that the very heavily sexualized messages that children are getting from online pornography and sexualized videos is impacting on their behavior, and it is changing the expectations they have around their relationships," Russell said.[22]

The 114,000 members of the Association for Supervision and Curriculum Development (ASCD), who are school superintendents, principals, teachers, and advocates from more than 127 countries, including 57 affiliate organizations, are dedicated to excellence in learning, teaching, and leading so that every child is healthy, safe, engaged, supported, and challenged.

The ASCD recommends that administrators make elimination of sexual harassment a top priority, educate students about how to deal with sexual harassment, and get parents involved in long-term behavior modification. Students need to know that teachers and administrators will help if they report harassment.[23]

New Normal will continue to make changes in the education systems to create safe schools worldwide by adopting protective policies, and supporting and holding students, families, teachers, and administrators accountable. Educators are accountable for discrimination, harassment, abuse, or sexual violence under their watch. Educators can be trained to leave gender bias and harassment behind. Education structures can be held accountable to build equity in opportunity and leadership roles. New Normal will make sure educators are equipped to prevent harassment and violence in schools and are supported by families and communities.

Media's Influence

Media is the main means of mass communication (broadcasting, publishing, and the internet) regarded collectively. All the messages people receive are coming through the media. Artificial Intelligence combined with social media is collecting data about social media users that businesses can use to market their products. The media's influence is immense and concentrated. Those who control media have an immeasurable impact on cultural change.

The messaging from social media about the role and place of girls and women has cemented cultural norms. New Normal will address whether and to what degree the media should be responsible for taking ownership of facilitating positive cultural change. If it is contributing to New Normal, the media must accept accountability to create content that does not sexualize or objectify people, create equality in media images, and remove stereotyping. The media and all involved must be responsible to use their power and influence for the good of the community. Consumers must take responsibility for the content of everything they allow into their brains. New Normal will require the media to equalize the playing field for content creators and leadership. And media owns responsibility to equalize opportunities and pay for all employed by the media.

Business

Seventy percent of women suffer sexual harassment on the job. The Equal Employment Opportunity Commission reports receiving 12,000 allegations of sex-based harassment each year, with women accounting for about 83 percent of the complainants. Roughly three of four people experiencing such harassment never tell anyone in authority about it. Instead, women "avoid the harasser, deny, or downplay the gravity of the situation, or attempt to ignore, forget, or endure the behavior."[24]

Human Resources guru Simon Casas, an HR consultant with over forty years of experience in business and over twenty-five years of HR experience, said in an interview, "We have a country full of employees who do not want to be held accountable, and employers who choose not to hold employees accountable for a variety of reasons."[25] Old Normal allowed employers to "play" at ending workplace harassment. Changes continue to happen, and employers need to be holding their employees accountable.

Mr. Casas said, "Personal choice and accountability is the key. Everybody knows what's right and what's wrong. Every action we take and every choice we make has a consequence. The consequences are the impacts on the various people involved."[26]

Businesses have legal, ethical, and economic responsibility to take reports seriously. New Normal consumers (their customers) are responsible to require change from the businesses they patronize. We will address this in chapter 15, "Marketplace Support." For now, it's important to ask yourself if you are a leader in business, if you work for a company, or if you do business with a company, what responsibilities do you own for the well-being of those who work for or with you?

Law Enforcement

In 2014, the Virginia legislature called for a count of untested rape kits. There were, it turned out, 2,902 kits in the state that had never gone to a lab. The oldest kit was from 1985:

> The state's attorney general, Democrat Mark R. Herring, had chaired a task force focused on sexual assault on college campuses; now, he wanted to take on the state's rape kit backlog. As the legislature passed a bill ensuring all future kits would be tested within 60 days, Herring secured $3.4 million in grants to pay for the testing of the older kits at a private lab. Then his office drafted another piece of legislation that would require law enforcement agencies to notify victims that their kits had been tested. The bill's chief patron was state Sen. Barbara A. Favola (D–Arlington).[27]

The law passed in 2017, and a backlog of hundreds of thousands of rape kits around the country remain untested. When Mariska Hargitay began acting as Olivia Benson on *Law & Order: Special Victims' Unit*, she learned of the staggering statistics about sexual assault, domestic violence, and child abuse in the United States. After receiving thousands of letters and emails from survivors, Hargitay started Joyful Heart Foundation to address the issue of sexual violence, and its Stop the Backlog initiative is making a difference.[28] She says,

> To me, the backlog is one of the clearest and most shocking demonstrations of how we regard these crimes in our society. Testing rape kits sends a fundamental and crucial message to victims of sexual violence: You matter. What happened to you matters. Your case matters. For that reason, The Joyful Heart Foundation, which I founded in 2004, has made ending the rape kit backlog our #1 advocacy priority.

The New Normal will require universal commitment to process evidence in a timely manner and to stop pressuring victims to decide not to press charges against the offender. The community needs to make sure that the laws are passed and enforced locally, nationally, and internationally. We must support law enforcement's responsibility and work toward eliminating violence against all victims of sexual violence.

Government

In April 2018, President Donald Trump signed the Allow States and Victims to Fight Online Sex Trafficking Act (FOSTA) bill, which passed the Senate in March with a 97 to 3 vote. FOSTA was endorsed by the Internet Association (major companies like Facebook and Google). FOSTA amends Section 230 of the Communication Decency Act, so protections for internet service providers no longer apply to civil or criminal charges of sex trafficking or to any conduct that promotes or facilitates prostitution.[29] In a March 21 article, Tom Jackman of the *Washington Post* reported:

> Linda Smith, founder of Shared Hope International, an anti-sex trafficking group, said she began providing research to Congress in 2007 about online sex trafficking, but the information wasn't taken seriously. "We were all waking up," Smith said. "Congress is not much different from the rest of the country. People are recognizing that these children are victims of crime and deserve justice. That vote is, I think, historic."
>
> A Senate subcommittee investigated Backpage and found that it was involved in editing prostitution ads on its site to remove references to underage girls, while allowing the ads to stay on the site. A *Washington Post* investigation last year revealed that Backpage representatives actively solicited ads from prostitutes who advertised on other sites and created ads for them on Backpage.[30]

Governments have responsibility for creating and maintaining a just, equitable, nonviolent society, yet there are governments that both support and undermine laws that address positive culture change. For New Normal to happen, people must hold their governments accountable and work through government to ensure nonviolence and equity for all.

It is the responsibility of all citizens to make sure that everyone has equal representation in government and to make sure that equal opportunity includes equal opportunity to financial support (for fair political processes) regardless of party or gender.

Religion and Civic and Community Responsibilities

A Catholic nun came forward in July 2018 to report the sexual abuse of religious sisters by priests and bishops. Cases have emerged in Europe, Africa, South America, and Asia, demonstrating that the problem is global and pervasive as a result of the power inequality in the Catholic Church between priests and nuns.[31] Reporting in an online article for APNews.com in July 2018, Nicole Winfield and Rodney Muhumuza wrote,

> Buoyed by the #MeToo movement and the growing recognition that adults can be victims of sexual abuse when there is an imbalance of power in a relationship . . . the sisters are going public in part because of years of inaction by church leaders, even after major studies on the problem in Africa were reported to the Vatican in the 1990s.[32]

At the Saint James Cathedral in Seattle, Washington, Fr. Michael G. Ryan's letter to the congregation and guests in the 2018 cathedral publication *In Your Midst* humbly addresses the sexual abuse scandals plaguing the Catholic Church:

Dear Friends . . . the Church is reeling from scandals that have caused many people to question their faith or even to stop practicing it altogether. I do not minimize even for a moment the feelings of betrayal, anger, and deep disillusionment people are feeling because of the sins and crimes committed by priests and bishops anointed to minister in the name of Christ. Not a day passes that I don't pray earnestly for the victims of this abuse and in those prayers I include all those whose faith has been shattered as a result. And I have no simple answers. Our Church leaders must deal not only with the sins and crimes themselves but with their underlying causes. They must find out how this has been allowed to happen and in doing so they must be completely honest and transparent. No laws, canons, or traditions, no matter how sacrosanct, should escape critical examination and review. Having said that, I would remind you that Christ entrusted his Church to human beings which is another way of saying that there will always be sinners as well as saints in the Church. I say that not to excuse anyone but simply because it is true. The Church is not something 'out there'—the Church is right here. The Church is all of us and it is the Body of Christ. My faith assures me that the holy yet sinful Church—so slow at times to wake up—is still Christ's Church, and no matter how many times we fail him, he will never fail us . . . He still finds a home among us. If there was ever a reason for hope, this is it!

Father Michael G. Ryan[33]

All the Fr. Ryans across the globe are needed, as voices calling for New Normal free from sexual violence. All religions must consistently start holding staff, volunteers, and members accountable for ending sexual abuse. Every religious community is responsible to makes changes to stop marginalizing and objectifying any of their members, from youngest to oldest, male and female.

Local Communities

To create New Normal, cities and towns must be accountable to make sure their streets are safe for women and girls. Females must be represented equally in leadership and law enforcement. Citywide structures must support the full participation of females in local business, law, and policymaking. The needs of single parents must be met so they can bring in the income their household needs to be economically sustainable. Local communities and neighborhoods need to come together to identify and implement changes to eliminate street harassment and violence.

Whose responsibility is it to start making these changes? I can start with myself. I invite you to do the same.

Questions for Thoughtful Consideration and Discussion

1. Who owns the responsibility for the safety of girls and women?
2. Are the victims to blame for trying to survive in the harshest of circumstances? Is the shame theirs to bear?
3. What does being under the influence of alcohol or other substances do to culpability for bad behavior?
4. What does the age of the victim have to do with the culpability of the offender?
5. What do you believe is the reason for Old Normal?
6. What do you intend to do to create change?
7. What is the next thing you'd like to learn in order to know how sexual harassment, abuse, and violence impact victims?
8. What beliefs are perpetuating Old Normal? What assumptions can be questioned?
9. What are the views of those who may not support change in the same way you see it, but who also would like to see a New Normal?
10. What can you do to be part of the solution?
11. What agreements can we create and make to help we the people choose a harassment-free, violence-free New Normal?

FOURTEEN

Creating Safe Cultures for Women

A woman told me about a time a male colleague saw her jogging (with no makeup), and how she overcame her awkwardness by saying, "Well, Don, you caught me without my makeup! Now we're intimate!"

She laughed, and I laughed in sympathy.

One morning I stopped by the school office, hoping to slip in and out without seeing anyone but the receptionist, but one of the dads I knew through the PTO came in the office. I felt embarrassed to be out in public without makeup. With no intention of offending anyone, I lightheartedly repeated that joke to him. It wasn't intended to be harassment, I was making light of my self-consciousness about not fitting the social standard at a school where all the moms were impeccably dressed and presented, but he didn't laugh. The awkward silence caught my heart as I realized he was offended. I actually sent a note apologizing to him and his wife.

Another time, a guy told me a joke in the presence of several other guys. He asked me, "Do you want to know how to make electricity?" He told me to place my hands against his hands, so I did. He asked, "Do you feel anything?"

I shook my head. He told me to put my toes up against his toes (with our shoes on), and I did.

He asked, "Do you feel anything?" I shook my head again. He laughed and said the punch line, "That's because it's not plugged in."

All the guys laughed out loud. Based on their reactions, I made the unfortunate mistake of thinking any guy would think that joke was funny, and a few months later, I retold it to an employee at a company party.

He was offended. He asked me if I thought that joke was funny.

I told him the guys who told it to me thought so. Not funny. #MeToo, Chris

Some might wonder where the discrimination is in Chris's stories because it was so subtle. The cultural requirement to wear makeup is discriminatory. Trying to fit in by repeating sexist jokes instead of saying "Not funny" is part of Old Normal culture. Joking can be a form of harassment. Responding differently based on who tells the joke can indicate gender discrimination. The jokes that circulate in a group are one of many elements that reflect the culture of the group. An appropriate definition of culture is "the way we do things around here."[1]

Cultures vary from place to place. According to SociologyGroup. com website's article "Basic Elements of Culture," culture is learned. Influencers, leaders, and generations pass or transmit culture to others and to the next generation. The powerful decide what culture they want. Even the most powerful of the powerless influence their culture.

Individual experiences augment what people receive from leaders and from the previous generation, allowing cultures to adapt.[2]

#MeToo stories transcend many cultures around the globe because the element of power and powerlessness is part of each story. Every story happened inside a culture, whether that was a workplace culture, a community culture, a national culture, a religious culture, or another kind of culture. Stories have been and continue to be submitted from people in many languages from a variety of countries with different norms, beliefs, values, and ways of dealing with or managing problems or calamities. What norms, beliefs, values, and ways of dealing with problems are prevalent in your culture?

One commonality among all #MeToo stories is the violation or absence of safety for all who experienced sexual harassment, abuse, or assault. Whether you're harassed on the street, groped on the subway, stalked online, or raped at a party, your sense of safety was taken from you, and it's not always easy to recover. Whether you've told a sexist joke, catcalled someone, manhandled another person at a nightclub, or been guilty (even if never charged or convicted) of date rape or sexual abuse, it's important to assess how you might have compromised your safety or the safety of others. Loss of one's sense of safety can lead to feeling powerless. Safety as a cultural norm can be a linchpin for change.

Agreeing on a Common Definition of Safety

Safety is the condition of being safe from *undergoing or causing* hurt, injury, or loss.[3] It seems obvious that when someone experiences harassment, abuse, or assault, they have been denied safety. This is my own perspective. I believe that a person committing the harassment, abuse, or assault is also denying and denied safety, because they have violated a cultural norm or value and therefore are misaligned with their community. I encourage readers to assess for themselves how these experiences may compromise safety for oneself and others. Safety is a basic human need, valued by every culture. It transcends cultures. Let's consider how cultures go about assuring safety.

Pinpoint What Supports Safety

Whether in a country, a company, or a family, cultures that value safety can support it in a number of ways. First, they clearly communicate shared values. Cultures can clash and tug at individual members. When leadership (power) lives out these values, a culture adopts that set of shared, strong values. When leaders' actions and words communicate *Do what I say, not what I do,* that culture doesn't adopt the stated shared values.

Safe cultures clarify required and expected behavior of all who are part of the culture. My observation from my own experience is that safe cultures also make it clear what the outcomes are for all who will and will not choose the expected behaviors. If the outcome for a behavior is unclear, the individual will lack awareness of the consequences of their behavior and, as a result, may choose to compromise the value of safety without such knowledge.

Cultures support values by sharing and rewarding behaviors that reflect their values. For example, a local middle school encourages good citizenship and shares positive attitudes about responsibility through signs and banners in the hallways and individual recognition. In cultures that value safety, every individual member buys in, owning responsibilities and accountabilities for safety.

Second, cultures can support safety by increasing the awareness of risks and dangers and educating all members of the community on prevention. Creating clear community agreements increases safety. Some cultures educate members through telling stories that help even the youngest members understand and avoid dangers.

In order to move to New Normal, communities need to examine their culture and how it supports the safety of each member. Communities can help create New Normal by committing to improve shared understanding and effective actions that protect safety for all members. They can also share responsibility for keeping track of each member of the community and how they're doing with adopting safe behaviors.

Creating a Shared Vision

A shared vision is a powerful cultural influence. When communities or organizations hold a shared vision, they work together better to make that vision reality. Tarana Burke's vision is steadfastly focused on all who shared their stories. She launched the website metoomvmt.org, providing resources for survivors of sexual violence and their allies. The #MeToo movement is planning training programs to teach leaders to start their own survivor support programs. It's also institutionalizing healing circles, an early element of the movement. In an October 2018 interview with Liz Rowley of *The Cut* online magazine, Ms. Burke said,

> I do think that in the next decade . . . we can shift how we talk about it, we can shift how we respond to it, we can shift how the culture understands it—because it's going to make a difference in the number of sexual assaults that we see. It's going to make a difference in the way people respond to survivors of sexual violence, and that difference is really everything.[4]

The following are a few organizations working toward the health of New Normal.

The National Sexual Violence Resource Center (NSVRC) is the leading not-for-profit organization (NPO) provider of information and tools to prevent and respond to sexual violence. The NSVRC envisions a world where diversity is celebrated and all people are treated with dignity and respect and have full autonomy over their own bodies and sexual expression.[5] The NSVRC translates research and trends into best practices that help individuals, communities, and service providers achieve real and lasting change. The center works with the media to promote informed reporting. NSVRC leads Sexual Assault Awareness Month (SAAM) every April to educate and engage the public in addressing this widespread issue.[6]

RAINN is the largest anti-sexual violence organization in the US. RAINN created and operates the National Sexual Assault Hotline in partnership with more than 1,000 local sexual assault service providers across the country and operates the DoD Safe Helpline for the Department of Defense. RAINN also carries out programs to prevent sexual violence, help survivors, and ensure that perpetrators are brought to justice. In 2018, RAINN helped more survivors than ever. "This year, we have seen the longest, sustained growth of people reaching out in our 24-year history. Sexual violence affects almost every family in America—and that's why it also takes every one of us to end it," said RAINN President Scott Berkowitz.[7]

RALIANCE, started in 2015 with an investment from the National Football League, is a national NPO partnership with the bold vision of ending sexual violence in one generation. RALIANCE makes prevention possible by advancing research, influencing policy, supporting innovative programs, and helping leaders establish safe workplaces and strong communities. RALIANCE partners with a wide range of organizations to improve their cultures and create environments free from sexual harassment, misconduct, and abuse. One of the partners, Sport + Prevention Center, engages the sport community as a partner in ending sexual and domestic violence. RALIANCE advocates for prevention funding and policies that put the needs of survivors first. The partnership has also awarded $2.3 million in grants to communities across the country.[8]

The Sheryl Sandberg & Dave Goldberg Family Foundation works to build a more equal and resilient world. The foundation holds the vision of bringing people together to support each other through two key initiatives, LeanIn.org, which empowers women, and OptionB.org, which helps people build resilience and find meaning after adversity.[9]

Thorn builds powerful technology products, leads new programs, maintains essential resources, and develops awareness campaigns to attack the issue of child sex trafficking from all sides. According to Thorn's website, with the help of Thorn's tools, law enforcement and investigators have been able to identify 5,791 child sex trafficking victims and rescue 103 children from situations where their sexual abuse was recorded and distributed. Thorn continues to build tools to tackle the toughest environments and empower the frontlines to stop abuse before it happens.[10]

Together for Girls is a global public-private partnership founded in 2009, which brings together national governments, UN agencies, and private sector organizations to prevent and respond to violence, as a fundamental step to achieving individual rights and well-being, gender equality, and sustainable development. The global partnership aims, using data as its guide along with action, advocacy, and communications, to raise awareness, promote evidence-based solutions, and galvanize coordinated action across sectors to end violence against boys and girls, with a special focus on sexual violence against girls. The growing partnership is currently active in more than twenty countries around the world.[11]

The United Nations Commission on the Status of Women (CSW) is the principal global intergovernmental body exclusively dedicated to the promotion of gender equality and the empowerment of women. Its 2019 priority theme was "social protection systems, access to public services and sustainable infrastructure for gender equality and the empowerment of women and girls."[12] A functional commission of the Economic and Social Council (ECOSOC), it was established on June 21, 1946. The CSW is instrumental in promoting women's rights, documenting the reality of women's lives throughout the world, and shaping global standards on gender equality and the empowerment of women.[13]

In its 2016 Global Plan of Action to strengthen the role of the health system within a national multisectoral response to address interpersonal violence (in particular against women, girls, and children), the director general of the World Health Organization, Margaret Chan, wrote,

> We know that much of violence is reinforced, condoned and promoted by social norms. For example, norms that deem that violence against women and girls is acceptable or promote views of masculinity premised on power and control over others, or sanction parents and teachers to use harsh discipline on children. We need to advocate for and support evidence-based prevention programmes to stop violence from happening in the first place. *We must work to end all forms of interpersonal violence, in particular violence against women and girls, and against children.* (italics mine)

There are many other organizations and people who are already envisioning New Normal. (For a more comprehensive list of organizations engaged in this work, visit www.lifebeyondmetoo.com.) In order to change cultural norms, diverse people must unite to outline and to gain acceptance and agreement from diverse cultures to work toward creating New Normal free of interpersonal and institutional violence.

How can we come together to agree on a vision that all can embrace? Leaders of diverse cultures must be given an opportunity to see that rotten roots produce dead trees. Only by doing the work will healthy roots cause the tree (their culture) to flourish, free from interpersonal and institutional violence. One possible shared vision statement for New Normal, adapted from the World Health Organization, is this:

> We envision and desire a world in which all people
> are free from all forms of violence and discrimination,
> the health and well-being of each person is protected and promoted,

the human rights and fundamental freedoms of each person is fully achieved,

and gender equality and the empowerment of women and girls are the norm.

Crafting a Strategy to Attain the Vision

In addition to a compelling vision, WHO has crafted a strategy from the perspective of global health services. The United Nations also has a strategy for women and children. Many other nations, states, organizations, and NPOs have strategies to advance a nonviolent, safe world. The world is watching to see how they will come together to create a unified vision and unified strategy.

I believe each person desiring New Normal must join the conversation and share information and strategies to accelerate change. Some will be vision casters, sharing the truth about the intolerability of Old Normal and a vision of the benefits of New Normal in every part of the world. Some will be innovators and problem solvers creating software, systems, apps, and more to facilitate change. Some will help keep information needed for change at hand for all to use justly. Some will be builders of organizations and structures where change takes place at the ground level.

Whatever your innate response to this opportunity to create New Normal, it is my sincere hope that you'll use the questions in each chapter of this book, and bring your own questions, to come together with your community and do the work it takes to create a future free from sexual harassment, abuse, and violence.

Creating SMART Goals

The WHO global plan of action has set a goal of accomplishing its strategy by 2030. As I type, that's one generation away. Many nations are starting to apply a public health approach to violence, especially violence against women and children. Prevention and victims' services are growing. Strengthening the role of, engagement of, and capacity of the global health system to address violence within a national, multisectoral response, however, is going to take a long-term approach. The WHO is aware that prevention and appropriate response to violence will require the kind of transformational change in the societies we have talked about in this chapter, notably changes of cultural norms.

Other organizations also have set strategies and goals. Collaboration is happening and will continue as the world comes to the awareness that Old Normal is no longer acceptable. In order for Old Normal not to be "sent away to the next town" to become someone else's problem, we need a united approach everywhere.

It's far beyond the scope of this book to outline a detailed strategy and SMART (specific, measurable, attainable, realistic, time-sensitive) goals for each person to create New Normal. Please visit www.lifebeyondmetoo.com for information about strategy and goal setting for change to bring about New Normal. I encourage each reader to consider the future you want to see and engage to the degree possible for you. You can start by setting personal goals for yourself and with your immediate family, to help move the needle for positive change. To download a free Goal Setting Worksheet, visit www.christinerose.coach/resources.

Accountability

Life can be overwhelming at times with its complexity, pace of change, and myriad of choices. As we work in our homes, our jobs, and our communities, we can disappear in the crowds and believe our absence makes no difference. Actually, the opposite is true. Your presence and connection are essential to positive change.

The founder and CEO of Cotential, Erica Dhawan, and business strategist Saj-Nicole Joni define *connectional intelligence* as the ability "to drive innovation and breakthrough results by harnessing the power of relationships and networks."[14] Powerful, professional coaching relationships drive results for my clients by offering them external accountability, plus awareness and strategy and helping them tap into their internal sources of accountability. For example, one of my programs, *WINS!*, offers weekly accountability for members to execute on their goals and offers community to encourage one another to press on. (Learn more at www.christinerose.coach/groups.)

There are many ways people can choose to become accountable. Whether through coaching or other relationships, connection can foster accountability, which can help people make giant leaps in creativity and progress. Internal accountability is powerful for those who are internally driven. Whether internally or externally motivated, in order to let go of Old Normal and create New Normal, we all must become adept at forming relationships, being influencers, and sharing this compelling vision clearly so that others get on New Normal's bandwagon. We need accountability.

Legal accountability is part of Old Normal. Obviously, the scope of sexual harassment, abuse, and violence demonstrates that current laws are not enough. More is needed to help each person honor the right of everyone else to a safe, violence-free life. If the roots of change are deeper than simply improving laws, communities must consider how to deepen accountability in the culture. Creativity and thought are needed to determine what structural supports are needed.

One example of an organization's increased accountability across cultures is from Rotary International, a "global network of 1.2 million neighbors, friends, leaders, and problem solvers who see a world where people unite and take action to create lasting change—across the globe, in our communities, and in ourselves."[15] They know that perpetrators of violence look like everyone else, that they can be adults or youth, and that zero tolerance is essential to create safe programs. The *Rotary Youth Protection Guide* offers guidelines to be followed by all Rotary members and volunteers (in cooperation with local laws) to protect the safety and well-being of youth in its programs.

Connect with your neighborhood or community organization, church, PTSA, book club, bunco group, town hall, or workplace (or any group) about the vision of New Normal. Look at what you're already doing to end Old Normal. Consider what else you might try and who else you might connect with in this work. Those with high connectional intelligence have gone before you, and there are many new relationships being nurtured and bringing forth brilliance in the work to advance a safe, violence-free, just world.

Questions for Thoughtful Consideration and Discussion

1. How did Chris experience harassment or discrimination?
2. How does sexist joking impact the culture?
3. How do diverse cultures around the globe all fail girls and women?
4. What is safety?
5. How do cultures influence your view of safety?
6. How does a shared vision impact the future?
7. What do you think about the vision statement for New Normal?
8. What part do you play in transforming cultural norms?
9. What is the next contribution you can make to facilitate positive change?
10. Who can you connect to who will help create accountability for respect and nonviolence?
11. How long will you tolerate disrespect, harassment, or violence or look the other way when it happens to someone in your circle?
12. What personal vision, strategies, goals, action steps, and accountability can you take to move the needle toward New Normal?

FIFTEEN

Marketplace Support

I was in equipment operations for a Fortune 500 company and was one of four women in the office and warehouse with about twenty-five males working in the warehouse. We had a new warehouse manager who had been promoted within. He and I were emailing back and forth regarding something work related. I am not even sure how it started, but in our email thread, I mentioned to Dave that the guy I had been dating off and on said he was no longer interested in dating me.

Dave, who was married and had just recently had his first child, quickly digressed, still through company email, and wrote that if I ever wanted to hook up, he knew of a spot in the warehouse where the cameras didn't record. And he had access to the service vans that weren't scheduled to go out that day.

I was completely appalled that he would write something like that to me, and that on top of that, he was dumb enough to do it through company email. I knew that Dave would be fired at some point if he continued with this kind of behavior, but I felt bad. He was young, and he and his wife just had a kid. I called and talked to the former manager who had just moved to a new position, because I had no clue what to do. I wanted Dave to know his actions were absolutely unacceptable, but I didn't want to ruin Dave's job or career. Joe offered to talk to him for me.

While I felt violated, the anger came after the fact. The next day I came to work filled with fury. I walked directly out to the warehouse and found Dave. I told him that if he ever said or wrote anything like that to me or any female again, I would have him fired in two seconds.

I talked to a girlfriend who also worked for a Fortune 500 company about this, and her reply blew me away. Her mom had told her that when she started working for corporate America, it was normal to be sexually harassed.

It might have been normal back then, but I am so grateful that the #MeToo movement was brought forward to make this not normal. Sexual harassment should never be normal.

#MeToo, Kay, age 35

Kay's story is all too common and has been for generations, but now others are catching on to courageously address their harassers. People like Kay are advancing New Normal in their workplaces. If employers haven't acted since #MeToo to proactively create a safer, more diverse, just, harassment-free workplace for their employees, they're living in Old Normal. It's past time to let go of Old Normal work conditions for your teams and to bring New Normal into your workplace.

Under federal law, employees are entitled to a safe workplace. Employers must provide a workplace free of known health and safety hazards. If you have concerns, you have the right to speak up about them without fear of retaliation.[1] Heather Bussing, who is an employment attorney and editorial advisory board editor at *HRExaminer* with over thirty years of experience in employment law, who teaches internet law and writes regularly about the intersection of people and technology, says,

> Employers also have a legal, ethical, and practical obligation to provide employees with a work environment that is free of harassment and discrimination. In many ways, it's a health and safety issue too. We know that sexual harassment causes depression, anxiety, PTSD, and can develop into other health issues as well. We also know that most harassment claims are not reported for fear of retaliation and the stress of having to deal with it.
>
> So, we need to take a different approach—to be more proactive, inspect conditions, test for danger, and make sure that everything is kept in good repair.[2]

Status quo is no longer tolerable. Employers that want to stay in business and be able to hire and retain top talent are dismantling toxic culture and conditions that perpetuate Old Normal in their companies.

Workplace Harassment Is Prevalent

In the US, of those who have reported harassment, 33 percent of women experienced harassment from male co-workers and 25 percent from men with influence over their work and career.[3] Globally, the percentage is higher in some countries and lower in others. The WORLD Policy Analysis Center at UCLA reported that sixty-eight countries have no workplace-specific laws against sexual harassment. For 424 million working-age women, including 235 million currently in the workforce, there is nothing legally that protects them against a predatory co-worker or boss or a discriminatory workplace.[4] Most keep the harassment to themselves.

While there certainly are claims by men against women, the vast majority of claims have been made by females who were harassed by males. The EEOC reported that in 2017 in the US, 25,605 complaints were filed on sex discrimination (November 2016 through October 2017).[5] Of the sex discrimination cases, approximately 10,000 sexual harassment complaints were filed. Of those, 16.5 percent of sexual harassment claims in the workplace were filed by men—and 83 percent were filed by women. The EEOC says at least 70 percent of sexual harassment cases are not reported, so it can be inferred that the incidence of harassment is much greater than the 10,000 reported.[6] Charges filed with the EEOC in 2108 alleging sexual harassment increased by more than 12 percent from fiscal year 2017.[7] The Women's Initiative reported in "Gender Matters" on the AmericanProgress.org website that

> the percentage of sexual harassment charges filed by women in each industry reporting to the EEOC is consistently higher than the percentage of women who work in the industry. Conversely, the percentage of men filing sexual harassment charges in each industry is consistently lower than the percentage of men who work in that industry.
>
> The data suggest even starker differences between women and men in their reporting of sexual harassment, when the rate of reporting is calculated to take into account the actual percentage of women and men working in that particular industry. For example, the data show that women—who constitute less than one-quarter of the transportation industry workforce—were ten times more likely to report sexual harassment to the EEOC than men in the transportation industry.[8]

Smart Business Addresses the Issue

With over forty years of experience in business and twenty-five years of experience in HR, Human Resources guru Simon Casas advises smart business leaders on the issue of sexual harassment and other discrimination cases. Smart businesses have already recognized that the status quo of holding an annual sexual harassment training and posting laws in the company break room is not enough to prevent harassment or to cover their assets in the event of a claim. They're already responding to #MeToo by doing more in the way of training and making reporting easier.

Mr. Casas says that most of the businesses he's worked with had effective nondiscrimination policies in place at the time an incidence of sexual harassment was reported. "Having the policies in place won't automatically stop bad behavior," he says. Most policies will be affected by the behavior of employees.

"You can never guarantee behavior of an employee," Mr. Casas cautions. He outlined some of the things a business owner or HR department needs to consider before and when harassment does occur. The following is a summary of his recommendations:

Firm policies need to be in place and clearly communicated to all employees from day one, even for small companies. Policies need to use language that puts the responsibility for the harassment solely on the predator. The whole organization needs to know that if sexual harassment occurs, it's not the target's fault, it's the predator's fault, and no matter what level they're at in the organization, the predator will be fired, not rewarded.

Policies should mandate bystander intervention and reporting. Employees must report all harassment. If it's not reported, there isn't much an employer can do, unless it's within a small company where everyone knows what's going on. For example, in a company with ten employees, two of whom are the owner and supervisor, if the other eight employees ("everyone") know about harassment happening, the case could then be made that leadership knows.

Keeping records of reporting harassment is important because in one case, after much investigation and in spite of a number of witnesses, nothing could be proven in court, as there were no records of the victim reporting the harassment.

The Equal Employment Opportunity Commission (www.EEOC. gov) website is a resource for those who get into litigation. Research the EEOC records for similar cases. It pays to have clear, zero-tolerance policies and simple, effective procedures for reporting and for your Human Resources to be highly responsive when reports are made.[9]

Protecting the Employee and the Business

Proactive, strong, safe cultures are essential not only to protect employees from harassment but also to protect the company from false claims, which are prevalent because of the ease of filing and the likelihood of a settlement. One attorney in Chicago told Mr. Casas, "I always know the law. I will always file for discrimination and harassment." Mr. Casas remarked, "It's become too easy to file a claim against an employer. It's going to end up settled (most of the time) if a Title 7 claim is filed. Even when the employer wants to terminate the employee, they'll be paying a settlement." Companies are investing in insurance in the event of claims, but the best insurance is to be proactive as leaders.

Leaders Set the Stage

In his TED Talk *Start with Why*, Simon Sinek said that all inspiring leaders think, act, and communicate in exactly the same way because each comes from a center of belief. They start not with *what* they do as an organization, nor *how* they do it, but with *why* their organization exists. Those businesses that start with a strong why, whose leaders hold clear visions and high standards of accountability for themselves and their companies, have already been leading change since #MeToo, instead of waiting for the laws to change.

Tolerance of harassment by leadership is the greatest contributing factor to its pervasiveness in a workplace. Inspiring leaders set the example that sexual harassment is not something that can be tolerated at any level in their workplace.[10] Smart business leaders are double checking policies to make sure they are fair. They're dropping requirements for nondisclosure agreements (NDAs) and putting 24/7 video training in their plants so not one employee can use the excuse that they didn't know what sexual harassment is or that it's against company policy and against the law. They're buying apps that make it easier for victims and observers to safely report harassment. The waves of consequences for offenders will not stop, as smart business leaders are requiring zero tolerance for perpetrators and immediate dismissal without pay. How your company leads on this issue is a factor you can ignore at your own peril or address successfully for a total team win.

Workplace Culture Initiatives

Organizations and industries are wise to start with culture and to continually assess, measure, monitor, and manage their cultures. It's got to be done from the inside out. According to Daniel Coyle's book *The Culture Code*, when you build purpose, vulnerability, and safety into a culture and maintain these key elements, your company culture can bring people together to create extraordinary results.[11]

Culture is built into organizational structure. Male-dominated "old boys' club" cultures with a dearth of females in leadership roles foster higher levels of sexual harassment. There's a dog-eat-dog competition for power, along with an inability of males in groups to recognize subconscious bias and sexism, and even when they do see sexual discrimination, it's rare for a man to call out a brother, which makes a male-dominant culture a high-risk workplace. Gender discrimination and harassment that creates a hostile work environment is common in such places where sexism is spoken, posted on the walls (porn calendars), and tolerated by leadership.

Male-dominated industries generate more discrimination and harassment against women. Lucy O'Brien, games and entertainment editor at IGN, interviewed several top women in gaming for a December 2017 article in IGN's online magazine. She writes,

> Sexism, harassment and inappropriate conduct in the workplace continue to be major issues for women throughout the (male-dominated)

video game industry, as they do for women in the tech world. . . . Many [women] . . . had experienced one of the above on a micro level, while some had experienced it to a major, life-changing degree. Nearly all had accounts of seeing it happen to someone else.[12]

Harassment and discrimination show up not only in sexual harassment cases, but in cultures that are biased against female employees, from the words they use in job postings to outdated family-leave policies, and even to locker rooms—where informal, casual conversations can happen for men but not for women. It's not just tech. This is true across the board for male-dominated industries.

Unconscious bias and discrimination can increase when women are promoted to leadership roles over males. Discrimination occurs when women are judged with a double standard if they act in ways that are necessary to fulfill the requirements of their roles (proactive, courageous, entrepreneurial, confident, assertive) if, in doing so, they're judged by males as not adhering to female gender stereotypes.[13] Women are less likely to be promoted to leadership roles, and research shows that the marketplace and society in general continues to favor men. For example, men have relatively more power than women in couples' (two-income earner relationships) early career negotiations, despite equal educational credentials. More frequently the male advances in his career and the female partner adjusts to fit his career goals, putting her behind the curve professionally.[14]

Power over a person's advancement or future in an organization can create ample opportunity for abuse. When organizations limit opportunities for gross inequality of power by creating flat organizational structures that include women in all levels of leadership roles, it produces fewer harassment cases. Businesses that make and keep a strong commitment to increase leadership opportunities for women and address the root causes of the gender pay gap also experience lower cases of harassment. They also grow more diverse, positive cultures.

Develop Diversity and Inclusion

To help businesses create equitable workplaces, Gender Equity Now has created the GEN Certification, "the national gold standard for gender equity in the US workplace." According to GEN,

> Businesses that are GEN Certified meet standards of excellence across five tenets of workplace culture. A composite assessment of employee experience and employer policies provides a data-driven standard of equity-centered work environments. The GEN Certification rewards business leaders who go beyond talk to meaningful action.[15]

According to the *2018 Pipeline Equity for All* report, 78 percent of CEOs in the United States say they prioritize gender equity, and only 22 percent of employees report regularly seeing information about gender being measured and shared.[16] Eighty-seven percent of CEOs marked themselves as highly focused on talent, diversity, and inclusiveness. So where does your company stand in regard to this discrepancy?

Eventbrite achieved parity on their board of directors in January 2019.[17] Consider what your company can do to move in that direction. If you're committed to New Normal, you will commit to the goal of increasing the number of women in leadership roles and at every level of your company.

One place to start is by continually filling the pipeline at all levels with more women, even if you have to get creative to find qualified candidates. Lisa Unwin, CEO and founder of She's Back, a London-based organization founded in 2014, works with organizations "to help them understand how to retain more women at all levels and how to re-engage with those who take a break. Research undertaken in 2015 by She's Back, the University of Edinburgh Business School, and sponsors from five different sectors, highlighted the scale of untapped potential in this particular talent pool."[18] Lisa offered the following advice to organizations looking for qualified, management-ready females who left companies or industries to raise children or start their own businesses: think outside the normal regarding resumes, CVs, and job descriptions when seeking candidates. Think about increasing flexibility for roles that don't really need a nine-to-five workday. Stay in touch and keep offering ongoing training or professional development opportunities.[19]

I would add, in hiring processes, companies can do a blind match of a prospective employee's innate nature to the role using assessments that measure innate value drivers that align with the role—for example, the Taylor Protocols Core Values Index (CVI), a highly reliable assessment with a repeat score accuracy rating greater than 97 percent.[20] (For a free version, visit http://bit.ly/crose-free-cvi.)

Also, fill the pipeline for profit-and-loss positions with more women. According to Discover.org, of the twelve most common C-Suite roles, women represent more than 50 percent of the hires in only one function, human resources. Marketing is the next most gender-diverse function, with an almost equal split of men and women. Most telling, however, is that women make up less than 10 percent of the four most senior-level roles at a typical Fortune 1000 company, chairman of the board, CEO, COO, and CFO.[21]

Design for Diversity and Inclusion

What can the leaders in the marketplace do to advance New Normal? Iris Bohnet, the Albert Pratt professor of business and government and academic dean of Harvard Kennedy School, behavioral economist at Harvard University, co-director of Women and Public Policy program, and adviser to governments and countries on the topic of gender design, advocates for "norm entrepreneurship" (a term coined by Cass Sunstein in 1996).[22] A norm entrepreneur is a person interested in changing social norms. I am convinced that many norm entrepreneurs will build on the notion of New Normal versus Old Normal and adopt change strategies to increase diversity and build a culture of inclusion at all levels which will reduce harassment. In her book *What Works: Gender Equality by Design*, Bohnet provides thirty-six tested practices to decrease gender bias and shift organizational culture to more inclusive. Bohnet recommends the following strategies among others:

- Change procedures/practices to challenge implicit bias.
- Create equal negotiation opportunities.
- Build leadership capacity through resources and use behavior design to support success.
- Create role models because people need to see others who look like them leading.
- Collect, track, and analyze data to understand patterns and make forecasts; measure to detect what is broken and design interventions.
- Evaluate your people free of demographic info, comparatively, and promote in batches; do not use unstructured interviews.
- Purge gendered language from ads and other company communications; pay for performance, not face time; make the job application processes transparent.
- Adjust risk when known differences in willingness to gamble might bias outcome; remove clues triggering performance-inhibiting stereotypes; make environments inclusive of different kinds of risk taking.
- Use gender-neutral designs; mitigate own gender bias toward self and others, do not share biased self-assessments with supervisors, give feedback to help others see their biases; pay for differential impact because of gender.
- On teams, maximize performance by combining average ability with complementary diversity of perspective and expertise; avoid tokenism.[23]

Build Trust

Don't pay lip service when it comes to diversity and inclusion. A 2018 survey conducted by PwC Research of 3,627 professional women (globally) revealed that most women don't trust what their bosses tell them about promotions or pay, and most are skeptical of their bosses' advice about what helps or hurts their careers.[24]

In addition to a commitment to diversity and to removing gender bias, positive company cultures must include trust, transparency, and the ability for each team member to communicate freely about (even negative) concerns. Harvard Business School professor Amy Edmondson, author of *The Fearless Organization: Creating Psychological Safety in the Workplace for Learning, Innovation, and Growth*, studies how companies with a trusting workplace perform better. Employees need to be able to offer input fron their own unique perspective, give candid feedback, openly admit mistakes, and learn from one another. (For information on testing for psychological safety in your company, visit www.christinerose.coach/programs.)

When an organization tolerates abuses of power, there is by default secrecy, which sets the stage for workplace harassment. Not only will companies that want to build a fearless organization create a trusting environment among team members, they will have zero tolerance for harassment and will require accountability for all team members to report gender-based discrimination and sexual harassment when they see it.

What about Small Businesses?

To the small business owner wondering how in the world to address this issue effectively with limited resources: be a learner. There are thousands of articles posted about how to proactively work to create a harassment-free company, including eight actionable steps outlined on LeanIn.org's website.[25] Do your research about what's required by law. Understand the power of your leadership and the power of culture.

Make it clear that harassment is not part of your company culture and that anyone can come to top management at any time with issues that impact the team.

In an interview, leadership development expert and adjunct professor at Northwest University Kim Martinez, DMin, recommended that small businesses "have a plan and think through the scenario ahead of time. What should the relationship of the boss look like when someone reports harassment?" Dr. Martinez also tells business leaders, "Educate yourself about language that may cause issues. Use disclaimers if you're uncertain. State up front, 'I need you to tell me if you are offended by anything I say.'"

Dr. Martinez advises purposeful communicating: "We can accidentally hurt people, and we need to make all our communications clear and positive." She also advises, "Accept that others may have triggers that you know nothing about. So even well-intentioned physical contact may be unwise. Some people are naturally more comfortable with physical contact than others. If you want to touch someone, ask ahead of time. We all have those moments when someone is sharing from their heart and we want to touch their arm or put a hand on their shoulder to give them a sense of support. Ask. "Is it okay if I put a hand on your arm" is not a weird question – it is a respectful question that acknowledges another person's right for personal space and our desire to give them support. If they say 'no.' Just smile, say 'okay,' and tell them that they have your support."[26] If you model this type of respect, you are setting the tone for your business as a place of respect and safety for all employees.

Lead by engaging regularly with your team, showing consistency between what you say and what you do. What will you do to solidify a plan of action to create a clear line of communication and know, across the company, how you'd deal with a harassment claim before it ever happens? If you're committed to New Normal (or even if you're lagging on a commitment to a world free from sexual harassment and violence), as a prudent entrepreneur, you will act to minimize any risk the damage such a claim could create for your small business's culture, reputation, relationships with clients and partners, or bottom line.

The Skewed Venture Capital Equation

According to PitchBook, only 2.2 percent of venture capital funding went to female-founded teams in 2017. But in a survey of 200 investors and lenders, 80 percent of respondents said they believe women- and minority-led businesses are getting sufficient capital. They also said they seldom see pitches from women or minorities. When they do fund those entrepreneurs, they offer about 20 percent of their average commitment. Where is the cognitive dissonance in the minds of mostly male investors and lenders?

Carla Harris, head of Morgan Stanley's Multicultural Client Strategy Group, said,

> If each one of them looked at three or four more deals from women and people of color, we will have made a difference. It may have been a marginal difference, but all you need is a couple of these large investors to start really making money in this space and it will catch on like wildfire.[27]

Angel investor Pip Wilson, CEO of amicable, wrote in *Entrepreneur Magazine*,

> An ever-growing body of data shows that female-founded companies grow faster than their male-founded counterparts. Female management is almost invariably more transparent, and diverse teams make more money and better decisions. Women are also more successful than men at winning seed-level crowdfunding, which is the most democratic way of raising capital. According to recent research, female-led crowdfunding campaigns were 32 percent more successful at reaching their funding target than male-led ones. The public, in

other words, backs female founders financially, which given the evidence is a smart investment, but VCs who are the presumed experts in investing are still operating as if there is something inherently toxic about female-founded companies.[28]

Although startups with at least one woman received more funding in 2018, the percentage of funding for women didn't change significantly. As movement toward New Normal continues, the marketplace will continue to adjust to increase opportunities for a diversity of entrepreneurs while increasing profits for investors and lenders.

Questions for Thoughtful Consideration and Discussion

1. What can employees like Kay do to minimize the risk of being harassed?
2. Whose responsibility is the harassment like Kay experienced?
3. What is the responsibility of the marketplace to build diverse, inclusive, and respectful workplaces?
4. Have you ever experienced or witnessed workplace harassment? What did you do?
5. Why are businesses leading the way with more trainings?
6. What does a diverse workplace do to reduce harassment?
7. What do business structures have to do with harassment?
8. Why are safe cultures important?
9. How do leaders influence the culture at and in their companies?
10. What is the cost of looking the other way when harassment happens?
11. How do trust, transparency, and honesty impact company cultures?
12. When is profit wrong?
13. What should a business do if their business partners tolerate harassment?
14. How can VCs and lenders increase their funding for women-led ventures?
15. How can you lead the work of New Normal in your workplace?

SIXTEEN

Powerful Nonviolence

Joanne was amazing. At nineteen, she was brilliant, gorgeous, and in great shape like an Amazon princess. We had been friends for a couple of years. I met her when we were freshmen in college. We had a "brother-sister" kind of relationship, as her sorority and my fraternity had some parties and functions together.

I'll never forget the night Joanne came to a party at my fraternity house. We chatted awhile, and then she disappeared. I thought she had left. I went up to my room around midnight. At two in the morning, I heard a knock at the door. I opened the door and there stood Joanne, looking like a dream come true.

She reached out to me and hugged me and held on to me. She wouldn't let go. Then she started crying. She came into my room, and she was bawling. She asked if she could stay the night. "Just hold me," she said.

I held her. For the longest time she kept bawling, and I asked her over and over, "What's wrong, Joanne?"

Finally, between the sobs and tears, she told me that one of my frat brothers had raped her. I believed her. Joanne was not the kind to cry rape. I told her to wait.

I went up to my frat brother's room and pounded on the door. He was a junior; I was a sophomore.

After a lot of noise, finally, he opened the door. "What's up, John?" he asked casually.

I tore into him and started beating him up. He headed for the door, and the fight continued outside. He threw some punches, but I hurt him pretty bad. He threatened to file an official report to the frat and to have me ejected. I told him, "Tim, if you report me, I'm going to report you. Everyone will know what you did to Joanne."

Tim never reported me to the frat, but everyone knew what had happened anyway. I lived in that house for another year with a rapist living above me. I avoided him whenever possible.

We never had another word between us, but I had swallowed my own whistle.

Joanne didn't want her family or sorority sisters to know. She didn't file a police report. She was afraid the girls would shun her and feared that her parents would try to take her out of school if they found out, and she wanted more than anything to get her degree. It was 1976; there wasn't really any mechanism for dealing with this situation. It broke my heart to see this young woman I'd admired and cared for so much be so deeply hurt. It pretty much goes without saying that she never came back to my fraternity house.

The irony is that for my first two years in college, I'd gone around to sororities before rushes with a group of sorority sisters and other frat brothers to talk about safety, and we told the incoming girls, "If you go to parties, stay on the main floor. If you go onto a sleeping floor or into one of the brothers' rooms, you'll basically be giving consent. None of the guys can be counted on to listen to you once you're on a sleeping floor."

#HerToo, John

John said that from the experience he had with his friend Joanne, the guilt and the resulting strain of relationships during his remaining time at the fraternity house led to eight years of drug and alcohol abuse. He said that it took some work, but he finally came to terms with it. This was just one man's perspective on being privy to a #MeToo story of someone he cared about. It had ended two friendships. Objectification and violence destroy human relationships.

Who Needs Relationships?

You need positive relationships if you want a long and happy life. Robert Waldinger, a psychiatrist at Massachusetts General Hospital and a professor of psychiatry at Harvard Medical School, is director of the Harvard Study of Adult Development and has studied the lives of men and their offspring over seven decades and has been including wives in the study for over a decade. A report on the study states,

> Over the years, researchers have studied the participants' health trajectories and their broader lives, including their triumphs and failures in careers and marriage, and the finding have produced startling lessons, and not only for the researchers.
>
> "The surprising finding is that our relationships and how happy we are in our relationships has a powerful influence on our health," said Robert Waldinger. "Taking care of your body is important, but tending to your relationships is a form of self-care too. That, I think, is the revelation."[1]

Very smart guys know that good relationships make life happier and help people live longer. Dr. Paul L. Corona, a certified leadership coach who trained under premier leadership coach Dr. Marshall Goldsmith, is a highly rated clinical professor of leadership in the Kellogg School of Management at Northwestern University and author of *The Wisdom of Walk-Ons: 7 Winning Strategies for College, Business and Life.* As another brilliant, educated man who knows that good relationships make people healthier and happier, Dr. Corona invested time to understand what makes for stronger relationships, and he invented and founded Lee's 3 Habits system, which helps motivated people build stronger relationships and achieve greater happiness. The three habits he promotes to build stronger relationships are ask more, listen more, and give more.[2] Without strong relationships we don't stand the same chance for happiness and success.

Where Do You Stand?

Where do you stand when it comes to speaking out and acting to prevent violence against women? What do the numbers say in terms of who the victims are? The United Nations defines violence against women as "any act of gender-based violence that results in (or is likely to result in) physical, sexual, or mental harm or suffering to women, including threats of such acts, coercion, or arbitrary deprivation of liberty, whether occurring in public or in private life."[3]

Global estimates published by WHO indicate that about 35 percent of women worldwide have experienced either physical or sexual intimate-partner violence or non-partner sexual violence in their lifetime. According to WHO,

> Men are more likely to perpetrate violence if they have low education, a history of child maltreatment, exposure to domestic violence against their mothers, harmful use of alcohol, unequal gender norms including attitudes accepting of violence, and a sense of entitlement over women.[4]

Data from thirty countries shows that of the nine million fifteen- to nineteen-year-old girls like Joanne who were victims of sexual assault in 2017. Only 1 percent reached out for professional help. Most have nobody to turn to, no voice to speak for them. UNICEF USA launched the #HerToo campaign to give a voice to these girls and women.[5] One in five women and one in seventy-one men in the US are victims of rape in their lifetimes.[6] Of victims of rape and sexual assault, nine of ten are female, and one of ten is male.[7] In eight out of ten cases of rape, the victim knew the perpetrator.[8] In some places, the percentage of people who are sexually assaulted is much higher.

There are an estimated 3.8 billion females on earth.[9] The way the world is now, over one-third of them, or over 1.25 billion, are or will be victims of violence perpetrated largely by males. The offenders are brothers, uncles, fathers, classmates, co-workers, and guys who join us at sports events, the local watering hole, the golf course, and the club.

If good relationships are key to men's happiness, health, and longevity, it's logical that men who value happiness, health, and longevity would value relationships and recognize that objectification and violence are destroyers of relationships. Sexual harassment and violence are repeated by perpetrators, even those who have spent time in jail. A key to move to New Normal is for men to recognize and commit to changes that will not only make them happier, healthier, and give them longer lives, but also will help to create a just, safe world.

Many Good Men

In fact, this is what most men are hungering for. Most men are not rapists, most men do not sexually harass women in their workplace, most men don't accost women on the street, and most don't abuse or pimp out their daughters, sisters, nieces, grandkids, kids in their scout troop or church group, or their neighbors' kids.

I heard from many men (and parents, both male and female) who are deeply concerned for the people (mostly women) in their lives whose traumatic stories have come out since October 2017. They expressed sadness, anger, and sometimes a sense of helplessness after hearing these stories, and they lacked the confidence to be supportive.

I've heard from men who are getting tired of reading or hearing how bad men are. They're hungry to be known as having good hearts and behaving with others' best interests in mind. The hashtag #notallmen came about in response to this.

This book is not about making anyone feel bad. Coaching is a judgment-free zone.

There is an ancient wisdom literature text that says, "There is none righteous, no, not one."[10] I've never met a perfect person. I'm far from perfect. I don't point fingers or throw stones. We all live in glass houses. I have found that as a result of decades of work looking inside, looking at the heart, looking at the past and the present, seeking forgiveness for my mistakes, forgiving others for theirs, and envisioning my best future, my relationships with myself and others are greatly improved. It is deeply respectful and rewarding, to myself and to others. A look inside clears the view.

An Open Window

One of the gifts of the #MeToo movement is an open window, a period of time for people to consider and discuss deeper human issues like value, purpose, gender, culture, sexuality, justice, responsibility, and more. This might feel more like a curse. Taking time for deep reflection may seem impossible; life is already so full. In our demanding world, reflection can feel more like a luxury than a necessity.

Men face competing calls for action, accomplishment, achievement, success, power, and status (whether on the ballfield, in the boardroom, or in the bedroom) that are strong, loud, incessant. The threat of fear and the shame of potentially appearing weak at any time or falling short of all the expectations put on men by others and society can overrule the call to reflect.

The voices of our families of origin and culture are so powerful, they can often drown out a person's own thoughts. These voices may be telling you that strength at all costs is essential. Only the strong survive. Rule. Fight back against anything that causes your force field to crack.

On the other hand, there may be voices that don't speak to you. A sixty-second commercial from a razor company about harassment and bullying was not well-received by a majority of men. A minority appreciated the reminder that young boys are watching and learning from the examples of the men in their lives. Other voices in the news, media, and in your community may not reflect your experience from your family of origin, your ethnic perspective, your economic situation, your cultural experience. Whether you agree or disagree with them, what others' voices can fail to offer you is the freedom to listen to *your own inner wisdom*, to recognize your innate strength, to define for yourself what strengths belong to humans at their best. This is where it may be beneficial to call for a time-out to reset.

Taking Some Time

Jonathan Milligan, a colleague in my Business Network International (BNI) chapter, told me that he got a lot from the Arbinger Institute's book *Leadership and Self-Deception*, because he took time to answer the questions that made him more self-aware. When do you afford yourself the gift of a little time out away from your family, those who depend on you, your friends, your culture, to get alone with your thoughts?

I encourage you to schedule and take time regularly to consider your own thoughts, values, and purpose, apart from what anyone else says. As a thought enters your mind, ask yourself, "Where did this thought originate? Is this in alignment with who I am as a person? Is this in alignment with my values? Is it true? Is it useful today?"

Here are some coaching questions for self-awareness, a key quality for strong leaders:

- Who am I? What makes me unique?
- What is my personal Why?

- What direction do I want to take my life?
- What are my dreams?
- How do I envision myself and my life in the next year? Five years? Ten? Twenty?
- What are the steps I need to take to make my vision a reality?
- What separates me from my vision for my life?
- What have I done/am I doing to align my life with my vision?
- What do I do that makes me feel great, proud, and happy in the long run?
- What do I do that makes me feel not-so-great, ashamed, sad in the long run?
- What is my sexual or gender identity, and what do I value about it?
- What do I value in myself?
- What do I value in the people who are in my life?
- Where does my life align with my values?
- Where are things not in alignment?
- What are my greatest fears?
- What makes me frustrated?
- What is the best way of dealing with fears and frustrations?
- How can I create or add to a solution for my fears and frustrations?
- Who am I when I'm at my best?
- What do I do when I fall short? What do I want to do?
- Have I sought forgiveness from those I have harmed? Is my slate clear?
- Do I carry bitterness? Have I offered forgiveness to those who've harmed me?
- Are my relationships edifying and positive for everyone involved? (If I don't know, is it safe to ask?)
- Who's in my corner who truly wants my best and holds me accountable?

- Who do I hold accountable? For what?
- Who's in my community? How does my community support me? How do I support my community?
- What is my place in Old Normal? What would my place be in New Normal?

In response to #MeToo, Benjamin Law, a writer from Sydney, Australia, tweeted on October 16, 2017, "Guys, it's our turn. After yesterday's endless #MeToo stories of women being abused, assaulted and harassed, today we say #HowIWillChange."[11]

Started in 2014, #HeForShe is the United Nations Global Solidarity Movement for Gender Equality. According to #HeForShe, over two million people have committed to gender equality. The world is at a turning point. People everywhere understand and support the idea of gender equality. They know it's not just a women's issue, it's a human rights issue. #HeForShe is an invitation for men and people of all genders to stand in solidarity with women to create a bold, visible, and united force for gender equality. The men of HeForShe aren't on the sidelines. They're working with women and with each other to build businesses, raise families, and give back to their communities.[12]

I'd like to invite you to consider not only how you will change how you relate to God, yourself, and others but also how you are a part of New Normal, where all people are honored and respected as human beings who share a world. What would you do first to reset? What needs to change for you to step into your best future?

Fear, Confusion, Chaos, and Questions

The past few years after #MeToo have brought the world into a time of fear, confusion, chaos, and questions. Here are some examples of questions I've heard:

How can I stop feeling frustrated and afraid of doing the wrong thing at work and in relationships? How do I handle the silence of co-workers in my workplace? Will I be able to enjoy sexual relationships? Does the risk of being assaulted while conscious or passed out from someone slipping me a mickey force me to stay home instead with a glass of wine or a drink with friends? Am I safe at home?

How can I be kind and not rude, without giving anyone the remote notion that I am interested in dating them or that they somehow have permission to touch my body? What do I do if I'm trying to be nice or friendly, and someone else believes I'm being a jerk, because they don't understand the motivation behind my words and take them as harassment?

Is losing a job because of a mistake someone made twenty years ago fair? Is suffering from PTSD or depression from an assault endured twenty years ago fair? Is getting raped and having to choose whether to report it, because one might lose a job in addition to suffering the ill effects of rape, fair? Especially since statistics show the offender will likely repeat their actions? ("Findings suggest it is very likely that a sexual offender has either previously sexually assaulted or will offend again in the future," said Rachel Lovell, PhD, a senior research associate at the Begun Center and co-leader of the Cuyahoga County Sexual Assault Kit Pilot Research Project.[13])

When can I compliment someone on what they're wearing? Should I or shouldn't I open a door for someone? How can I work late and not worry about getting home safely? When is it okay ask someone on a date? Can I decline a request to wash the dishes in the break room (not in the job description) or decline a request for sexual favors (definitely not in the job description) and not have to worry about getting fired without cause? What should I do when I'm saddled with the lion's share of unpaid work on top of having to earn half the family income? What do we do with all the questions about discrimination, harassment, abuse, and sexual violence? To leave them unanswered is to live in fear.

It is wise to examine reasons and deeper motivations behind our fears. What automatic negative thoughts come to mind? It is a choice to keep or let go of those thoughts. You can choose to replace negative thoughts with positive action thoughts that will move you out of fear and into confidence, strength, and peace with all those you interact with on a daily basis.

Words to the Innocent

If you're a person who has never objectified anyone; never sexually objectified anyone (including online); never perpetrated or witnessed any sexual harassment, abuse, or violence or looked the other way or remained silent about it; have always supported victims and those organizations trying to help them; have always supported laws and organizations that help victims and level the playing field for those who need it; have always been an ally in the workplace for those facing discrimination; have worked to counter implicit bias in your home, workplace, and society; have worked to create a culture of equity and justice in your home, workplace, and society—thank you! You're exceptional. You deserve a holiday in your honor! Your respect of yourself, of women (and all victims), and your value for all people is essential in the transition to New Normal free of violence and of recriminations. You're a role model for those who either don't know better or don't do better, for those who've been brainwashed by culture into seeing other humans as objects to be used. So far.

That all being true, it would probably not hurt to dig a little deeper. Did you know that a majority of self-confessed rapists (who described to researchers the sexual behavior that they did, and it's rape) actually believe that when they sexually penetrated someone without their consent, it wasn't sexual assault?[14] Another thing that men who have raped and who don't believe what they did could be called rape have in common is that they don't believe they're the problem.[15] The same may be true of harassment, silence, and looking the other way and cultural tolerance for these things. There's a hidden dynamic of denial by the person who did those things and the silence of the person they did them to. Denial might be pretty easy for some, but reality is better.

If you've faced reality and come out completely innocent, you can be a strong ally. How might you continue to broaden your perspective about gender-based discrimination, sexual harassment, abuse, and violence? What questions can you ask yourself that will help you to continue in the path you've walked, in spite of the culture working overtime to drag you into sexual objectification of others? What can you do, or continue to do, to lead change that would usher in New Normal, a more just and safer world for all people?

A Message to the Not-So-Innocent

If you're someone who has ever objectified anyone or sexually objectified anyone (including online); has ever perpetrated sexual harassment, abuse, or violence; has ever looked the other way or remained silent about it if you have witnessed these things; has not always been a support for victims and those organizations trying to help them; has not always supported laws and organizations that help victims and level the playing field for everyone; has not worked to counter implicit bias in your home, workplace, or society; and has tolerated injustice or discrimination in your home, workplace, or society . . . welcome to the club. Me too.

Thank you for reading this book and for considering the results that your actions or your inaction has had on others. Nobody's asking you to shout your failures from the rooftops. We already know that there are no perfect people. Those in the 90 percent of all who've been victims, the females in your life, and females in general (about half the people in the world) are grateful for your open-mindedness and honesty with yourself. This alone is commendable and will be impactful!

This is not about heaping judgment on anyone. Jesus said to a crowd of judgers seeking to condemn a person who was found guilty, "He that is without sin among you, let him be the first to cast a stone . . ."[16]

This is about checking in to determine who really wins by choosing to live in Old Normal, which is clearly damaging to self and to others.

Is it possible there is a better way that will lead to more life and peace, health, and happiness? What can you do to help the future be safer for all? Where can you get support and accountability to make changes? Only you can choose for yourself how you want your future to go. Please know that your actions impact not only your own health and happiness but also those whose lives connect to yours and those with whom you interact.

You are unique, one of a kind. There never has been, and there never will be, any other person exactly like you. Like Dr. Rick Warren, author of the bestseller *The Purpose Driven Life*, I believe that you're not an accident or a mistake. You are here for a purpose. Science agrees that your DNA is unique. No one else has your fingerprints or your iris pattern, not even if you're an identical twin. As a completely unique person, you have incomparable value. You are not a commodity. The same is true of each individual on earth who has unique DNA, fingerprints, irises, a voice.

I've never met a perfect person, so I can guess with some accuracy that you may have made some mistakes in your life, as we all have. Some of them may be huge, but we are all more than the sum of our past mistakes.

No one is beyond the ability to change, because we all get to choose. Some are more aware of their choice than others. Along with Dr. Warren's book, I recommend *Man's Search for Meaning* by Dr. Victor Frankl as a way to understand how powerful you are in your ability to choose. As a free agent with your choices ahead of you, I address you from the coaching perspective that honors your right to choose and to face the consequences of your choices.

To learn about healing and transformation available for anyone who's not perfect, I recommend *The Book of Forgiving: The Fourfold Path for Healing Ourselves and Our World* by Archbishop Desmond Tutu,

Nobel Peace Prize winner, Chair of the Elders, and Chair of South Africa's Truth and Reconciliation Commission, and his daughter, the Reverend Mpho Tutu. Most people need both healing and transformation to be forgiven and to forgive.

Firm Requests

Another thing I do as a coach is make firm requests of my clients based on what they've revealed about themselves and their goals. After listening carefully to the client and hearing what they say they want, I sometimes repeat what they're communicating in the form of a request. It is given with the clear reminder that this is a request, not a command. A request is something the client can take or leave. A request may be modified by the client. The client alone is taking responsibility for their response to the request and whether or not they choose to accept it or fulfill it.

People share common traits and needs, and it is on this common ground that I offer some firm requests. I don't believe these requests will in any way harm anyone. I do believe that they will help everyone. I don't believe these requests require anyone to change their belief systems, to compromise cultural values, to deny or hide their character or gender or to deny their rights. I believe if you can read this (or listen to it), we can agree that this is an appropriate time to make the following *eight firm requests* (if we don't agree, please stop reading for now and come back to this part later):

1. If you objectify others, if you turn people into things for your use or profit, please stop now. If you're not sure, ask them. They'll tell you.
2. If you sexualize people, please stop now. See them as the whole humans they are.
3. If you act in predatory ways toward anyone (viewing them as a target to consume), please stop now.

4. If you minimize or hide the damage of objectification and sexualization of yourself or others, please stop now.

5. If you look the other way when others are harassed or harmed, please stop now.

6. If you have work to do to bring forgiveness and restoration to your relationships with others, please start now.

7. If you can add anything to the shift to New Normal that will allow each person to live in human dignity and safety, please start now.

8. If you're mocking this list of requests (this will apply to some readers), please seek psychological and perhaps spiritual counseling. Your lack of compassion and narcissistic tendencies are keeping you from fully living, and they put you at risk of damaging others. You are steeped in Old Normal.

The reason for these requests is for your own benefit and for the well-being of every person on earth. You're one of us. Commit to change and commit to becoming a change agent. You decide when, where, and how. Today, you have an opportunity to step up and take advantage of the culture changes. The window is still open.

Strength in Integrity

Strength is admirable. People build strength and integrity by aligning their actions with core values. They also build strength in several other ways: aligning with people who support their values, maintaining boundaries that support their values, overcoming fears that impact their values, and committing publicly to behaving in alignment with their values.

While each person is responsible for their own actions, peer pressure can increase the risk of sexual harassment and violence. Peer pressure to abuse substances (alcohol, drugs), to be sexually active, and to buy the lies that consent is not necessary and that people are objects to be used, prizes to be won, or the enemy to be conquered. Peers can encourage choices that later cause regret, sadness, or shame.

The good news is that peer pressure can also be used to reduce the risk of sexual harassment and violence. Choose peers who are leading the way as they maintain appropriate boundaries, relate to their peers (regardless of gender) as equals, commit to nonviolence, and overcome fear of others' judgment or reprisal if they don't go along with the group. Peer pressure can influence you to make healthy choices that leave you and everyone else feeling happy and confident and grateful for the positive results for yourself and others.[17] In New Normal, positive peer pressure that begins in infancy and childhood will unravel and remove from current and future generations, centuries or even millennia from now, the cultural conditioning that has created the Mess of Old Normal.

As a coach, I ask clients questions that help them clearly look at the present and envision the best future possible, not only for themselves but for all whose lives they can impact. Here are some questions you might consider, not all at once but over time, to personally look at your present and your best future.

Questions for Thoughtful Consideration and Discussion
1. Who was responsible for Joanne's rape?
2. What was John's responsibility?
3. What might increase the likelihood of victims reporting violence?
4. How would you describe your relationships? Would others describe them the same way?
5. How do you interact with co-workers? With strangers in public? With your family and friends?
6. In what ways may you be contributing to Old Normal?
7. What kind of person do you want to be?
8. What are you holding on to in terms of judgment or need for forgiveness (for yourself or others)?
9. What is gender equality?
10. What would it take to attain a goal of gender equality in the world?
11. What do you stand to gain or lose by allowing the status quo to continue?
12. What would commitment to nonviolence look like for you?
13. What do you stand to gain or lose by engaging in New Normal?

SEVENTEEN

Intrepid Survivors

On the night I was first raped, I had done everything I was told would keep me safe. I picked the route to my dorm that took me past all of the "rape stations"—the towers of pale-blue and white lights with emergency buttons that promised a fast response time if pressed. I had my keys and rape whistle at the ready. Per my usual habit, I locked my door behind me. I wasn't afraid that night; I was incandescently happy. I was in love.

I changed into pajamas, curled up with a good book, and waited. When I heard the special knock on the door, I opened it to the face of the boy I loved so much.

Then he raped me.

I felt betrayal, heartbreak, fear, pain—and then nothing. As my soul watched my own rape happen beneath me, I slowly accepted that I was dead, and God had forgotten me.

I have no concept of how long I was disassociated from my body, but eventually I felt the painful pricks of a sleeping limb waking up, and I was back. He was gone.

I tried to make sense of what had happened to me, but every time my mind returned to the assault, I would feel numbness creeping up my limbs, so I forced the memories down, almost as afraid of how I had survived as I was of the attack.

Looking to my left, I saw the rape whistle I had been given my first week of college, sitting just out of my reach as it had the whole time. I ripped it off the key ring and smashed it, torn between anger and a vast sense of detached, dark nothingness that would become as familiar to me as anything I'd ever felt. . . . Until I finally told someone what had been done to me. Then there was nothing but pain. It took a great deal of time after sharing my story, but finally, slowly, I've recovered peace.

#MeToo, Oksana

I'm writing now directly to people like Oksana who have experienced discrimination, sexual harassment, abuse, and violence, whether or not you shared your #MeToo stories. For those who have, thank you for speaking up. Your courage to share your #MeToo story is changing the world. By now you already know about some of the things that have changed since October 2017. Perhaps you attended a march, stood along the side of a long road, or took other action in protest. Your intrepid willingness to join the collective voice created a collective power that made every story count. Things will never be the same again. While some are sitting squarely in the midst of Old Normal, we are looking down from a transition point to New Normal. The collective power of those desiring change is growing and converting to action.

You Are Not Alone

Sexual discrimination, harassment, and violence create shame for victims, and shame isolates. Shame says, "I am unworthy." Shame commands, "Don't look at me. Don't judge me. Don't hurt me more than I've already been hurt." Some of us have never shared our stories with anyone. For some the sense of shame that the event caused at that time has prevented us from sharing with family and friends about the pain we have suffered. Some of us have carried the hurt and bear the scars alone, not even sharing them in the #MeToo movement. Sometimes shame is magnified by a culture that is not supportive of victims of violence. Blame and recrimination from those close to you may have added to an already very heavy burden. I want you to know first and foremost that #MeToo told the truth: You are not alone. You don't have to carry your burden alone anymore. I'm with you in this. Speak your truth.

The Truth Changes Us

The act of courageously sharing your story is changing you as well. Speaking (and writing) the truth allows us to see it more clearly. As we witness the truth about how another has harmed us, whether with a trusted counselor or with a friend or family member we trust, may we all come to understand that others' misbehaviors imparted a shame that is not ours to bear.

According to Dr. Bessell van der Kolk in *The Body Keeps the Score*, "as long as you keep secrets and suppress information, you are fundamentally at war with yourself," and "getting perspective on your terror and sharing it with others can re-establish the feeling that you are a member of the human race."

Maybe you have believed one of these common lies as a result of your experience: You're worthless. You're vile. You're a piece of trash. What's wrong with you? Why weren't you strong enough to keep this from happening? You weren't smart enough to protect yourself.

Some of us have bought these lies (and worse) because of how someone else treated us. That shame from hurts others inflicted on us is not our shame to bear. It's their very real guilt. We can come to terms with the hurts, express and release the pain and deepest emotions, and heal from the pain so that our souls are whole and healthy. If we haven't had an opportunity to do so yet, we can overcome the shame.

Overcoming Shame

A person's choice to demean, harass, abuse, or assault someone is never caused by their victim. It's always the thoughts, words, and actions of the offender. Shame shows up for the victim, though, in insidious questions like, What did I (or she) wear or do or say to deserve this? People shame victims, but that doesn't mean the victim has to accept or hold on to that shame.

Researcher Brené Brown says, "If you put shame in a Petri dish, it needs three things to grow exponentially: secrecy, silence, and judgment. If you put the same amount in a Petri dish and douse it with empathy, it can't survive. The two most powerful words when we're in struggle: me too."[1] The secrecy, silence, and judgment we have lived through as survivors who harbored these stories and did not share them have been dismissed, like darkness in the room when someone turns on a light. We've said and heard "Me Too."

As we recognize this truth, we are freed to release whatever shame has stuck with us from the story we lived through. By reaching out to one another in empathy, we are becoming a force to be reckoned with. We are not victims. We are intrepid survivors and more than overcomers.

Dealing with Mistrust

When people are harmed by others, they learn to refuse to trust, so they can be sure no one hurts them again. We make a subconscious decision not to trust anyone. The lies that creep in and trap us sound like:

"I will never let someone get close to me again. I will never hug anyone again. It's safer to never attract any attention. I will be invisible. From now on, I'm wearing all black, wearing shapeless clothes . . . at least then nobody notices my body. I'll never get married. I'll never have children, because they'll just be hurt like I was. Kindness is just someone trying to butter me up before the kill. Men (women) are all the same."

To accept people's failure and establish appropriate boundaries is not the same thing as building walls so that nobody else can touch our hearts. Mistrust is an iron cage we lock ourselves in. The problem is that even if the offender is long gone, the people we love, the people closest to us, are the ones who get hurt repeatedly when they bang against our iron cages. Offenders are quick to get you to drop your boundaries. Safe people honor your boundaries. It's vital for healthy relationships to trust the right people.

In *Beyond Boundaries*, Dr. John Townsend writes,

Trust is the oil that keeps the relational machinery running smoothly. It is not a luxury. It is vital. . . . Trust is necessary for healthy and full relational lives. What is more, it is beautiful. Trust is the ability to be vulnerable with another person. When you trust someone, you feel certain this person will keep your best interests in mind. You believe that they are who they say they are. You feel that the deepest parts of you will be safe with them. You expect that they will be there for you no matter what and that they will love you even when you are not so loveable.[2]

So examining our inner thoughts about trust and discerning who is actually safe are both important things to do. If you need help to develop discernment, check out *Safe People: How to Find Relationships That Are Good for You and Avoid Those That Aren't* by Dr. Henry Cloud and Dr. John Townsend. *The Power of the Other*, also by Dr. Cloud, helps leaders (and we all have the capacity to influence others and be leaders) to discern the types of people we're in relationship with and to choose to invest in and lead from safe, healthy, deep, and authentic relationships.

Come on out of that iron cage. You are not alone, and you're not better off alone.

Extinguishing the Flames of Rage

You've been hurt, an injustice has happened, and you feel enraged. Rightly so. Feeling the anger and venting can help you feel better for the short term, but it also can increase the anger over the long term and not actually address the underlying causes. One of the hormones the brain produces during anger arousal is norepinephrine, which can act as an analgesic, numbing the pain in your brain.[3] Anger also produces the hormone epinephrine, an energy or adrenaline rush that surges through the body.[4]

Anger can help someone who's felt powerless to feel powerful. The problem is that the underlying sense of powerlessness isn't gone when the rage dissipates. And we can use anger (subconsciously or consciously) to keep from feeling vulnerable in our relationships.[5] If someone's too close, we can get angry. If someone's too distant, we can get angry and pick a fight, which at least produces engagement in the relationship.

What has worked for me to let go of the anger?

Forgiveness.

In the last chapter, we addressed the need to seek forgiveness. I'm not asking you to seek forgiveness for being victimized! Far from it!

Choosing to forgive all who have discriminated against me, harassed me, abused me, and assaulted me was the key to releasing bitterness and anger, and therefore restoring emotional, psychological, and physical health. Scientific studies confirm that in addition to helping to let go of anger, forgiveness is associated with lower use of medications and alcohol, lower blood pressure, and fewer physical symptoms of disease.[6] As the saying goes, holding on to anger is like drinking poison and hoping someone else will die.

How does one forgive?

Forgiveness is not denying the reality of your experience. Forgiveness is not glossing over an offense or forgetting it. Forgiveness is not saying it's unimportant or it doesn't matter. Forgiveness is not letting an offender or group of offenders off the hook. Forgiveness is not failing to hold them accountable for their crimes. Forgiveness is not re-establishing relationship.

Forgiveness makes a conscious, deliberate decision to release feelings of resentment or vengeance (judgment, revenge) toward a person or group who has harmed you, whether or not they deserve it. Forgiveness empowers you to be honest with yourself about pain you suffered or shame you endured without letting that pain or shame define you in any way.

Receiving and extending forgiveness is part of a healthy human experience. As a person of faith and a person who's lived close to sixty years (and never met a perfect person), I believe that anyone who truly thinks they're perfect is, at best, deceiving themselves. I also believe what the Jesus-follower named John wrote: "If we confess [speak out loud in agreement with another] our sins [imperfection, falling short], [God] is faithful and just [holy] to forgive us our sins and to cleanse us from all unrighteousness [wrongdoing]."[7] I find this promise gives me strength to confess my own wrongs and to forgive others, whether or not they admit to their offenses or commit to change.

Although I'm far from perfect, my faith assures me of receiving God's gift of forgiveness for all the times I have failed. I believe that having been forgiven, I need to forgive others who have harmed me. A letter from another of Jesus's followers, Paul, contained the following advice: "Be kind and compassionate to one another, forgiving each other, just as in Christ, God forgave you."[8]

To those who are agnostic or atheists, you're still a person with a choice. You can choose to hold on to anger or to tap into the power of forgiveness. In my humble opinion, forgiveness is healing. I know I have benefited from both receiving and offering forgiveness. No matter your beliefs, if you are willing to forgive those who have harmed you, you can find healing for yourself. By forgiving others, I have been able to let go of the rage and move on with my life. So can you.

What to Do with Residual Trauma

My abusers died long ago. In spite of the fact that the abuse ended nearly four decades ago, some experiences, sounds, and even tastes make me sick to my stomach and make my skin crawl. Bodies change as a result of threat or actual trauma, and both the experience and the remembrance of traumatic, emotional events cause us to experience sensations in the body as a response to the trauma.[9] These gut feelings I had and still carry, although not as many, served as warning signals and were part of my trauma.

Generally, when people are able to feel their body's visceral warning signs, trust them, and consciously respond (having agency as a person), they're able to have a sense of control over their bodies, emotions, and self.[10] Traumatized people survive by disconnecting from gut feelings and numbing awareness. Numbness replaces self. They hide inside. They often are not able to identify feelings.[11]

Some who are traumatized become so disconnected from themselves they're unable to feel pleasure or pain. This happens during the event as the brain protects the victim from the trauma and after the event as a result of the brain's conditioning. The disconnection from feelings and sensations affects people in different ways.

Removing residual trauma and regaining emotional and physical awareness are possible. Those whose trauma prevents them from connection to self and agency over their life can pursue a variety of types of treatments. Some treatment methodologies I've heard of over the past decade include traditional therapies, EMDR, yoga, massage, neurofeedback, art therapy, theater therapy, and life integration therapy. Mindfulness practices can also help a person to recover self. I encourage you to do your own research and determine what will work best for you to remove residual trauma and offer you freedom from visceral pain and emotions that have remained in the body long after the trauma has occurred.

Becoming Resilient

Resilience is "an ability to recover from or easily adjust to misfortune or change."[12] "Resilience is the product of agency: knowing that what you do can make a difference," Dr. van der Kolk asserts.

In an interview, Dr. Madelyn Blair, PhD,[13] who is on faculty at Columbia University's IKNS program, said that knowing who you are is key to resilience. In her work with executives and managers, Dr. Blair asks them to write their personal stories. Those stories help her clients to see themselves more clearly. In her interview, Dr. Blair said, "In the sharing and telling of your story you connect with truths. Awareness of choice (agency) is essential."

Dr. Blair referred to Victor Frankl's book *Man's Search for Meaning*, stating, "Between the stimulus and the response, if we choose to be aware of it and seize the moment, there exists a moment of time to think. In that moment we have the ability to choose our response."

At the moment of trauma, and even afterward, we may be stripped of our ability to choose. At times, the trauma in the body may put us in autopilot and increase our risk of losing that sense of choice. The truth is that we don't live in yesterday. So today, we have the ability to respond and make choices that align with our purpose, values, vision, mission, and goals. Sometimes it's necessary to get help to move to this sometimes-infinitesimal place of choice. Dr. Blair said, "It's in the clarity of purpose that you gain confidence, you can determine your actions and responses and choose in the moment what is most important." For those of us who have stories, no matter how limited or nonexistent our apparent choices may have been at the time, the gift is that we can now choose to use them to grow our resilience.

Reputation Management

Other people aren't always as careful with our stories as we'd like, and even use our stories against us to perpetrate additional harm. For this reason, it's important to be careful with your stories and with whom you choose to share them. While recognizing the risk of more harm, consider your options. If you believe that it will bring you the best results, report illegal discrimination, harassment, abuse, and sexual assault (of yourself or others) to the correct person at your workplace, if it's job-related, and to the authorities. For specific advice about what to do when you've experienced workplace discrimination and harassment in the US, check out the Equal Employment Opportunity Commission's website, www.eeoc.gov. You might also want to read *Be Fierce* by Gretchen Carlson.

Even if others fail to believe you, fail to be tender with you when you're already emotionally wounded, or fail to bring the offender to justice, there is a benefit to reporting crime. The justice system is made up of people who fail, but without a victim's willingness to blow the whistle, Old Normal will continue to prevail, and someone else will likely be hurt by the person who hurt you.

When it comes to sharing your stories with others, discretion is advised. At the speed of light, the rumor mill destroys reputations and lies before there's time to verify the facts. It is unwise to share the details of your story with anyone who is not safe. In the book *Why Am I Afraid to Tell You Who I Am?*, John Powell describes five levels of communication: level five is polite (cliché) conversation. Level four is sharing facts and information about others. Information giving. Level three is sharing ideas, opinions, and decisions. Level two is communicating about your feelings about a situation, experience, or person. Level one is self-disclosing, being completely open and honest with another person.[14] Your level-one stories deserve to be told only to trusted people. If they haven't reached level-one trust and communication with you, they haven't merited your disclosure of heartfelt emotions or traumas.

Now I'm going to address those who have perpetrated harm and have paid for it by being fired or asked to resign. You can't undo the past, but your reputation in the future will be based on your behavior. To improve your reputation, change what you think and consistently change what you do now and in the future. You must also do what you can to mitigate the damage you've done to others. Do not take this responsibility lightly, or assume that it can be instantaneous. Apologizing without acknowledging the pain and harm you caused to the other is worse than remaining silent. You may sincerely apologize and still never regain someone's trust. Even if they are open to the possibility of relationship, rebuilding trust takes time and consistency in future behaviors. Tell the truth to yourself and to others. *Leadership and Self-Deception* by the Arbinger Institute is a great resource for those who are interested in clearing their reputation and proactively moving forward.

Hurt People Hurt People

There's a saying that goes, "Hurt people hurt people." Somewhere along the line, someone harms a person, uses them, objectifies them, and takes out their base emotions on them. Rather than going through the process of forgiving, the victim internalizes the damage and acts in ways that perpetrate the damage on others.

It takes humility and sincere sorrow to process harms done to you, and to come to grips with the truth about any harms you've inflicted on yourself or others. It takes repentance, which is a willingness to come face-to-face with the real damage you've done to yourself or another and the commitment to make a 180-degree turn to change your behavior, to stop objectifying yourself or others, and to act in sincere consideration for your own well-being and the well-being of others. Repentance requires keeping that commitment.

The Healing Power of Gratitude

I've wrestled with the command in the first book of Paul to the Thessalonians (chapter five, verse 18): "In everything give thanks: for this is the will of God in Christ Jesus concerning you."

Everything? Really?

The truth is, I am not thankful for the pain I've suffered in my life, and I think I'd have to be mentally ill to believe gratitude for being harassed or assaulted is in any way called for. I'm not thankful for abuse in any form. I'm not thankful for the damage that took decades to sort through and heal from. I'm not thankful for any evil that harassers and abusers inflict on people. This command didn't make any sense to me for the longest time. I couldn't think about the experience without feeling emotional pain, which never left, so I stuffed it.

"The brain is like Velcro for negative experiences," psychologist Rick Hanson is fond of saying, "but Teflon for positive ones . . . acquiring a big pile of negative experiences in implicit memory banks naturally makes a person more anxious, irritable, and blue. Plus, it makes it harder to be patient and giving toward others."[15] This described me because I couldn't look back without getting stuck in the negativity. But I had read about the healing power of gratitude:

> In 2007, Robert Emmons began researching gratitude through a psychological lens. He found that expressing gratitude improves mental, physical and relational well-being. Being grateful also impacts the overall experience of happiness, and these effects tend to be long-lasting. Benefits of gratitude include:
>
> - Improved physical, emotional, and social well-being,
> - Greater optimism and happiness,
> - Improved feelings of connection in times of loss or crises,
> - Increased self-esteem,

- Heightened energy levels,
- Strengthened heart, immune system, and decreased blood pressure,
- Improved emotional and academic intelligence,
- Expanded capacity for forgiveness,
- Decreased stress, anxiety, depression, and headaches,
- Improved self-care and greater likelihood to exercise, and
- Heightened spirituality—the ability to see something bigger than ourselves.[16]

I wanted an increased sense of connection and relief in my life. So I thought hard until I found a few things to give thanks about. I considered the verse from 1 Thessalonians from a new perspective: what, if anything, could I find to give thanks for in the terrible situations I've faced?

Among many things, I'm grateful for the public library that was on my way home from school, a refuge for me for many years. I'm also grateful I was finally able to talk about my traumas with trusted professionals and with family members who have their own stories. I'm grateful for those who have researched to understand how human brains and emotions work and for authors who have helped me heal significantly. I'm thankful for new, developed therapies that can release trauma and for healing. I'm grateful for the deeper level of compassion that I have gained for others who have been harmed and for the power of forgiveness that brings peace. I'm grateful for many wonderful years of life and for the people in my life. I'm grateful for hope for a better tomorrow.

I'm never going to give thanks for what is clearly evil, but I will look for ways to find the pieces of light, the hidden blessings, in all dark situations. I've found the healing power of gratitude, and I encourage you to find gratitude for yourselves, no matter what your story is.

Moving Forward in Hope

For those whose discrimination, harassment, and sexual violence stories happened recently, and for those whose stories are recently resurfaced after being buried for ages, let me encourage you with the truth. There is healing.

Reach out to safe people and share in a safe community. If you can, talk to a professional or read professional resources. Check out the resources page at www.lifebeyondmetoo.com. Take the time to care for yourself as an investment in your future.

You are intrepid and your future is much more than that of just a survivor. Your courage can also place you in a position of service to others who are struggling. Together, we can continue to raise our voices and to move forward in hope for New Normal.

Questions for Thoughtful Consideration and Discussion

1. Why does it take courage to share a #MeToo story?
2. What is the power of a collective voice?
3. What does shame do to a person?
4. How do you overcome shame?
5. What are the building blocks of trust?
6. How do you handle unresolved anger?
7. What reasons are there to forgive people who harm you?
8. What are the risks of holding the anger?
9. What does agency have to do with resilience?
10. How does someone who was not given a choice regain their agency?
11. Who is it safe to share a #MeToo story with?
12. What does gratitude do for a person?
13. What's your next step?

EIGHTEEN

Hope for New Normal

Envision #MeToo redefined as a way to share positive life stories in contrast to Old Normal. Imagine with me a #MeToo story from someone who has lived in New Normal her entire lifetime. It might read something like this:

In a land where during #OldNormal millions of girl children used to be aborted and killed at birth, I was born to two loving parents who very much wanted me in their family. In fact, they planned me and were delighted to learn that I would be a girl. Both worked outside the home and were looked up to as leaders in our community. They took turns working from home and working at their offices.

I have many happy childhood memories. My parents taught me the community value: to love people and use things, not the other way around. My brothers, sisters, and friends included me in childhood games. When finished with schoolwork, I was permitted to play in the neighborhood with friends until dark. We all went home to our houses and met up with brothers and sisters who'd been busy with their schoolwork and playing, to cook and eat together and talk about our days and what we'd learned. We shared chores and looked after my grandparents together.

School was for every child, and teachers were highly respected. I was encouraged to read at a very young age and was included in primary school from age four. I loved learning with friends. I have a very curious and inquisitive nature, and school increased my curiosity and rewarded me for asking and finding the answers to my questions. I decided at age twelve that I wanted to be a scientist. I was awarded a scholarship to a secondary school and graduated with honors. When I reached the age of independent travel by car, my parents taught me the importance of each person who might be my passenger or in another vehicle and to make sure to honor others at all times wherever I went.

In post-secondary, friends met up in groups to go to movies, see plays and concerts, dance, play sports, or stay in and play games. We were careful to honor one another in our thoughts, words, and actions, and to engage in activities that didn't diminish or objectify people. We had one another's backs, making sure all were safe at all times. We took responsibility to get educated and to vote for good leaders as soon as we were allowed at age eighteen.

When I turned twenty-one, the legal age to drink alcohol, my parents and I went out for dinner and ordered a bottle of wine. We talked about the responsible use of alcohol and the value of maintaining self-control. My parents had modeled moderation in their consumption of alcohol. I don't recall ever in my life seeing anyone noticeably impaired from drinking or the use of drugs, which I had read was common in #OldNormal.

When I graduated from college, I was hired by a research lab. We had about a fifty-fifty split between males and females at every level of the company. I loved working there with excellent mentors and role models. After five years, I left to start my own company in order to bring my ideas to the marketplace. I found plentiful seed funding from angel investors who believed in me, and we succeeded in our venture.

I met a wonderful life partner, and together, we decided to unite to have children of our own. Others didn't wait to have sexual unity because they were over the age of consent and decided to engage, but we waited until we were ready to parent and to choose to keep our sexual union exclusive.

I sold the company when the opportunity came. After our wedding, we started a new business, a company where we could share the work and share the childcare. We enjoyed meaningful sexual unity, and over time, we had three children who grew strong. We taught our children from birth to love people and use things, with honor and respect, as our parents and elders taught us. They saw us live this way at home and at work.

As a parent of both girl and boy children, I thought about what I'd studied in school about Old Normal and how difficult times were for those people back then. Those days were so barbaric. They were filled with broken people and broken hearts.

Thinking about my life brings me great joy. I'm so grateful that the #MeToo movement brought clarity about the Mess of #OldNormal and brought the awareness people needed to shift to #NewNormal. I am so grateful for the joy of community we have now with honor, respect, and love for each member.

#NewNormal, Eve, age 40

You are a valuable member of community. Your place in the world is unique; your thoughts, ideas, and brilliance are special and very much needed when coming up with an answer for the Mess as big as Old Normal. Your vision is important.

If you could envision New Normal where #MeToo stories of discrimination, harassment, abuse, or violence no longer existed, what would it look like? How would people interact? What would make it safe? What would make it just? What would make it joyful?

What would make it possible? How would the world attain it? What would the process be like to make the individual and structural changes in motivation and the support needed to get there? Who would be responsible for making those changes? How would they be held accountable? What would the costs or trade-offs be? What values would be held highest?

Owning Our Part

People can change. Organizations can change. Institutions can change. Cultures can change. Each person can be involved in making change happen. How can we go about making sure that we are contributing to and not impeding or delaying positive change? What part of change is yours? What ownership in the movement toward New Normal would you like to take on in your own life? In your community?

Six Keys to Change

Earlier I offered a suggested list of Six Keys to Change. This was offered as one person's suggestion, to take or leave or change as you wish. What would you want to do to implement Six Keys (such as these) in your personal life, your family, your place of work, your communities, your government, and your leadership or more? As a coach, I would like to encourage you to engage in conversations by using the following questions and coming up with your own to create change:

1. Value all individuals equally.

How would we ensure each person can grow into the fullness of who they are without another's bias or self-centeredness warping or limiting their potential? How would we teach our children that each person is, as individual, precious and equally valuable as everyone else?

What would we have to do to make sure we stop stereotyping, dividing, judging, disabling, or devaluing anyone?

2. Initiate peace.

How would we teach our children that our inalienable rights to life, liberty, and the pursuit of happiness are not lost because of any circumstance of birth (color, creed, gender, race, age, geographic location, different abilities, etc.)? How could we teach our children that nothing gives us the right to infringe upon or devalue another's right to life, liberty, and the pursuit of happiness? How do we get people to stop acting with contempt and violence against people?

What would we need to do so that anytime any action of an individual, group, organization, or community doesn't lead to peace, the community is able to step in and justly help them make corrections?

3. Demonstrate respect for all humans.

How do we teach our babies that humans, at every point in life from first heartbeat to last, each and every one, are never objects to satisfy our personal needs or desires? What will it take to assure that all people are honored as an equally valuable life force and community member, worthy equally of respect, each bearing incalculable innate worth? How do we change the culture and teach our children that people are not things to objectify, harass, use, or control, to do what we want with, for ourselves? What will it take for each of us to stop objectifying people?

4. Clarify consent.

How will we ensure that people honor one another by assuring there is responsible, mature, mutual consent at every point in any sexual encounter with any other human being?

How do we recognize and honor each person's age, ability, gender, sexual identity, beliefs, ethnic origin, citizenship, and consciousness so that human sexuality is honored and clarity of mutual consent is seen as essential in any respectful relationship?

What will it take to put an end to any verbal or physical (or other type of) engagement with another person about any sexual matter, which is an unwelcome intrusion if consent has not been obtained at that time for that interaction? What needs to be done to teach and ensure all know that to obtain consent, the person we seek consent from must be capable of offering consent physically, emotionally, cognitively, and rationally, from an adult perspective? What can we do to stop the unacceptable abuse of power and the violation of another's basic human rights?

What will it take for humans to stop using other people's bodies without consent?

5. Accept complexity.

How can people honor basic human desires and needs for sexual expression, including scientifically observed and verified innate gender differences and similarities, as each person brings to community the multidimensional aspects of their entire person? What will it take to stop believing or acting upon the lie that anyone has a right to, in any slightest way, place a limit on the fullness of another's individuality by viewing them as nothing but an object of personal sexual gratification? How do we ensure the next generation and those following know and live by the truth that people are much more than their gender or sexuality? What will it take for people to stop sexualizing people?

6. Embrace accountability.

How will individuals be held accountable to communities? What will it take for all humans to commit to zero toleration of negative behaviors (in ourselves, and in others) that allow for sexual discrimination, harassment, abuse, or any violence? How will we ensure that negative behaviors are called out by the community and those perpetrating negative behaviors stop? How will the community fully support those who are harmed? What needs to happen to deal with perpetrators so they actually are motivated and supported to stop offending? When will we as a society of human beings stop tolerating, excusing, ignoring, overlooking, or failing to hold people (including self) accountable for unacceptable Old Normal behaviors?

I mentioned the name of this book at an event in January 2019, and a woman told me about a time when she and her husband were dining with friends, and one friend shared her #MeToo story that had happened at work.

"I could hardly believe her," the woman told me. "I'd never heard of #MeToo, and I have never once experienced anything like what she was talking about anywhere I worked. I had no idea anyone could ever treat a co-worker so poorly." Eventually, her friend convinced her that she was telling the truth.

Prior to hearing her friend's #MeToo story, this woman's circle looked somewhat like what New Normal might look to anyone. She'd lived in a bubble of protection, where firsthand stories of discrimination and harassment, abuse and assaults, and attempted assaults had been nonexistent. She'd encountered Old Normal culture but never up close.

If you've been in a bubble, it may be hard to believe there is an Old Normal or to see any need for changes. If you live up close and personal to, or in the carnage of Old Normal, it's hard to believe there's hope for a better future. If you've lived in a bubble, you might think we're almost or already there. Perspective is everything.

Hope for New Normal

I dream of a world at peace, where all humans are honored. I dream of a world where no child is disposable and all children are wanted even before they were purposefully conceived. A world where all children are equally valued and have equal opportunity to grow healthy, productive lives of contribution to community. I dream of a world where all children play and learn and grow fearlessly in safety.

I dream of a world where all children are loved, nourished, and have equal access to and engagement in quality education. I dream of a world where all are able to contribute and be rewarded justly in the marketplace and out of it. I dream of a world where unpaid work is shared by all joyfully, and there are none who are disadvantaged by carrying a heavier burden of unpaid work.

I dream of a world where sexuality is viewed as a beautiful, miraculous gift, where people voluntarily come together for intimacy, unity, and procreation. I dream of a world where nobody is used. Where consent is always ascertained and agreed upon, and there is never a doubt about whether a sexual expression is desired. I dream of a world where sexual discrimination and harassment do not exist. Where people are invested in caring for and honoring other humans with their thoughts, words, and actions. I dream of a world where there is no gender discrimination, no objectification (or resulting self-objectification), no such thing as sexual abuse, sexual assault, or attempted sexual assault.

I dream of a world where leaders live and teach and help their communities to live and teach deep respect and honor among all members of community. A world where none are excluded for any reason, and all are seen for the miracles that we are.

Let's make it so.

I'd like to close by returning full circle to my first #MeToo story. Imagine what it might have been like if, instead of living in the Mess of Old Normal, I was living in New Normal on that day when I walked home from my friend's house after kindergarten.

Angel, New Normal

An autumn breeze blew rust-mottled maple leaves across a driveway. I hurried around the corner out of Sandy's neighborhood and then onto a narrow path next to the tall chain-link fence. I had never walked it alone before, but I knew the path was the short way home, and my mother had told me in the morning it would be safe to go that way.

From two classrooms away, I heard basketballs hitting the pavement in the breezeway. I turned the corner and noticed two tall boys playing. They looked like giants compared to my brothers, almost as big as my uncle. I hurried toward the south wall when one of the boys let his ball bounce away.

He smiled and spoke to me: "Hey, little girl! How are you doing? It's late and it's about to be dark. What's your name? Are you okay?"

I nodded. "My parents call me Angel. I just was playing at a friend's house. I'm walking straight home like my mom said to do."

The boy moved kindly toward me and held out one hand, taking my small hand in his much bigger one. "My name is Jimmy. This is Tommy. Would you like to make a basket?"

I nodded. Tommy handed me a ball, and Jimmy picked me up and took me right up to the net. I threw the ball up in the air. *Swish!* My ball went right in, and Jimmy put me down gently.

"Be safe, Angel," Jimmy said as he picked up his basketball.

I skipped all the way home. For years after that, whenever I went to visit Sandy or anyone else after school, Tommy and Jimmy looked out for me and greeted me.

#NewNormal, Angel

Questions for Thoughtful Consideration and Discussion

1. What kinds of feelings do you have after reading the #NewNormal story?
2. What have you learned from this book?
3. What do you agree with or disagree with?
4. Who will you share this book with?
5. Do you think people can change our cultures?
6. If not, what should be done about the discrimination and violence against women?
7. If so, how might you contribute to the work toward creating New Normal?
7. What power do you hold to create change?
8. What could you do to inoculate the next generation against Old Normal?
9. How can you continue or further this discussion?
10. What is the next step you will take to be a change agent?

Endnotes

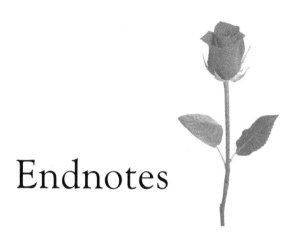

Chapter 1

1   Todd M. Johnson and Brian J. Grim, *The World's Religions in Figures: An Introduction into International Religious Demography* (London: J. Wiley and Sons Ltd., 2013).

2   This quote was attributed to Edmund Burke by John F. Kennedy in a speech to the Canadian parliament in 1961: http://www.presidency.ucsb.edu/ws/?pid=8136. But it appears nowhere in any of Burke's published works, https://tartarus.org/martin/essays/burkequote.html.

Chapter 2

1   https://www.poetryfoundation.org/poems/45870/concord-hymn.

2   https://twitter.com/alyssa_milano/status/919659438700670976?lang=en.

3   https://www.cbsnews.com/news/metoo-more-than-12-million-facebook-posts-comments-reactions-24-hours.

4   https://www.cbsnews.com/news/metoo-more-than-12-million-facebook-posts-comments-reactions-24-hours.

5   https://www.cbsnews.com/news/metoo-more-than-12-million-facebook-posts-comments-reactions-24-hours.

6   "How #MeToo Really Was Different according to the Data," *Washington Post*, January 22, 2018, https://www.washingtonpost.com/news/the-intersect/wp/2018/01/22/how-metoo-really-was-different-according-to-data.

7   https://www.foreignaffairs.com/articles/2018-03-06/how-metoo-became-global-movement.

8   http://justbeinc.wixsite.com/justbeinc/the-me-too-movement-cmml.

9   https://www.ted.com/talks/tarana_burke_me_too_is_a_movement_not_a_moment?language=en.

10   https://www.newyorker.com/culture/culture-desk/the-power-of-yesallwomen.

11   https://www.newyorker.com/culture/culture-desk/the-power-of-yesallwomen.

12   https://www.newyorker.com/culture/culture-desk/the-power-of-yesallwomen.

13   https://www.thedailybeast.com/three-years-later-a-look-at-the-bringbackourgirls-catch-22.

14   https://www.thedailybeast.com/three-years-later-a-look-at-the-bringbackourgirls-catch-22.

15   https://www.timesupnow.com/.

16   https://www.timesupnow.com/.

17   https://www.facinghistory.org/educator-resources/current-events/black-womens-activism-and-long-history-behind-metoo.

18   Statistics cited in this paragraph are from https://endsexualviolencect.org/resources/get-the-facts/woc-stats/.

19 https://www.seattletimes.com/seattle-news/homeless/survey-reveals-high-rates-of-sexual-assault-among-native-american-women-many-of-them-homeless/.

20 http://www.stopstreetharassment.org/resources/2018-national-sexual-abuse-report/.

21 https://leanin.org/www.who.int/en/news-room/fact-sheets/detail/violence-against-women.

22 https://www.spiked-online.com/2017/12/18/meet-the-women-worried-about-metoo/.

23 https://www.nytimes.com/2018/10/08/us/politics/heidi-heitkamp-kevin-cramer-metoo.html.

24 https://www.nytimes.com/2018/10/08/us/politics/heidi-heitkamp-kevin-cramer-metoo.html.

25 https://www.huffingtonpost.com/entry/me-too-lets-men-off-the-hook_us_59e4e3a2e4b04d1d518390d2.

26 https://www.rollingstone.com/culture/culture-news/why-the-harvey-weinstein-allegations-could-change-our-culture-119273/.

27 https://www.huffingtonpost.com/entry/me-too-lets-men-off-the-hook_us_59e4e3a2e4b04d1d518390d2.

28 https://www.bustle.com/p/the-metoo-movement-doesnt-represent-me-heres-why-2933098.

29 https://courses.lumenlearning.com/boundless-sociology/chapter/social-movements.

30 https://www.nytimes.com/2018/10/08/us/politics/heidi-heitkamp-kevin-cramer-metoo.html.

31 *Oprah Magazine*, vol. 19, umber 3, p. 140, italics mine.

32 https://www.businessinsider.com/steve-bannon-oprah-women-take-charge-of-society-2018-2.

33 Jimmy Carter, *A Call to Action: Women, Religion, Violence and Power* (NY: Simon and Schuster Inc., 2014), http://www.simonandschuster.com/books/A-Call-to-Action/Jimmy-Carter/9781476773964.

34 https://www.vox.com/2018/3/20/16955588/feminism-waves-explained-first-second-third-fourth.

Chapter 3

1   Accessed October 1, 2018. https://www.eeoc.gov/laws/types/harassment.cfm.

2   Accessed October 1, 2018. From https://www.eeoc.gov/laws/types/sexual_harassment.cfm.

3   EEOC: Title VII of 1964 Civil Rights Act text: https://www.eeoc.gov/laws/statutes/titlevii.cfm. Description: https://www.eeoc.gov/laws/types/sexual_harassment.cfm. Facts about Sexual Harassment: https://www.eeoc.gov/eeoc/publications/fs-sex.cfm. Justice Department (enforces against state and local governments): https://www.justice.gov/crt/overview-employment-litigation.

4   Accessed October 7, 2019, https://news.bloomberglaw.com/daily-labor-report/rise-in-sexual-harassment-claims-has-eeoc-looking-for-answers

5   Accessed October 4, 2018, https://www.vox.com/identities/2018/2/21/17036438/sexual-harassment-me-too-assault-hollywood.

6   Accessed October 4, 2018, https://www.vox.com/identities/2018/2/21/17036438/sexual-harassment-me-too-assault-hollywood.

7   Accessed October 4, 2018, https://www.vox.com/identities/2018/2/21/17036438/sexual-harassment-me-too-assault-hollywood. Accessed October 1, 2018, http://www.stopstreetharassment.org/.

8   Accessed October 1, 2018, http://www.stopstreetharassment.org/.

9   Accessed October 7, 2109, Merriam-Webster Dictionary, https://www.merriam-webster.com/legal/sexual%20abuse.

10 "Definitions of Child Abuse and Neglect," Summary of State Laws, National Clearinghouse on Child Abuse and Neglect Information (US Department of Health and Human Services).

11 "Definitions of Child Abuse and Neglect," Summary of State Laws, National Clearinghouse on Child Abuse and Neglect Information (US Department of Health and Human Services).

12 https://www.counseling.org/docs/disaster-and-trauma_sexual-abuse/long-term-effects-of-childhood-sexual-abuse.pdf.

13 "Child Maltreatment Survey 2013," Administration for Children & Families, Children's Bureau (United States Department of Health and Human Services, 2015).

14 "Child Maltreatment Survey 2013," Administration for Children & Families, Children's Bureau (United States Department of Health and Human Services, 2015).

15 "Child Maltreatment Survey 2013," Administration for Children & Families, Children's Bureau (United States Department of Health and Human Services, 2015).

16 "Child Maltreatment Survey 2013," Administration for Children & Families, Children's Bureau (United States Department of Health and Human Services, 2015).

17 Dr. Dan B. Allender, *The Wounded Heart*, 1990, Revised 1995, 2008.

18 Jennifer J. Freyd, *Betrayal Trauma: The Logic of Forgetting Childhood Abuse* (Harvard University Press, 1996).

19 Accessed October 4, 2018. https://www.scientificamerican.com/article/sexual-victimization-by-women-is-more-common-than-previously-known/.

20 https://www.rainn.org/statistics/scope-problem, accessed 10/04/2018.

21 "National Intimate Partner and Sexual Violence Survey Summary Report" (National Coalition against Domestic Violence, 2011), 19.

22   Accessed October 4, 2018, https://www.rainn.org/about-sexual-assault.

23   National Research Council, *Estimating the Incidence of Rape and Sexual Assault* (Washington, DC: National Academies Press, 2013).

24   Lynn Langton and Jennifer L. Truman, "Criminal Victimization 2013" (September 14, 2014): 7, retrieved March 26, 2015.

25   C. R. Yung, "How to Lie with Rape Statistics: America's Hidden Rape Crisis," *Iowa Law Review*, no. 1197 (2014).

26   Accessed October 4, 2018, https://www.vox.com/identities/2018/2/21/17036438/sexual-harassment-me-too-assault-hollywood.

27   Freyd, *Betrayal Trauma*.

28   Accessed October 8, 2019, https://www.nsvrc.org/node/4737

Chapter 4

1   https://www.vox.com/identities/2018/2/21/17036438/sexual-harassment-me-too-assault-hollywood.

2   P. 8, http://www.stopstreetharassment.org/wp-content/uploads/2018/01/Full-Report-2018-National-Study-on-Sexual-Harassment-and-Assault.pdf.

3   Jason N. Houle, et al., "The Impact of Sexual Harassment on Depressive Symptoms during the Early Occupational Career," *Society and Mental Health*, no. 1.2 (2011): 89–105. https://www.ncbi.nlm.nih.gov/pmc/articles/PMC3227029/.

4   Houle, et al., "The Impact of Sexual Harassment on Depressive Symptoms during the Early Occupational Career."

5   https://www.washingtonpost.com/national/health-science/sex-harassment-can-make-victims-physically-sick-studies-reveal/2018/02/07/1e018f3a-05f5-11e8-b48c-b07fea957bd5_story.html.

6   https://www.chicagotribune.com/lifestyles/health/ct-sex-harassment-victims-health-20180208-story.html.

7   https://www.chicagotribune.com/lifestyles/health/ct-sex-harassment-victims-health-20180208-story.html.

8   http://www.stopstreetharassment.org/wp-content/uploads/2018/01/Full-Report-2018-National-Study-on-Sexual-Harassment-and-Assault.pdf.

9   http://www.stopstreetharassment.org/wp-content/uploads/2018/01/Full-Report-2018-National-Study-on-Sexual-Harassment-and-Assault.pdf.

10   https://www.upi.com/Archives/1988/11/22/Survey-shows-sexual-harassment-in-Fortune-500-Companies/5490596178000/.

11   The Cost and Consequences of Sexual Violence in California, California Coalition Against Sexual Assault, http://www.calcasa.org/svcostreport/

12   https://blogs.scientificamerican.com/voices/harassers-arent-brilliant-jerks-theyre-bad-scientists-and-they-cost-all-of-us/

13   Dr. Dan B. Allender, *The Wounded Heart: Hope for Adult Victims of Childhood Sexual Abuse* (NavPress, 1990) (rev. 1995, 2008).

14   https://www.endsexualviolence.org/where_we_stand/costs-consequences-and-solutions/.

15   https://www.endsexualviolence.org/where_we_stand/costs-consequences-and-solutions/.

16   Eric Beauregard and Roxanne Lieb, eds. James Q. Wilson and Joan Petersilia, "Sex Offenders and Sex Offender Policy" (NY: Oxford University Press, 2011), 345–367.

17   https://www.nsvrc.org/statistics.

18   https://deploymentpsych.org/disorders/sexual-assault-main.

Chapter 5

1   https://www.nytimes.com/2018/01/25/learning/lesson-plans/the-reckoning-teaching-about-the-metoo-moment-and-sexual-harassment-with-resources-from-the-new-york-times.html.

2 http://www.pewresearch.org/fact-tank/2018/10/11/how-social-media-users-have-discussed-sexual-harassment-since-metoo-went-viral/

3 https://metoorising.withgoogle.com.

4 https://www.ted.com/playlists/582/the_conversation_around_sexual_assault.

5 https://www.nbcnews.com/better/health/breaking-silence-talking-young-kids-about-sexual-assault-consent-ncna914726.

6 Accessed October 20, 2018, http://stopsexualassaultinschools.org/january-campaign/.

7 Accessed October 20, 2018, http://stopsexualassaultinschools.org/who-we-are/.

8 Accessed October 23, 2018, https://www.usatoday.com/story/news/politics/2018/09/28/ruth-bader-ginsburg-metoo-sexual-assault/1455888002/.

9 https://hbr.org/podcast/2018/03/work-after-metoo.

10 https://hbr.org/podcast/2018/03/work-after-metoo.

11 Justine Hamran and Benjy Hansen-Bundy, "What 1,147 Men Really Think about #MeToo," *Glamour*, May 30, 2018, https://www.glamour.com/story/men-metoo-survey-glamour-gq.

12 https://www.glamour.com/story/men-metoo-survey-glamour-gq.

13 Accessed October 25, 2018, https://nypost.com/2018/02/03/a-male-backlash-against-metoo-is-brewing/.

14 Accessed December 31, 2018, https://www.wired.com/story/brett-kavanaugh-hearings-himtoo-metoo-christine-blasey-ford/.

15 Accessed October 20, 2018, https://www.economist.com/united-states/2018/10/20/measuring-the-metoo-backlash.

16 https://www.cnn.com/2018/10/02/politics/trump-scary-time-for-young-men-metoo/index.html.

17 Jeremy Diamon, "Trump Says, 'It's a Very Scary Time for Young Men in America,'" CNN, updated October 2, 2018, https://www.

cnn.com/2018/10/02/politics/trump-scary-time-for-young-men-metoo/index.html.

18   Accessed October 25, 2018, https://www.cnn.com/2018/10/02/politics/trump-scary-time-for-young-men-metoo/index.html.

19   https://t.co/4PVdYZCKDc.

20   *Jetzt Magazine of the Suddeutsche Zeitung* (Munich, Germany), October 18, 2018, https://www.jetzt.de/gender/metoo-debatte-wieder-hashtag-unsere-sprache-beeinflusst, accessed October 17, 2018.

21   https://www.foxnews.com/entertainment/lindsay-lohan-women-speaking-out-about-metoo-experiences-look-weak.

22   https://www.worldcrunch.com/opinion-analysis/full-translation-of-french-anti-metoo-manifesto-signed-by-catherine-deneuve.

23   https://deadline.com/2018/01/catherine-deneuve-metoo-criticism-backlash-france-1202239864/.

Chapter 6

1   https://www.nytimes.com/2018/09/28/us/me-too-men.html.

2   https://mic.com/articles/187292/the-media-is-officially-in-the-metoo-movement-for-the-long-haul#.JejPurueI.

3   https://mic.com/articles/187292/the-media-is-officially-in-the-metoo-movement-for-the-long-haul#.JejPurueI.

4   Eliza Ennis and Lauren Wolfe, Media_and_MeToo_Womens_Media_Center_report.pdf.

5   https://www.thestar.com/news/canada/2017/12/20/public-conversation-on-sexual-harassment-named-canadian-press-news-story-of-2017.html.

6   https://www.thestar.com/news/canada/2017/12/20/public-conversation-on-sexual-harassment-named-canadian-press-news-story-of-2017.html.

7   https://www.girlup.org/mexico-also-say-metoo/#sthash.FR3aSW3w.dpbs.

8   Elmer O'Toole, "How to have a #MeToo conversation," *Irish Times*, December 23, 2017, https://www.irishtimes.com/culture/film/how-to-have-a-metoo-conversation-1.3333696, accessed March 7, 2019.

9   https://www.genus.se/en/newspost/swedish-metoo-movement-greatest-impact-amongst-the-nordic-countries/.

10   https://www.reuters.com/article/us-africa-women-sexcrimes/metoo-challenges-taboo-against-admitting-sexual-abuse-in-africa-idUSKBN1CP1CG.

11   https://saih.no/artikkel/2018/2/the-metoo-campaign-from-a-south-african-point-of-view.

12   https://www.aljazeera.com/blogs/europe/2018/03/russian-media-metoo-moment-180324215606821.html.

13   https://news.harvard.edu/gazette/story/2017/12/metoo-surge-could-change-society-in-pivotal-ways-harvard-analysts-say/.

14   https://www.americantheatre.org/2018/08/21/theatretoo/.

15   https://www.wired.com/story/music-industry-me-too/.

16   https://www.wired.com/story/music-industry-me-too/.

17   https://theconversation.com/metoo-in-the-art-world-genius-should-not-excuse-sexual-harassment-91554.

18   https://www.allvoices.co/howitworks.

19   https://www.hotelmanagement.net/operate/metoo-and-hotel-industry.

20   https://www.newyorker.com/culture/annals-of-gastronomy/one-year-of-metoo-a-modest-proposal-to-help-dismantle-the-restaurant-industrys-culture-of-sexual-harassment.

21   Vanessa Fuhrmans, "What #MeToo Has to Do with the Workplace Gender Gap," *Wall Street Journal*, updated October 23, 2018, https://www.wsj.com/articles/what-metoo-has-to-do-with-the-workplace-gender-gap-1540267680.

22 https://www.theglobeandmail.com/business/careers/leadership/ article-metoo-moves-the-harassment-conversation-into-the- executive-suites/.

23 https://www.theglobeandmail.com/business/careers/leadership/ article-metoo-moves-the-harassment-conversation-into-the- executive-suites/.

24 https://www.wsj.com/articles/ big-investors-seek-a-metoo-clawback-1537754820.

25 http://www.latimes.com/politics/la-pol-ca-legislature- harassment-response-20180903-story.htm.

26 http://www.latimes.com/politics/la-pol-ca-sexual-harassment- sacramento-one-year-later-20181017-story.html.

27 https://www.huffingtonpost.com/entry/half-of-states- address-sexual-misconduct-issues-as-me-too-claims-mount_ us_5b842476e4b072951514f352.

28 State Responses to #MeToo Lean toward Transparency, Fairness, https://www.apnews.com/152a22794cc5412aa666483dd851dbca.

29 https://www.washingtonpost.com/politics/2018/08/08/ women-just-broke-new-record-most-nominees-female-governor- candidates/?noredirect=on&utm_term=.ec2673e58292.

30 https://www.theatlantic.com/politics/archive/2018/07/ the-25-candidates-for-2018-sunk-by-metoo-allegations/565457/. ps://www.economist.com/united-states/2018/09/27/ american-politics-after-a-year-of-metoo.

31 Accessed November 7, 2018, http://cnn.it/2DubO9O.

32 Sarah Margon, "Giving Up the High Ground," *Foreign Affairs Magazine*, March/April 2018, https://www.foreignaffairs.com/ articles/united-states/2018-02-13/giving-high-ground.

33 https://www.cnbc.com/2018/12/28/new-state-laws-in- california-elsewhere-inspired-by-metoo-movement.html.

34 https://www.nytimes.com/2018/06/28/arts/what-is-next-metoo- movement.html.

35 https://www.abc.net.au/news/2018-05-12/united-nations-admits-metoo-critics-dont-think-actions-enough/9751226.

Chapter 7

1   Peter J. Denning and Robert Dunham, *The Innovator's Way: Eight Essential Practices for Successful Innovation* (Cambridge, MA: MIT Press, 2012), 339.

2   Denning and Dunham, *The Innovator's Way*, 319

3   Virginia Lynn Ramseyer Winter, "Sexual Objectification of Women" (PDF, dissertation, submitted to the graduate degree program in the School of Social Welfare and the graduate faculty of the University of Kansas, 2015). https://books.apa.org/education/ce/sexual-objectification.pdf.

4   https://time.com/4029029/10-questions-with-brene-brown/.

5   https://www.dosomething.org/us/facts/11-facts-about-human-trafficking.

6   https://www.state.gov/j/tip/laws/index.htm.

7   Trafficking Victims Protection Act (TVPA) of 2000, Pub. L. no. 106-386, Section 102(A), 114 Stat. 1464.

8   https://www.dosomething.org/us/facts/11-facts-about-human-trafficking.

9   https://www.dosomething.org/us/facts/11-facts-about-human-trafficking.

10   https://www.dosomething.org/us/facts/11-facts-about-human-trafficking.

11   https://www.unodc.org/documents/data-and-analysis/glo-tip/2016_Global_Report_on_Trafficking_in_Persons.pdf.

12   https://www.unodc.org/documents/data-and-analysis/glo-tip/2016_Global_Report_on_Trafficking_in_Persons.pdf.

13   https://www.state.gov/documents/organization/282804.pdf.

14   https://www.state.gov/documents/organization/282804.pdf.

15   https://www.nobelprize.org/prizes/peace/2018/press-release/

citation, MLA style: The Nobel Peace Prize for 2018, NobelPrize. org., Nobel Media AB 2018, October 2018. https://www.nobelprize. org/prizes/peace/2018/press-release/.

16 https://www.humanrightsfirst.org/resource/ human-trafficking-numbers.

17 https://www.thorn.org/ child-sexual-exploitation-and-technology/.

18 Rein Fuchs, "Why America Should Legalize Prostitution," *Business Insider*, November 13, 2013, https://www.businessinsider. com/why-america-should-legalize-prostitution-2013-11.

19 https://www.businessinsider.com/ why-america-should-legalize-prostitution-2013-11.

20 https://www.netnanny.com/blog/ what-serial-killers-and-murderers-think-about-pornography/.

21 https://fightthenewdrug.org.

22 See 18 USC. § 1460; 18 USC. § 1461; 18 USC. § 1462; 18 USC. § 1463.

23 https://www.justice.gov/criminal-ceos/citizens-guide-us-federal-law-obscenity (See 18 USC. § 1465; 18 USC. § 1466).

24 (18 USC. §2252(b)).

25 (18 USC. §1466A(a)).

26 (18 USC. §2256(2)(A)).

27 https://www.dictionary.com/browse/lascivious.

28 From NCMEC National Center for Missing and Exploited Children, child sexual exploitation page. http://www.missingkids.com/theissues/cse/exploitation.

29 From NCMEC National Center for Missing and Exploited Children, child sexual exploitation page. http://www.missingkids.com/theissues/cse/exploitation.

30 https://nbcmontana.com/news/nation-world/ south-korean-women-protest-against-spy-cam-porn.

31 https://www.businessinsider.com/
why-america-should-legalize-prostitution-2013-11.

32 https://fightthenewdrug.org/real-average-age-of-first-exposure/.

33 http://thenovusproject.org/the-facts.

Chapter 8

1 Gilda Lerner, *The Creation of Patriarchy* (New York: Oxford University Press, 1987).

2 https://www.unwomen.org/en/what-we-do/
leadership-and-political-participation/facts-and-figures.

3 https://www.unwomen.org/en/what-we-do/
leadership-and-political-participation/facts-and-figures.

4 https://www.cnbc.com/2019/03/04/the-us-ranks-75th-in-womens-representation-in-government.html.

5 Susan Brownmiller, *Against Our Will: Men, Women and Rape* (NY: Simon & Schuster, 1975), 31–113.

6 Brownmiller, *Against Our Will*, 31–113.

7 https://treaties.un.org/Pages/ViewDetails.
aspx?src=TREATY&mtdsg_no=XVIII-10&chapter=18&clang=_en#12.

8 Paraphrasing Judith Shklar, *American Citizenship* (Cambridge, MA: Harvard University Press, 1998), 2.

9 Sidney Verba, et al., *Voice and Equality: Civic Voluntarism in American Politics* (Cambridge, MA: Harvard University Press), 18.

10 Deondra Rose, *Citizens by Degree: Higher Education Policy and the Changing Gender Dynamics of American Citizenship* (NY: Oxford University Press, 2018).

11 https://www.biblegateway.com, Micah 6:8 NIV: "He has shown you, O mortal, what is good. And what does the Lord require of you? To act justly and to love mercy and to walk humbly with your God."

12 https://www.biblegateway.com, Romans 3:23 NIV: "For all have sinned and fall short of the glory of God."

13 Genesis 1:27, 28, 31.

14 Carter, *A Call to Action and Power*, 19.

15 https://qz.com/1392837/the-dalai-lama-to-buddhist-sex-abuse-victims-you-have-given-me-ammunition/.

16 https://www.nytimes.com/2018/07/11/nyregion/shambhala-sexual-misconduct.html.

17 https://www.biblegateway.com, Galatians 3:28 NIV.

18 https://www.crin.org/en/library/publications/holy-see-child-sexual-abuse-report.

19 https://www.thehindubusinessline.com/news/world/pope-begs-for-gods-forgiveness-for-sexual-abuse-scandal/article24786804.ece.

20 https://www.washingtonpost.com/news/magazine/wp/2019/06/03/feature/the-crusading-bloggers-exposing-sexual-assault-in-protestant-churches/.

21 https://www.bbc.com/news/uk-england-london-45270364.

22 https://www.theguardian.com/commentisfree/2018/apr/27/india-abuse-women-human-rights-rape-girls.

23 https://www.independent.co.uk/voices/sexual-abuse-metoo-muslim-woman-its-my-duty-to-speak-out-a8094796.html.

24 https://www.theguardian.com/commentisfree/2010/apr/25/middle-east-child-abuse-pederasty.

25 https://www.facebook.com/groups/1503695826381063/.

26 https://www.haaretz.com/opinion/.premium-the-jewish-world-s-metoo-crisis-is-much-deeper-than-shavit-and-cohen-1.6316456.

27 Carter, *A Call to Action*, chapter 3.

28 https://religionnews.com/2018/04/16/american-atheists-terminates-its-president-over-sexual-misconduct-allegations/.

Chapter 9

1   https://www.merriam-webster.com/dictionary/war.

2   UNICEF, "Gender Discrimination across the Lifecycle," https://www.unicef.org/sowc07/docs/sowc07_panel_1_1.pdf.

3   https://www.ncbi.nlm.nih.gov/pmc/articles/PMC3867633/.

4   https://www.ncbi.nlm.nih.gov/pmc/articles/PMC3168620/.

5   https://www.pop.org/63-million-women-india-missing-11-million-missing-due-sex-selective-abortion/.

6   https://www.pop.org/63-million-women-india-missing-11-million-missing-due-sex-selective-abortion/.

7   https://www.sociology.org/female-infanticide-killing-the-little-girls-of-the-world/.

8   WHO | Intimate partner violence during pregnancy, www.who.int/reproductivehealth/publications/violence/rhr_11_35/en/.

9   https://insights.ovid.com/crossref?an=00006250-201111000-00013.

10 https://www.aclu.org/blog/womens-rights/pregnancy-and-parenting-discrimination/employees-who-have-babies-are-still.

11 Accessed October 8, 2019, https://archive.siasat.com/news/male-dominated-india-sex-discrimination-begins-womb-416579/.

12 https://www.lifesitenews.com/news/india-has-killed-63-million-of-its-daughters-through-sex-selection-abortion.

13 http://www.bbc.co.uk/ethics/abortion/medical/infanticide_1.shtml.

14 https://www.theguardian.com/global-development/2018/jan/18/sexual-assault-and-harassment-rife-at-united-nations-staff-claim.

15 "2017 Report of the Secretary-General on Conflict-Related Sexual Violence," 4.

16 "2017 Report of the Secretary-General on Conflict-Related Sexual Violence," 4.

17 "2017 Report of the Secretary-General on Conflict-Related Sexual Violence," 5.

18 "2017 Report of the Secretary-General on Conflict-Related Sexual Violence."

19 https://www.un.org/sexualviolenceinconflict/wp-content/uploads/reports/sg-reports/SG-REPORT-2017-CRSV-SPREAD.pdf.

20 https://www.un.org/sexualviolenceinconflict/wp-content/uploads/reports/sg-reports/SG-REPORT-2017-CRSV-SPREAD.pdf.

21 https://www.ctvnews.ca/world/south-sudan-rebels-raped-girls-seized-others-as-wives-un-report-1.4139636.

22 https://s3.amazonaws.com/rdcms-aaa/files/production/public/FileDownloads/pdfs/issues/press/upload/2015-CoGEA-Award.pdf.

23 http://www.cornellpress.cornell.edu/book/?GCOI=80140100164210.

24 Peggy Reeves Sanday, "The Socio-Cultural Context of Rape: A Cross-Cultural Study," abstract, the Society for the Study of Psychological and Social Issues online library, https://spssi.onlinelibrary.wiley.com/doi/abs/10.1111/j.1540-4560.1981.tb01068.x.

25 Peggy Reeves Sanday, "Rape Prone versus Rape-Free Campus Culture," abstract, Violence Against Women 2, no. 2 (June 1996): 191-208.

26 "Sexualization of Women," https://www.livescience.com/20773-sexy-advertising-increasing.html.

27 https://www.deseretnews.com/article/865567072/Toddlers-and-Tears-The-sexualization-of-young-girls.html.

28 https://www.sciencedaily.com/releases/2017/01/170124111520.htm.

29 Stephanie V. Ng, MD, "Social Media and the Sexualization of Adolescent Girls," *American Journal of Psychiatry Residents' Journal* (March 10, 2017), https://ajp.psychiatryonline.org/doi/10.1176/appi.ajp-rj.2016.111206.

30 https://www.newstatesman.com/laurie-penny/2014/01/
why-patriarchy-fears-scissors-women-short-hair-political-statement.
31 https://www.psychologytoday.com/us/blog/meet-catch-and-
keep/201502/5-research-backed-reasons-we-wear-makeup.
32 https://www.theatlantic.com/business/archive/2015/08/
the-makeup-tax/400478/.
33 https://www.psychologytoday.com/us/blog/meet-catch-and-
keep/201502/5-research-backed-reasons-we-wear-makeup.
34 http://www.cosmetic-business.com/de/News/
cosmetics-for-kids-the-young-market-of-the-future/148615.
35 J. E. Workman, et al., "The Role of Cosmetics in Attributions
about Sexual Harassment," *Sex Roles: A Journal of Research* 24, no.
11-12 (June 1991): 759–769.
36 https://www.theatlantic.com/business/archive/2015/08/
the-makeup-tax/400478/.
37 https://www.apa.org/action/resources/research-in-action/share.
aspx.
38 https://www.brookings.edu/blog/
brown-center-chalkboard/2018/04/23/
how-our-education-system-undermines-gender-equity/.
39 https://en.unesco.org/themes/women-s-and-girls-education.
40 http://www.edchange.org/multicultural/papers/genderbias.html.
41 https://www2.ed.gov/about/offices/list/ocr/docs/tix_dis.html.
42 https://www.athleticscholarships.net/scholarships-women-title-
ix.htm.
43 https://www.biography.com/people/maria-mitchell-9410353.
44 https://www.shrm.org/shrm-india/pages/women-in-tech-time-
to-lead-the-way.aspx.
45 https://www.economist.com/briefing/2018/07/05/
culture-and-the-labour-market-keep-indias-women-at-home.
46 https://www.economist.com/briefing/2018/07/05/
culture-and-the-labour-market-keep-indias-women-at-home.

47   https://ourworldindata.org/
women-in-the-labor-force-determinants.

48   https://www.payscale.com/data/gender-pay-gap.

49   https://www.pay-equity.org/day.html.

50   https://www.wherewomenwork.com/
PrimeEmployersforWomen.

51   https://www.weforum.org/agenda/2017/11/
why-iceland-ranks-first-gender-equality.

52   WSJ.com, "Parsing the Gender Pay Gap," Opinion, November 22, 2018.

53   WSJ.com, "Parsing the Gender Pay Gap," Opinion, November 22, 2018.

54   WSJ.com, "Parsing the Gender Pay Gap," Opinion, November 22, 2018.

55   https://www.aauw.org/article/aauw-top-research-of-2018/.

56   Louis Hyman, *Temp: How American Work, American Business, and the American Dream Became Temporary* (NY: Viking Press, 2018).

57   Hyman, *Temp*, 60.

58   Email from GEN dated Tuesday 11/27/2019 to Giving Tuesday prospective donors.

59   Sally Helgesen and Marshall Goldsmith, *How Women Rise* (New York: Hatchette Books, 2018).

60   https://www.oxfam.org/en/even-it/
why-majority-worlds-poor-are-women.

61   Dubravka Ritter, "Do We Still Need the Equal Credit Opportunity Act," discussion paper (Federal Reserve Bank of Philadelphia, 2012), 37–38.

62   https://www.phil.frb.org/-/media/consumer-finance-institute/
payment-cards-center/publications/discussion-papers/2012/D-
2012-equal-credit-opportunity-act.pdf.

63 https://www.oxfam.org/en/even-it/
why-majority-worlds-poor-are-women.

64 https://www.oxfam.org/en/even-it/
why-majority-worlds-poor-are-women.

65 https://www.forbes.com/sites/reenitadas/2018/04/12/womens-
healthcare-comes-out-of-the-shadows-femtech-shows-the-way-to-
billion-dollar-opportunities/#4ec0c7296159.

66 https://www.hrw.org/news/2017/04/05/
us-ends-funding-global-womens-health-agency.

67 https://www.healthecareers.com/article/salary/
gender-pay-gap-healthcare.

68 https://www.healthecareers.com/article/salary/
gender-pay-gap-healthcare.

69 https://www.healthecareers.com/article/salary/
gender-pay-gap-healthcare.

70 https://www.healthecareers.com/article/salary/
gender-pay-gap-healthcare.

Chapter 10

1 https://digiday.com/marketing/sobering-findings-one-five-
young-women-media-advertising-sexually-harassed/.

2 https://www.adweek.com/brand-marketing/4as-study-finds-
most-women-advertising-have-experienced-sexual-harassment-and-
discrimination-172943/.

3 https://www.fastcompany.com/40542243/a-week-in-advertis-
ings-double-edge-sword-of-gender-equality.

4 https://adage.com/article/agency-viewpoint/
year-s-resolve-time-wage-equality/302262/.

5 https://www.nytimes.com/2018/01/25/arts/music/music-
industry-gender-study-women-artists-producers.html.

6 https://www.nytimes.com/2018/01/25/arts/music/music-
industry-gender-study-women-artists-producers.html.

7   https://www.forbes.com/sites/pauleannareid/2018/08/24/this-founder-is-changing-the-tune-of-gender-inequality-in-the-music-industry/#ada76d174098.

8   https://www.wgea.gov.au/wgea-newsroom/music-industry-not-such-sweet-song-women-0.

9   https://www.theguardian.com/inequality/2017/oct/12/tonights-live-music-acts-will-mostly-be-male-only-whats-holding-women-back.

10   https://medium.com/thrive-global/the-lack-of-women-in-the-music-industry-6f275030aad2.

11   https://radiichina.com/women-promoters-at-the-vanguard-of-chinas-electronic-music-scene/.

12   https://www.deseretnews.com/article/700177458/BYU-study-Sexualized-song-lyrics-increasing-dramatically.html.

13   https://www.theodysseyonline.com/response-to-rap-music-and-the-over-sexualization-of-women.

14   https://www.theodysseyonline.com/response-to-rap-music-and-the-over-sexualization-of-women.

15   Phone Interview, Rese Knickerbocker, January 25, 2019.

16   Lisa Respers, "Times Up Takes Aim at R. Kelly" (France, CNN Entertainment), updated April 30, 2018. https://www.cnn.com/2018/04/30/entertainment/r-kelly-times-up/index.html.

17   https://genius.com/Maddie-and-tae-girl-in-a-country-song-lyrics.

18   http://www.unwomen.org/en/news/stories/2014/9/geena-davis-study-press-release.

19   Kate Harding, *Asking for It: The Alarming Rise of Rape Culture and What We Can Do about It* (Boston: DaCapo/Lifelong, 2015), 184.

20   Harding, *Asking for It*.

21   Faye H. Dambrot, et al., "Television Sex Roles in the 1980s: Do Viewers' Sex and Sex Role Orientation Change the Picture?"

abstract, *Sex Roles: A Journal of Research* 19, no. 5-7 (September 1988): 387–401, https://link.springer.com/article/10.1007/BF00289844.

22 Dambrot, et al., "Television Sex Roles in the 1980s," https://link.springer.com/article/10.1007/BF00289844.

23 https://www.huffingtonpost.com/2015/06/18/how-feminist-tv-became-the-new-normal_n_7567898.html.

24 https://www.huffingtonpost.com/2015/06/18/how-feminist-tv-became-the-new-normal_n_7567898.html.

25 https://www.theguardian.com/tv-and-radio/2018/feb/27/tv-industry-diversity-women-people-of-color-decline.

26 https://broadly.vice.com/en_us/article/43gwpb/the-woman-teaching-the-world-how-to-erase-film-industry-sexism.

27 https://www.cbc.ca/news/technology/women-online-harassment-1.3490249.

28 https://www.theguardian.com/commentisfree/2018/jan/24/video-games-industry-metoo.

29 https://www.finder.com.au/sex-in-mass-effect-andromeda-adds-one-night-stands.

30 https://www.nytimes.com/2016/04/01/sports/soccer/uswnt-us-women-carli-lloyd-alex-morgan-hope-solo-complain.html.

31 https://mic.com/articles/121847/5-inequalities-female-athletes-still-face-even-if-they-re-world-champs#.2e6lTQq8O.

32 https://mic.com/articles/121847/5-inequalities-female-athletes-still-face-even-if-they-re-world-champs#.lqQjXi6Tt.

33 http://www.endvawnow.org/en/articles/30-sexual-harassment-in-sport.html.

34 https://www.nytimes.com/2018/04/10/sports/cheerleaders-nfl.html.

35 Time.com/money/5127457/nfl-cheerleaders-career-pay-salary/.

36 https://www.statista.com/statistics/675385/average-nfl-salary-by-team/.

37 "Here's How Aly Raisman Described Her Experience with Dr. Larry Nasser in Her New Book," Bostonglobe.com/sports, November 12, 2017.

38 https://www.ranker.com/list/professional-athletes-who-went-into-politics/celebrity-lists.

39 https://www.unwomen.org/en/what-we-do/leadership-and-political-participation/facts-and-figures.

40 https://www.unwomen.org/en/what-we-do/leadership-and-political-participation/facts-and-figures.

41 https://www.forbes.com/sites/janetwburns/2017/09/22/2016-proved-women-are-great-for-business-yet-still-being-pushed-out/#3188ecdd188b.

42 Harding, *Asking for It*, 170.

Chapter 11

1 http://www3.weforum.org/docs/WEF_GGGR_2017.pdf, p. 28.

2 http://www3.weforum.org/docs/WEF_GGGR_2017.pdf, p. 10 table 3.

3 http://www3.weforum.org/docs/WEF_GGGR_2017.pdf, p. 10 table 3.

4 Frances Hesselbein, Marshall Goldsmith, and Sarah McArthur, eds., *Work Is Love Made Visible: A Collection of Essays about Finding Your Purpose from the World's Greatest Thought Leaders* (Hoboken, NJ: John Wiley & Sons Inc.), 231.

5 *Work Is Love Made Visible*, 232.

6 http://www3.weforum.org/docs/WEF_GGGR_2017.pdf, p. 27.

7 https://www.nbcnews.com/news/sports/steph-curry-responds-9-year-old-asking-curry-5-shoes-n941841.

8 http://www3.weforum.org/docs/WEF_GGGR_2017.pdf.

9 https://www.weforum.org/agenda/2017/11/women-leaders-key-to-workplace-equality/.

10 http://www3.weforum.org/docs/WEF_GGGR_2017.pdf.

11   http://www3.weforum.org/docs/WEF_GGGR_2017.pdf, pp. 27–28.

12   http://www3.weforum.org/docs/WEF_GGGR_2017.pdf.

13   Kerry Patterson, et al., *Influencer: The Power to Change Anything* (VitalSmarts LLC), 97. The authors quote Bandura's work, which is summarized in this abstract, https://www.uky.edu/~eushe2/Bandura/Bandura1999PSPR.pdf.

14   Patterson, et al., *Influencer: The Power to Change Anything*, 97.

15   https://www.adweek.com/brand-marketing/schweppes-brazil-made-a-dress-that-measures-how-often-women-get-groped/.

16   A. Bandura, "Moral Disengagement in the Perpetration of Inhumanities," *Personality and Social Psychology Review*, Special Issue on Evil and Violence (1999): 193–209.

17   https://news.harvard.edu/gazette/story/2017/04/over-nearly-80-years-harvard-study-has-been-showing-how-to-live-a-healthy-and-happy-life/.

Chapter 12

1   https://www.endpolio.org/.

2   Influencer: The Power to Change Anything, 77.

3   https://seths.blog/2018/12/respect-difficult-problems/.

4   https://www.leadershipnow.com/leadingblog/2017/04/conflict_without_casualties.html.

5   Influencer: The Power to Change Anything, 78.

6   Influencer: The Power to Change Anything, 78.

7   https://www.un.org/press/en/2008/sc9364.doc.htm.

8   https://obamawhitehouse.archives.gov/the-press-office/2014/04/29/fact-sheet-not-alone-protecting-students-sexual-assault.

9   https://www.ed.gov/news/press-releases/us-department-education-releases-list-higher-education-institutions-open-title-i.

10   https://theweek.com/speedreads/795343/betsy-devos-new-rules-campus-sexual-assault-cut-investigations-save-money.

11   https://treaties.un.org/Pages/ViewDetails.aspx?src=TREATY&mtdsg_no=IV-8&chapter=4&lang=en.

12   https://www.ohchr.org/EN/HRBodies/CEDAW/Pages/Membership.aspx.

13   https://www.globalfundforwomen.org/womens-groups-in-drc-demand-justice/#.XAxaj2hKhM1.

14   https://www.securitycouncilreport.org/atf/cf/%7B65BFCF9B-6D27-4E9C-8CD3-CF6E4FF96FF9%7D/CAC%20S%20RES%20 1820.pdf.

15   "The Elusive Peace: Ending Sexual Violence during and after Conflict," report (US Institute of Peace, December 2018), https://reliefweb.int/report/world/elusive-peace-ending-sexual-violence-during-and-after-conflict.

16   https://www.simplypsychology.org/katz-braly.html.

17   https://www.psychologytoday.com/us/blog/nurturing-self-compassion/201709/the-psychology-behind-racism.

18   https://www.simplypsychology.org/katz-braly.html.

19   https://psychcentral.com/news/2010/08/11/long-term-effects-of-stereotyping/16675.html.

20   https://psychcentral.com/news/2010/08/11/long-term-effects-of-stereotyping/16675.html.

21   https://www.simplypsychology.org/katz-braly.html.

22   https://www.essence.com/news/alabama-9-year-old-kills-herself-after-racist-bullying/.

23   https://www.pbs.org/kcts/preciouschildren/diversity/read_teaching.html.

24   https://www.pbs.org/kcts/preciouschildren/diversity/read_teaching.html.

25   http://www.discoveryeducation.com/teachers/free-lesson-plans/understanding-stereotypes.cfm.

26 https://www.aclu.org/teach-kids-not-stereotypes.

27 https://iwantrest.com/story/.

28 Ray Miller-Still, "High Volume of Calls Made to Assault Centers," *Enumclaw Courier-Herald*, November 7, 2018, pp. 1, 11.

29 Ray Miller-Still, "High volume of calls made to assault centers," *Enumclaw Courier-Herald*, November 7, 2018, 2018, pp. 1, 11.

30 Ray Miller-Still, "High volume of calls made to assault centers," *Enumclaw Courier-Herald*, November 7, 2018, 2018, pp. 1, 11.

31 Ray Miller-Still, "High volume of calls made to assault centers," *Enumclaw Courier-Herald*, November 7, 2018, 2018, pp. 1, 11.

32 https://www.wsj.com/articles/france-prepares-to-get-tough-on-firms-that-pay-women-less-1542542400?.

33 https://www.wsj.com/articles/france-prepares-to-get-tough-on-firms-that-pay-women-less.

34 Parul Sinha, et al., "Structural Violence on Women: An Impediment to Women Empowerment," https://www.ncbi.nlm.nih.gov/pmc/articles/PMC5561688/.

Chapter 13

1 http://www.actionaid.org/2013/02/whos-responsible-safety-women-and-girls-our-cities.

2 https://www.stltoday.com/news/local/crime-and-courts/ferguson-police-investigating-reported-rape-of--year-old-woman/article_b26f4cfd-0f44-59ac-80b8-f588e27e0c43.html.

3 https://www.stltoday.com/news/local/crime-and-courts/ferguson-police-investigating-reported-rape-of--year-old-woman/article_b26f4cfd-0f44-59ac-80b8-f588e27e0c43.html.

4 https://www.news18.com/news/india/100-year-old-woman-brutally-raped-in-bengal-youth-in-police-custody-1918409.html.

5 https://www.kansas.com/news/local/crime/article91157157.html.

6   https:/ https://www.kansas.com/news/local/crime/article91157157.html /abc13.com/man-gets-life-sentence-times-4-for-raping-3-month-old-baby/3036828/.

7   https://abc13.com/man-gets-life-sentence-times-4-for-raping-3-month-old-baby/3036828/.

8   https://www.nytimes.com/2018/07/07/world/asia/myanmar-rohingya-rape-refugees-childbirth.html.

9   Accessed January 3, 2019, http://www.endvawnow.org/en/articles/299-fast-facts-statistics-on-violence-against-women-and-girls-.html?next=300.

10   Ray Miller-Still, ed., "We All Know Sex Offenders," *Courier Herald*, April 25, 2018, 7.

11   https://fox59.com/2018/11/19/its-a-joke-man-who-raped-dying-teen-gets-less-than-3-years-in-prison/.

12   "We All Know Sex Offenders," 7.

13   Alexandra Styron, *Steal This Country: A Handbook for Resistance, Persistence, and Fixing Almost Everything* (NY: Viking, 2018), 126–127.

14   http://www.ox.ac.uk/research/research-impact/grandparents-contribute-childrens-wellbeing.

15   https://www.publicsafety.gc.ca/cnt/rsrcs/pblctns/fmls-rsk/index-en.aspx.

16   https://www.publicsafety.gc.ca/cnt/rsrcs/pblctns/fmls-rsk/index-en.aspx.

17   https://www.gse.harvard.edu/news/uk/17/10/what-parents-can-do-stop-sexual-harassment.

18   https://www.gse.harvard.edu/news/uk/17/10/what-parents-can-do-stop-sexual-harassment.

19   https://centralasiainstitute.org/top-10-reasons-to-support-girls-education/.

20   "Top Ten Reasons to Support Girls Education" (Central Asia Institute, April 8, 2013), https://centralasiainstitute.org/top-10-reasons-to-support-girls-education/.

21   https://www.aauw.org/research/crossing-the-line/.

22   https://www.theguardian.com/society/2016/aug/08/sex-offences-in-schools-reported-to-police-trebles.

23   http://www.ascd.org/publications/educational-leadership/nov93/vol51/num03/What-to-Do-To-Stop-Sexual-Harassment-at-School.aspx.

24   https://www.psychologytoday.com/us/blog/the-compassion-chronicles/201711/why-dont-victims-sexual-harassment-come-forward-sooner.

25   Phone interview, Simon Casas, September 5, 2018.

26   Phone interview, Simon Casas, September 5, 2018.

27   https://www.washingtonpost.com/news/style/wp/2018/02/20/feature/decades-worth-of-rape-kits-are-finally-being-tested-no-one-can-agree-on-what-to-do-next/?noredirect=on.

28   http://www.joyfulheartfoundation.org/about-us/our-story.

29   https://www.theverge.com/2018/4/11/17223720/trump-signs-fosta-sesta-sex-trafficking-section-230-law.

30   https://www.denverpost.com/2018/03/21/sex-trafficking-websites-bill-white-house/.

31   https://www.apnews.com/f7ec3cec9a4b46868aa584fe1c94fb28.

32   https://www.chicagotribune.com/news/nationworld/ct-vatican-metoo-nun-abuse-20180727-story.html.

33   Accessed December 28, 2018, http://www.stjames-cathedral.org/Pubs/Midst/IYM%20December%202018.pdf.

Chapter 14

1   http://www.academia.edu/34859400/Andrew_Hopkins_and_the_sociology_of_safety.

2   http://www.sociologygroup.com/
elements-of-culture-basic-elements-of-culture/.

3   https://www.merriam-webster.com/dictionary/safety.

4   https://www.thecut.com/2018/10/tarana-burke-me-too-
founder-movement-has-lost-its-way.html.

5   https://www.nsvrc.org/about/
national-sexual-violence-resource-center.

6   https://www.nsvrc.org/about/
national-sexual-violence-resource-center.

7   https://www.rainn.org/.

8   http://www.raliance.org/wp-content/
uploads/2018/12/2018report_FINAL508.pdf.

9   www.sgff.org.

10 https://www.thorn.org/impact-report-2017/.

11 https://www.togetherforgirls.org/about-us/.

12 http://www.unwomen.org/en/csw.

13 http://www.unwomen.org/en/csw.

14 https://www.psychologytoday.com/
us/blog/the-romance-work/201503/
the-brave-new-world-connectional-intelligence.

15 https://www.rotary.org/en/about-rotary.

Chapter 15

1   https://www.osha.gov/workers/index.html.

2   https://www.saba.com/blog/
creating-a-harassment-free-workplace.

3   https://abcnews.go.com/Politics/unwanted-sexual-advances-
hollywood-weinstein-story-poll/story?id=50521721 .

4   http://fortune.com/2017/11/17/sexual-harassment-legal-gaps/.

5   https://www.eeoc.gov/eeoc/statistics/enforcement/charges.cfm.

6   https://www.americanprogress.org/issues/women/
news/2018/08/06/454376/gender-matters/.

7   https://www.eeoc.gov/eeoc/newsroom/release/10-4-18.cfm.

8   https://www.americanprogress.org/issues/women/news/2018/08/06/454376/gender-matters/.

9   Phone interview, Simon Casas, September 5, 2018.

10   https://spssi.onlinelibrary.wiley.com/doi/pdf/10.1111/josi.12086.

11   Daniel Coyle, *The Culture Code: The Secrets of Highly Successful Groups* (NY: Random House, 2018).

12   https://www.ign.com/articles/2017/12/20/women-in-video-game-development-in-2017-a-snapshot.

13   https://www.rci.rutgers.edu/~search1/pdf/Eagley_Role_Conguity_Theory.pdf.

14   https://gendersociety.wordpress.com/2017/04/27/gender-inequality-and-the-two-body-problem/.

15   https://thinkgen.org/gen-certification/.

16   https://www.pipelineequity.com/press/equity-report-finds-7-percent-gender-equity-increase-results-3-percent-revenue-bump/.

17   http://fortune.com/2018/11/09/eventbrite-reaches-50-50-gender-split-on-board-of-directors/.

18   https://thriveglobal.com/stories/it-s-time-to-change-your-strategy-on-hiring-women/.

19   https://thriveglobal.com/stories/it-s-time-to-change-your-strategy-on-hiring-women/.

20   Taylor Protocols Core Values Index Assessment, http://bit.ly/crose-free-cvi.

21   http://pages.discoverorg.com/rs/845-NAZ-184/images/DiscoverOrg%20Gender%20Diversity%20Report_vFinal.pdf.

22   Iris Bohnet, *What Works: Gender Equality by Design* (Cambridge, MA: Belknap Press of Harvard University Press, 2016), 252–253.

23   Bohnet, *What Works, Gender Equality by Design*, 252–253.

24   https://www.pwc.com/gx/en/about/diversity/iwd/international-womens-day-pwc-time-to-talk-report.pdf.

25 https://leanin.org/sexual-harassment.

26 Phone interview, Dr. Kim Martinez, March 6, 2018.

27 https://www.bloomberg.com/news/articles/2018-12-11/morgan-stanley-calls-out-investor-bias-against-women-minorities.

28 https://www.entrepreneur.com/article/298145.

Chapter 16

1 https://news.harvard.edu/gazette/story/2017/04/over-nearly-80-years-harvard-study-has-been-showing-how-to-live-a-healthy-and-happy-life/.

2 www.lees3habits.com.

3 https://www.who.int/news-room/fact-sheets/detail/violence-against-women.

4 https://www.who.int/news-room/fact-sheets/detail/violence-against-women.

5 https://www.unicefusa.org/stories/standing-hertoo/34986.

6 M. C. Black, et al., *The National Intimate Partner and Sexual Violence Survey (NISVS): 2010 Summary Report* (2011), retrieved from the Centers for Disease Control and Prevention, National Center for Injury Prevention and Control, http://www.cdc.gov/ViolencePrevention/pdf/NISVS_Report2010-a.pdf.

7 https://www.nsvrc.org/statistics.

8 https://www.nsvrc.org/statistics.

9 https://countrymeters.info/en/World.

10 Romans 3:10 KJV.

11 https://twitter.com/mrbenjaminlaw/status/920035649817690112.

12 https://www.heforshe.org/.

13 https://case.edu/socialwork/about/news-publications/research-reveals-new-insights-into-rapist-behavior-assists-rape-investigations-and-prosecutions.

14 https://www.nytimes.com/2017/10/30/health/men-rape-sexual-assault.html.

15 https://www.nytimes.com/2017/10/30/health/men-rape-sexual-assault.html.

16 John 8:7 KJV, https://www.biblegateway.com/passage/?search=John+8%3A7&version=KJV.

17 https://www.accreditedschoolsonline.org/resources/peer-pressure/.

Chapter 17

1 Bessel van der Kolk, MD, *The Body Keeps the Score: Brain, Mind, and Body in the Healing of Trauma* (New York: Penguin Press, 2015), 99.

Dr. Brené Brown, TED Talk. https://www.ted.com/talks/brene_brown_listening_to_shame/transcript?language=en.

2 3 John Townsend, *Beyond Boundaries* (Grand Rapids: Zondervan, 2011).

3 https://www.psychologytoday.com/us/blog/evolution-the-self/200807/what-your-anger-may-be-hiding.

4 https://www.psychologytoday.com/us/blog/evolution-the-self/200807/what-your-anger-may-be-hiding.

5 https://www.psychologytoday.com/us/blog/evolution-the-self/200807/what-your-anger-may-be-hiding.

6 https://www.psychologytoday.com/us/blog/evolution-the-self/200807/what-your-anger-may-be-hiding.

7 https://www.biblegateway.com/passage/?search=1+John+1%3A8-10&version=NKJV.

8 https://biblehub.com/ephesians/4-32.htm.

9 Van der Kolk, *The Body Keeps the Score*, 99.

10 Van der Kolk, *The Body Keeps the Score*, 99.

11 Van der Kolk, *The Body Keeps the Score*, 99.

12 https://www.merriam-webster.com/dictionary/resilience.

13   Dr. Blair is founder of Pelerei, a boutique consulting firm which specializes in organizational learning, knowledge management, narrative intelligence, storytelling, and gender.

14   https://www.habitsforwellbeing.com/five-levels-communication/.

15   https://www.rickhanson.net/take-in-the-good/.

16   https://www.huffpost.com/entry/the-transformative-power_b_6982152.

Bibliography

Allender, Dan B. *Healing the Wounded Heart: The Heartache of Sexual Abuse and the Hope of Transformation*. Grand Rapids, MI: Baker Books, 2016.

Bohnet, Iris. *What Works: Gender Equality and Design*. Cambridge, MA: Belknap Press of Harvard University Press, 2016.

Brown, Brené, PhD., LMSW. *Dare to Lead: Brave Work, Tough Conversations, Whole Hearts*. NY: Random House, 2018.

Brownmiller, Susan. *Against Our Will: Men, Women and Rape*. Reprint, NY: Ballantine Books., Inc., 1993 of NY: Fawcett Books/Random House Publishing Inc, 1975.

Carlson, Gretchen. *Be Fierce: Stop Harassment and Take Your Power Back*. NY: Center Street/Hachette Book Group, 2017.

Carter, Jimmy. *A Call to Action: Women, Religion, Violence, and Power*. NY: Simon and Schuster, 2014.

De Hart, Jane Sherron. *Ruth Bader Ginsburg: A Life*. NY: Alfred A. Knopf, 2018.

Gay, Roxanne, ed. *Not That Bad: Dispatches from Rape Culture*. New York, NY. Harper Collins, 2018.

Greene, Lucie. *Silicon States: The Power and Politics of Big Tech and What It Means for Our Future*. Berkeley, CA: Counterpoint, 2018.

Harding, Kate. *Asking for It: The Alarming Rise of Rape Culture—and What We Can Do about It*. NY: Da Capo Press/Perseus Books Group, 2015.

Holmes, Kat. *Mismatch: How Inclusion Shapes Design*. Cambridge, MA: MIT Press, 2018.

Hyman, Louis. *Temp: How American Work, American Business, and the American Dream Became Temporary*. NY: Viking, 2018.

Kelly, Megyn. *Settle For More*. NY: HarperCollins Publisher, 2016.

Matthews, Nancy. "Feminist Clashes with the State: Tactical Choices by State-Funded Rape Crisis Centers," in *Feminist Organizations: Harvest of the New Women's Movement,* edited by Myra Marx Ferree and Patricia Yancey Martin, 291–305. Philadelphia: Temple University Press, 1995.

McGuire, Danielle L. *At the Dark End of the Street: Black Women, Rape, and Resistance*. New York, NY: Vintage Books, 2010.

Oluo, Ijeoma. *So You Want to Talk About Race*. NY: Seal Press, 2018.

Reinelt, Claire. "Moving onto the Terrain of the State: The Battered Women's Movement and the Politics of Engagement." In *Feminist Organizations: Harvest of the New Women's Movement,* edited by Myra Marx Ferree and Patricia Yancey Martin, 84–104. Philadelphia: Temple University Press, 1995.

Stryon, Alexandra. *Steal This Country: A Handbook for Resistance, Persistence, and Fixing Almost Everything.* NY: Viking, an Imprint of Penguin Random House LLC, 2018.

Van der Kolk, Bessel. *The Body Keeps the Score: Brain, Mind, and Body in the Healing of Trauma.* New York, NY: Penguin Books, an Imprint of Random House LLC, 2014.

About the Author

Christine Rose is founder and CEO of Christine Rose Coaching & Consulting, a coaching firm in the greater Seattle area dedicated to facilitating and accelerating transformation for individuals and organizations, helping business leaders grow their leadership skills, teams, and companies since 2015. Her passion is to bring the power of love to every encounter, to help people to create positive changes in their lives and in the world.

Ms. Rose is an award-winning Certified Psychological Safety Coach in partnership with Amy Edmondson's The Fearless Organization and Noomii.com, a Taylor Protocols CVI™ certified strategic growth coach to business leaders and executives from a variety of industries and NPOs, a speaker and author. A mom of two adult daughters, she's a member International Coaching Federation(ICF) and Forbes Coaches Council, seen and heard on Forbes.com, National Business Radio, Public Affairs Radio with Gary Shipe (Hubbard Radio), ACC News Talk Radio, CUTV Global News Radio with Jim Masters and Doug Llewelyn, and a popular guest on podcasts including Life Transformation Radio and That Special Touch of Excellence.

Prior to founding Christine Rose Coaching & Consulting, Ms. Rose served as Development Director at Attain Housing. A graduate of Georgetown University's School of Business Administration and Coach U's Advanced Corporate Coaching Program, Ms. Rose holds a Fundraising Management Certificate from the University of Washington. She's served as a coach for ICF Global in the United Nations Ignite Global program coaching NPO executives, and is a board member (2020-2022) and satellite group facilitator for ICF Washington. Ms. Rose also serves on the boards of the global NPO Educational Communities Worldwide, Tacoma-based Urban Business Support, and on the advisory board of Attain Housing in King County.

While she's not celebrating her clients' transformations, and sometimes while she is, Christine loves the Seattle Seahawks, smooth jazz, reading, hiking the beautiful Pacific Northwest trails, live theatre, decaf coconut milk lattes, Washington wines, Seattle Chocolates and travel.

Follow Life Beyond #MeToo or join our Community on Facebook –
www.facebook.com/lifebeyondmetoo

Follow Coach Christine on Facebook –
www.facebook.com/christinerose.coach

Follow Coach Christine on Instagram –
www.instagram.com/coachchristinerose

Contact Christine to speak to your organization or faith community –
www.christinerose.coach

CPSIA information can be obtained
at www.ICGtesting.com
Printed in the USA
LVHW022107290120
645191LV00018B/1517

9 781683 147886